The Life of Eric Gill

Eric Gill photographed by Howard Coster (Crown Copyright Reserved).

TO

JOAN AND RENÉ HAGUE

this book

is affectionately dedicated

Contents

Illustrations

ILLUSTRATIONS BETWEEN PAGES 262 AND 263

Acknowledgments

The publishers are grateful to the following for permission to use illustrations in this book: Mrs René Hague for plates 3, 4, 7, 13, 14, 19, 20, the engravings between pages 262 and 263 and the illustrations on pages iii, 143 and 189; the Monotype Corporation for plate 18 and the drawings on page 185; the Victoria and Albert Museum for the engravings on pages 212 and 213; Mr David Jones for plate 8; Mr S. Samuels for plate 9; the Tate Gallery for plate 15; Elbert Holbrook for plate 16; the Central Office of Information for the frontispiece; the British Broadcasting Corporation for plate 11; the City Art Gallery, Manchester, for plate 12; and Edward Sweetland for plate 17. The publishers also acknowledge with gratitude the assistance of Mr Evan Gill in making available a large number of illustrations.

Preface

The material for a life of Eric Gill falls under the following heads:

1. His published writings, including his own *Autobiography* and a selection from his letters, both published after his death in 1940.
2. His diaries and private papers, all of which have been placed unreservedly at my disposal, through the courtesy of his brother, Mr Evan Gill, and his daughter Mrs René Hague.
3. The testimony of those who knew him and who have given me all the help I asked for.

I should like, therefore, to express my particular gratitude to Mr Evan Gill, without whose meticulous devotion to his brother's life and work the writing of this book would have been impossible: his *Bibliography* of Eric Gill's writings and of the principal criticism on his work, and his *catalogue raisonné* of his Inscriptions, have both proved invaluable sources. To Mr and Mrs René Hague, whose assistance and encouragement have been seasoned with much kind hospitality; to Dr Cecil Gill; to Mr and Mrs Denis Tegetmeier; and to Mrs Enid Clay and Mrs Angela Skelton. All these are members of Eric Gill's family.

Among his friends I must record a special debt to Mr Walter Shewring, who has shown in his own published work how well he understood what Eric Gill stood for; Mr Douglas Cleverdon, who made available to me the complete material for the *Profile* of Eric Gill broadcast by the BBC in 1961; Mr David Jones; Mr Austen St Barbe Harrison; Father Brocard Sewell, O. Carm.; Mr Donald Attwater; Mr S. Samuels; and Mr Philip Hagreen. Others to whom I am indebted in varying degrees include His Eminence Cardinal Heenan; Sir Edward and Lady Maufe; Sir Roger Stevens; Mr Leslie French; Mr Graham Carey; Mr Stanley Morison; Sir John and Lady

Rothenstein; Father Martin d'Arcy, S.J.; Father Bede Bailey, O.P.;
Father John-Baptist Reeves, O.P.; Dr Flood; Miss Faith Ashford;
Mr T. F. Burns; the late Dr Charles Burns; Mr Michael Richey; Mr
Philip Mairet; Miss Helena Hall; Mr George Speaight; Father Con-
rad Pepler, O.P.; Mrs Susan Falconer; Mrs Helen Davies; Mrs
Priscilla Roworth; Mr Laurie Cribb; Mr Joseph Cribb; Dom
Theodore Baily, O.S.B.; Monsignor John McQuillan; Mrs Clemency
Stanes; and Monsignor Sutton. I must also thank my secretary, Mrs
Brayne, who has typed a difficult MS with unfailing accuracy and ex-
emplary speed.

If anyone suggested that Eric Gill's influence has not ceased to
diminish since his death, I should not be disposed to disagree. Nevertheless I do not think that this biography needs any better excuse than
the influence he exerted during his lifetime and the quality of the man
himself. That quality was such that his fame may well outlast his
fashion – although it is worth recalling that eighteen years after his
death 6,000 visitors found their way to the Lecture Hall of Monotype
House in Fetter Lane to see the exhibition of his work in lettering.
Nothing is more impervious to time than a good inscription and in
this respect it is quite safe to speak, with Beatrice Warde, of the
'diuturnity' of Eric Gill. I knew him over a period of ten years,
though not intimately. I admired his writing and his workmanship in
stone, and I shared his religious beliefs; but I was not personally engaged in the battles he fought, and I was not committed to his
opinions. I hope, therefore, that those who were so engaged and so
committed will forgive a detachment, not of the heart but of the
head, which in no way tempers the affection in which I held him. Nor
have I any expert knowledge of the many disciplines – typography,
wood-engraving, and stone-carving – of which he was a master. I am
quite incapable of estimating the soundness of his views on monetary
reform. His work in all these domains was abundantly discussed
during his lifetime; and where he invited controversy the debate will
continue for as long as men are concerned about the meaning and the
conduct of human life. My purpose has been to paint a portrait and
to tell a story. Eric Gill drew his own portrait in his *Autobiography*;

and there, too, he told us a large part of his story. But there were many gaps, and a self-portrait can never be the same, even when it is self-critical, as a portrait drawn by a candid friend. Moreover, Eric Gill, perhaps because he was writing against time, chose to depend upon nothing but the material of memory.

His importance, at a time when in Britain as elsewhere men had lost their bearings, was in the exact sense of the word prophetic. Whether you regarded him as a John the Baptist or a Jeremiah; whether you believed or not that his prophecy had substance; whether you thought him inspired or merely opinionated; whether you considered him a sublime failure and an amateur revolutionary – he could not be ignored. Such men are rare in Britain. You have to look back to Carlyle and Ruskin and William Morris to trace his pedigree, and in more recent times only Chesterton and, in France, Péguy and Bernanos were engaged in a polemic so unrelenting and so profound. Where Péguy looked for the 'harmonious city' Eric Gill looked for the 'unanimous society', in which all men were of one mind, however various their functions, because the truth had made them free. Some people would have described this as Utopia; for others it would have been very far from Utopian. Gill no more believed in Free Thought than he believed in Free Love, though he thought with every muscle of his mind and loved with every muscle of his body. He passed for an individualist, but the last thing he wanted was to be different from everyone else. He could never quite understand why everyone else was different from him. He was a revolutionary and even an iconoclast, but he would have built upon old foundations. Like Péguy, of whom he had hardly heard, and like Chesterton, who was his friend, he claimed his sanction from the teachings of the Catholic Church, but the Church has clearly failed to endorse his more radical conclusions. His condemnation of the modern world may go down to history as a lonely and exaggerated protest, but if the ultimate catastrophe should befall us, his will be the last word. It will only be regretted by any chance survivors that he is not here to inscribe our tombstone.

Benenden, 1965

Artists are those who know how to make something useful.

SOCRATES

Work is sacred, leisure is secular.

ERIC GILL

Ce qu'il y a de mauvais dans la machine, ce n'est pas la machine,
c'est l'esprit bourgeois.

JACQUES MARITAIN

Ex Ore Infantium.
The child said: First I think,
Then I draw my think.
The art student said: First I look,
Then I draw my look.
The child is simply a young person;
The art student is a more or less inaccurate photographer.

ERIC GILL

Without philosophy man cannot know what he makes;
without religion he cannot know why.

ERIC GILL

All human perversity, or vice, consists in wishing to enjoy what we ought
to use, and to use what we ought to enjoy.

ST AUGUSTINE

La création artistique n'imite pas celle de Dieu, elle la continue:
l'art procéde d'un instinct spontané comme l'amour, et il doit
être cultivé comme l'amitié.

RAISSA MARITAIN

PART ONE

London, Brighton and South Coast

1882-1907

I

Arthur Eric Rowton Gill – to give him his full name for the first and last time – was born at No. 32 Hamilton Road, Brighton, on February 22, 1882. He was baptized by his father, the Reverend Arthur Tidman Gill, Assistant Minister to the chapel of the Countess of Huntingdon's Connexion in North Street. This was an appropriate initiation for a baby who – in the larger understanding of the word – had non-conformity in his blood. Perhaps it would be truer to say that Eric was possessed with a deep hunger to conform, but only found one thing worth conforming to – and even that was not always a comfortable conformity. He was the second child of his parents, and the eldest son.

Mr Gill, in his beard and square black cap, looked like any one of the great Victorians; and although he was not quite that, the great Victorians were his gospel. He always voted for Mr Gladstone, and admired Tennyson, Carlyle, Frederick Maurice, F. W. Robertson, Dean Farrar, George Macdonald, and Charles Kingsley. He treasured particularly Macdonald's *Diary of an Old Soul* with a reproduction of 'The Light of the World' on the fly-leaf and his own transcription of Macdonald's poem 'To my friends'. When Tennyson died in 1892 he recorded 'the death of my greatest Poet-Friend', and took his eldest daughter Enid to the funeral in Westminster Abbey. Enid was named after Tennyson's heroine, and Eric himself after 'Eric – or little by little'. This might not unfairly be described as starting life with a handicap.

Mr Gill was Victorian in his moral earnestness, his emotionalism, and his large untroubled masculinity. He expected, and received, submission. His voice throbbed with a rich *vibrato* when he was preaching, or declaiming *In Memoriam*. He was poor for the same reason that his son for much of his life was relatively poor, because he thought that work was more important than wealth. He taught Eric to fear God and to sharpen pencils properly – and both lessons were valuable. Mrs Gill had French blood in her veins – an ancestor had accompanied Louis XVI on the flight to Varennes – and Eric's pitiless logic may have owed something to this remote connection. But in all other respects Eric was typically English, and even in some respects typically Victorian; never more so, indeed, than when he was wishing the British Empire at the bottom of the seas that it claimed to rule, or lambasting Victorian conventions.

He would stand before the world as a man with two or three imperative ideas, which the world regarded as obsessions. But he was always concerned with the doing – the translation of the idea into act. He was the very reverse of a dreamer. If you wanted to put something down on paper, you had to sharpen your pencils properly. It was as easy – or as difficult – as that. And so he was more interested in playing games than in learning lessons. If you worked out a sum correctly or got a date right, you merely proved your knowledge; but if you kicked a goal or hit a boundary, you had achieved something as visible as sculpture. You had done more than show your knowledge of how the thing ought to be done – although you had done that as well. It is ironical that Eric, who was so often derided as a theorist, was in fact so eminently practical a person. Indeed, he was observant rather than imaginative, and what he began to observe from a quite early age were, quite simply, the facts of life.

I have not put the words into inverted commas, because there are more facts in life than the facts which are generally put in inverted commas. Nevertheless Eric was quick to put them there himself when he wanted to narrow his scrutiny. And so he came to realize that what he had been taught to conceal as an 'organ of drainage' was easily transformed into a 'pillar of fire'.[1] This may seem to us lordly language for nasty habits, but although Eric would not have commended the habits, he was struck by the inherent contradiction in a convention – it was hardly a point of view – which regarded the same object as at once too disgusting and too sacred to be spoken of. He would work the matter out in his own way, and his solutions were as

[1] *Autobiography*, 1940.

disconcerting, on occasion, to other people as they were cheerfully satisfying to him. I only mention the matter here to show that although Eric developed, he developed in a straight line. He was consistent with himself, even when he changed his ideas. He is there, every bit of him, in those early years at Brighton, with the towering, patriarchal father, the teeming family, and the mother handing on the clothes to Cicely, Irene and Max, Romney, Madeleine, Gladys, Evan, Vernon, Kenneth, Angela and Cecil. These were the names by which the children were known, but Vernon had also been christened Kingsley, and Kenneth also Carlyle. Perhaps there were moments – one doesn't know – when Mrs Gill put her foot down. She had not put it down very often since the day when Mr Gill had captured her from a mid-Victorian concert platform. The precise circumstances of the romance were never disclosed.

Eric, at the age of six, had light brown hair, blue eyes, and a neat little nose which the other members of the family would describe as 'snub' when they wanted to tease him. He wore sailor suits, embroidered with an anchor in front, which were passed on from 'rich Aunt Lizzie' on Blackheath. He was a cheerful and plucky child. On one occasion Mr Gill produced a 'burning glass' from his pocket and held it over Eric's little palm until he cried out in pain. Mr Gill then said sternly: 'I am ashamed that you, the son of a Christian clergyman, should wince. There was once a Roman boy who held his hand in the fire till it burnt.' Other members of the family privately thought the Roman boy had been an ass.

Religion would be as important in Eric's life as sex or 'making'; indeed, more important because it would inspire the practice and the preaching of both. He was not a particularly pious boy, he tells us,[1] but another jotting from his father's notebook is a reflection of the evangelical simplicity in which the family were brought up:

Eric told me that when he goes to bed:

I put my arm round Jesus – although I can't see him – and I stroke his head, and I said I'd jump out of bed so that he might have all the bed; but

[1] *Autobiography*, 1940.

then I remembered Jesus was always with me, so it would be no use to keep out – so I stayed in bed, and I put my arms round him again, and it makes me feel so happy.

Eric was only 7 at the time, and already patiently attending service at the Countess of Huntingdon's chapel. Selina, Countess of Huntingdon (1707–91) had quarrelled with her Bishop and founded a number of chapels up and down the country. Her Connexion was the most aristocratic, but it was not the most eccentric, of dissident sects. Apart from its freedom from episcopal interference, it followed the doctrines and liturgy of the Church of England. Its tone was evangelical. Although the altar remained at the east end, the pulpit was placed in front of it, and emphasis was on the word rather than on the sign. The preacher was vested in a black gown of ample proportions, and his sermon rarely lasted for less than forty minutes. The Gills sat in the front row of the gallery, just above their father's reading desk – an intolerable exposure. Good behaviour was more than a moral or social obligation; it was a matter of family *amour propre*. One couldn't let down the side.

Eric's grandfather and great-uncle had both been Congregationalist missionaries in the South Sea Islands, and his father had been brought up as a Congregationalist. So the Countess of Huntingdon's Connexion – although each congregation elected and paid for its own ministers – was a dangerous step nearer to the Church of England. Eric's richer relatives were all Congregationalists, but he preferred the Book of Common Prayer – however self-expressively interpreted – to the extempore licence of the Congregational chapel to which he was sometimes taken on Blackheath. Mr Gill had himself been ordained as a Congregationalist minister, but his congregation had forced him to resign because he had preached against the doctrine of Hell. He had then been struck by the absurdity of a shepherd receiving his doctrine from his sheep, and the Countess of Huntingdon's Connexion at least guaranteed him a doctrine handed down from above. From the Anglican point of view the Connexion was in schism, but it was not in heresy. When Eric came to consider these

1. Rev. A. T. Gill and Mrs Gill,
Eric's parents.

2. Eric Gill aged 22 (1904).

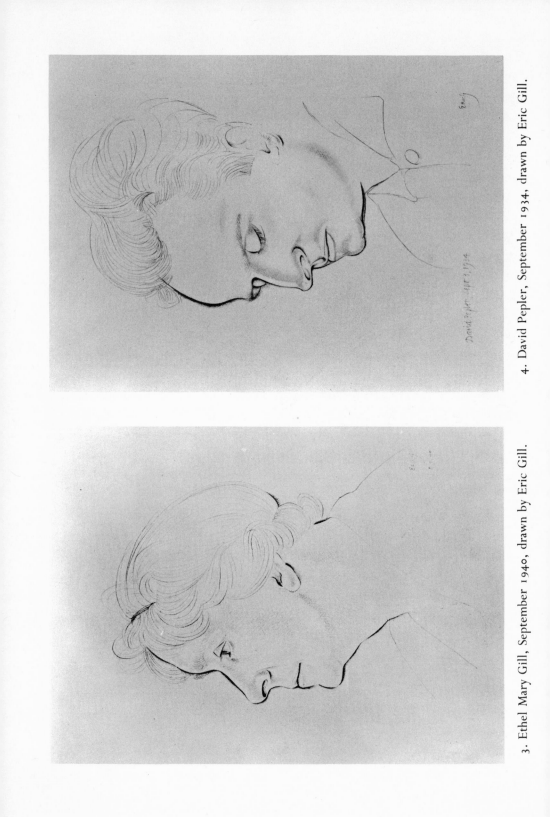

4. David Pepler, September 1934, drawn by Eric Gill.

3. Ethel Mary Gill, September 1940, drawn by Eric Gill.

matters for himself, he never toyed with anything so second-rate as a private religion of his own.

The family moved to Cliftonville Road, and afterwards to Preston View, Highcroft Villas, in Dyke Road Drive. The back garden of the house overlooked the sidings of the railway station – an appropriate nursery for one who was to spend so much of his life on the London, Brighton and South Coast Railway. Eric, with his sisters, was sent to a kindergarten school kept by the Misses Browne, quite near by. They were the daughters of 'Phiz', the illustrator of Dickens; so presumably they did not discourage the boy from drawing. Already, at the age of 10, he was editing a Monthly Magazine of Fun and Frolic with Enid and Cicely. This was priced at 1d, and it was liberally illustrated with locomotives, windmills, suspension bridges, telegraph wires, disappearing carriages, goods trains, horses and traps. The number for March 1892 also contained advertisements for Van Houten's cocoa, Baker's Hosiery, Pears Soap and Mellins Food. There was a picture of the Brighton Paddle Steamer and 'the house I shall build for us to live in in Preston'. Another illustration, called 'A Picture of Everything', was a surrealist compendium of everything that mattered to Eric at that time; a bridge, a tunnel, some houses and railway lines, a football, a windmill and some troops.

From 1891–2 Mrs Gill had the help of Helena Hall, a girl of 18, who remained a valued friend of the family. She would help Eric with his homework, and he would give her pictures of his engines which she stuck up on the wall of her room. But the family were too poor to keep her long, and Mrs Gill had once more to make her immense rice puddings by herself. She also made all the children's clothes, and when the twins – Evan and Vernon – arrived unexpectedly one Sunday afternoon, the baby linen was in desperately short supply.

A large family can amuse itself, and one of the Children's Programmes (c. 1893) is an indication of contemporary taste. The deaths of Nelson, Harold, and Mary Queen of Scots were reproduced in tableaux; Jack and Jill were shown in three postures – going up the hill, falling down, and tucked up in bed. Then refreshments were served, followed by the singing of 'All things bright and beautiful', and the recital of 'The Destruction of an Army' by Eric and 'A Psalm of Life' by Cicely.

Among the younger brothers, Max and Romney were inseparable, and Eric was rather left out on his own. Another jotting of Mr Gill's leaves us a picture of him 'finding his way home when we thought he had lost it – and us – very bravely. May he find his way thus bravely "Home" at the last – nay, may he never be in danger of losing it.' There are further sketches of Enid playing with Eric's bricks; and of a thorn taken from Eric's finger 'with much sorrow and crying'; and the note of a prize awarded him – perhaps the first prize he ever got – for pulling out a tooth by himself; and the record of him heedlessly running 'up against the second lamp post in Stanford Road' and receiving 'an ugly wound on the forehead' and losing 'much blood on the pavement'.

When he had learnt all that the Misses Browne and Helena Hall could teach him, he was sent to Arnold House School at 51–2 Cromwell Road, Hove. This was the successor to Western College where his father had taught in the 1880s. Since the children of the English middle classes spend so much of their time in learning how to use every language except their own, and since Eric had no aptitude for foreign tongues, and never much taste for foreign ways, he was not a particularly bright pupil. He sat for a scholarship at Bradfield, but was floored by the Latin papers, although he managed the arithmetic and the algebra pretty well. Certainly his schooling did him no harm, even if it only taught him what was wrong with schools. Since the school in question disappeared, and the headmaster became a cigar merchant, it was not perhaps a very good school. And no lesson in the classroom taught him as much as the sight of Ranjitsinhji batting at Hove.

'Does the county cricketer,' asks Neville Cardus, 'realize what he looks like in the eyes of a boy; what an obligation he has not to let down and abuse young faith and vision?';[1] and Eric watched 'Ranji' – in 'Ranji's' own phrase – transform 'the single-stringed instrument

[1] *Cricket*, 1930.

into the many-chorded lyre'. The memory of this – of its grace and power and discipline – never left him. 'Even now,' he wrote shortly before his death, 'when I want to have a little quiet wallow in the thought of something wholly delightful and perfect, I think of "Ranji" on the County Ground at Hove.'[1] Eric realized that games were played, as lessons were taught, for the wrong reasons. What mattered was not how many matches you won, but the skill required in the winning or losing of them. 'That boy is easily led' was not a pleasant remark for a schoolboy to overhear from one of his teachers, and it caused Eric some temporary heart-burning. But he came to appreciate its truth. He was a leader himself, because he respected leadership. *Sine auctoritate nulla vita* – this was as true in art as it was true in religion. Eric Gill was sometimes described as a rebel; but like his father he rebelled in the name of authority.

Mr Gill's rebellion took him further than the Countess of Huntingdon's Connexion. After all, if one were taking one's religion on authority, there were better authorities than the Countess of Huntingdon. It was at least possible that in a dispute between the Countess and the Church of England, the Church of England might have been in the right. And so in 1897 Mr and Mrs Gill joined the Church of England. Some people said that they did so for snobbish reasons; church was always better 'class' than chapel. As a curate in North Street Mr Gill had an income of £150 a year, supplemented by the fees for teaching a single private pupil, a few subscriptions, and odd cast-off clothes from relations and friends. It was not very much on which to bring up a family of eleven, with the eldest only 16. If the Gills hoped for easier conditions in the Establishment, they could have been forgiven for making a ready pact with episcopacy. It was even rumoured that the Bishop of Chichester refused to accept Mr Gill as a candidate for Holy Orders because he doubted the sincerity of his conversion. His successor, however, Bishop Wilberforce, was less unworthily sceptical and received him as a student at Chichester Theological College. Whatever Mr Gill may have hoped – or other people have believed that he was hoping for – the change brought him

[1] *Autobiography*, 1940.

no material advantage. But for Eric it opened the windows on to a new world.

His first intimation of the move was on a Sunday morning when his father, without a word of explanation, took him into St Peter's Church, a dignified building in the Steyne. It seemed an uncomfortable place to worship in when you compared it with the cushioned ease of the Countess' conventicle. No reason was given for the visit – perhaps Mr Gill wanted to hear the sermon – but very soon the family were attending services at the old parish church of Preston – quiet, essential Anglicanism with its congregation of all and sundry, and the sunlight streaming through the coloured glass. Here the Liturgy supported the preacher; not the other way about. There was the possibility of contemplation, if by contemplation one means the surrender of personality to a mystery infinitely larger than oneself. Naturally this was beyond Eric's understanding at the time, and beyond his criticism also; but there was a whiff of adventure about the place, and the children were at one with their father and mother in preferring it to the sectarianism in which they had been reared. So Mr Gill preached his last sermon in North Street; the hat was passed round; the tradesmen's bills were paid; and in due course the family saw him off to Chichester. It is safe to guess that Eric had an expert eye for the locomotive.

2

Eric was by now 15 and locomotives had become a serious interest. He used rulers and compasses, but measurement and proportion were calculated by the eye alone. English locomotives were elegant and powerful machines, but Eric was interested by their purpose rather than their prettiness. He was only concerned with their shape in so far as this was dictated by the work they had to do. In fact he played with the idea of becoming a railway engineer long before he thought of becoming an artist in lettering or stone. But when his father took him to see a friend who was an engineer (not of locomotives) he was confused by the diagrams of stresses and strains, and the talk of reservoirs and hydraulics. A locomotive was a very individual thing, and in his long life of making Eric was always fashioning the individual object. This was in part a reflection of his own individuality, though he did not understand individuality as it was understood by the modern world.

The family remained at Brighton while Mr Gill was studying at the Theological College, and one day Eric bicycled over to see him. The visit inspired a new train of momentous comparisons. He suddenly saw Brighton – his Brighton – for what it was; a meaningless congerie of slums and suburbs, camouflaged by a Regency façade. But Chichester was a city with meaning. It had a market and cathedral. It was reasonably planned, with its four main intersecting streets, built upon the Roman design, and reminiscent of the Roman order. It was beautiful because it made no pretensions to be picturesque. The villages he passed on the way, or which lurked in the hollows of the Downs – Shoreham and Steyning, Bramber and Beeding, Patcham and Poynings – these too belonged to nature and to man in a way that Brighton did not. Chichester was 'something as human as home and as lovely as heaven'.[1] Eric knew enough about home to know that

[1] *Autobiography*, 1940.

it was lovable, and he had heard enough about heaven to believe that it was lovelier still.

But a great sorrow came now to cross this vision of relative beatitude. His favourite sister Cicely died on January 18, 1897, at the age of 14. She was only a year younger than Eric, and her death stood up before him as a fact of life instead of a 'fact of natural history'.[1] Nothing remained of their close companionship but the text on her grave in the cemetery – ΤΑΛΙΘΑ ΚΥΜΙ;[2] it was a beautiful text, but it could not restore the dead to life. And so the move to Chichester came not only to open a vision but to fill a void. Mr Gill was ordained and given a curacy at the Subdeanery Church, St Peter's in West Street. He received a salary of £90 a year – little more than half of what he had earned in Brighton, so the imputations of mercenary motive were effectively belied. The family were now living at 2 North Walls, and buildings took the place of locomotives as the target of Eric's observation. He still did not measure his drawings, but his father had taught him the laws of perspective. Accuracy was always his aim – to draw a thing as it was, not as it might be or ought to be. His main interest was in churches, and especially in Chichester Cathedral. Here again it was the public purpose, not the private appeal, which inspired him. What was a cathedral for? He would not, of course, have put it as clearly as that; but beyond the look of the thing – and the look was lovely – were the things that went on inside it. What he would afterwards define as the liturgical sense was already awakening within him.

Mr Gill himself had a talent for oil-painting. 'Ah my boy,' he would say, 'I ought to have been an artist.' Recognizing Eric's talent, he sent him as a whole-day student to the Chichester Technical and Art School. In the Fitzwilliam Museum, Cambridge, there are two ink and wash drawings of his done about this time – in 1898. One of them is a view of Chichester Cathedral from the West Pallant, and the other is of St Richard's Walk. They are quite unlike any other drawings of his that I have seen – very exact, but with the romantic

[1] *Autobiography*, 1940.
[2] Maiden sleeping.

overtones of a Victorian print. He also made a sketch of Portfield church for the cover of the Parish Magazine – the first job for which he was paid. Although he had won a Queen's Medal for perspective drawing, the object of the Art School was clearly to produce art masters rather than artists; and all Eric's devotion to his teacher – George Herbert Catt – could not reconcile him to this dismal prospect. Meanwhile he developed an enthusiasm for church music, sitting by the hour in the cathedral choir-stalls, playing football with the choirboys, and making friends with the head verger. He was given the keys of the cathedral and came to know it by heart, climbing up the spire, wandering through the clerestories, and listening to the music, unperceived, from whatever Gothic altitude he could reach. The experience was of decisive importance, because it not only directed his musical taste along paths which it would never leave, but taught him, as nothing else could have taught him, how a cathedral was made and what it was meant for.

He found two other friends at court. One was the Prebendary, Richard Codrington, who invited him to tea; and in return Eric and Max, in their Sunday clothes, swept away from the Prebendary's flower bed the bricks fallen from his garden wall. Codrington was an erudite antiquarian who, nevertheless, ridiculed the idea that modern Gothic should try to look like its ancestor. Possibly he had in mind the ravages of Viollet-le-Duc. The other was the assistant organist of the cathedral, Osmund Daughtry, who cured Eric of his enthusiasm for Mendelssohn and Stanford, and introduced him to Beethoven and Mozart, Handel and Bach, Corelli and Purcell, and earlier masters of English church music. This was the music that Eric enjoyed to his dying day, and in 1898 the introduction to it was 'as new and exciting and almost as unexpected' an experience as 'the city of Chichester after a childhood in Brighton'.[1]

His third passion was lettering. He had begun with the careful lettering of locomotives' names. After all, names were important; they gave a thing identity. And this led on to handwriting. Eric, with his native and as yet hardly recognized itch for reform, started

[1] *Autobiography*, 1940.

addressing his father on paper as 'Father' – a return to bare essentials which offended Mr Gill a good deal. Of course Mr Catt had the most extravagantly decorative ideas of lettering on which Eric was later to look back with disgust. In calligraphy, as in so much else, the Victorians could not leave a good thing alone. But at the time he did his best to imitate the swirls and squibbles which were supposed to differentiate art from utility in what was certainly among the most useful of the arts. Nevertheless, Eric's preoccupation with lettering had even more important consequences than his interest in architecture; and it preceded by some time his interest in sculpture. He was happy in his work, but he was not happy in himself. A tentative and adolescent love affair with a girl at the Art School got him into trouble with Mr Catt, who may also have realized that Eric had no intention of following in his own footsteps. Moreover, the complacency of cathedral Anglicanism was no more inspiring than the embarrassing fervour of the Countess of Huntingdon's Connexion. The boy became restless and dissatisfied, questioning and rebellious. Fortunately at this difficult moment Dr Codrington secured him a place in the office of W. H. Caroe, architect to the Ecclesiastical Commissioners in London, and at the same time Mr Gill went to a curacy at St John's, Bognor. Chichester, for all its charm, had proved no abiding city after all.

3

The offices of the architect to the Ecclesiastical Commissioners, Mr Caroe, were at 8A Whitehall Place,[1] Westminster. Eric worked with several others in the basement. 'So far I like the work very much indeed', he wrote to Robert Heaps, Lay Vicar of Chichester Cathedral.

The chaps in the office are all right on the whole though some are rather fast. One thing must be said for them, and that is they are extremely good-natured on the whole. I have a permit to sketch in the Abbey which of course is quite close. I have been working there all this afternoon. I very frequently go there during my dinner hour. I go to St Paul's to hear the music which I like very much there. They are in very good training just now, I think. (June 9, 1900)

Eric had been taken on as an apprentice at a specially low premium and he had only 10s a week for his meals and incidental expenses. He lodged at 68 Victoria Road, Clapham – the Church Club, next to St Saviour's Church. These were supposed to be respectable surroundings, and Dr Codrington's brother, Oliver, lived near by. Eric's mood – a common one at his age – was one of uncertainty and revolt. The Ecclesiastical Commissioners were the capitalist face of the Church of England; their interest in architecture was purely commercial. Eric was still saddled with his upbringing – a good enough upbringing of its kind – and he joined his parents, who had now become Liberal Unionists, in cheering on Sir Redvers Buller in his remarkably unsuccessful and doubtfully justified campaigns. He even found himself drilling with the Queen's Westminster Volunteer Corps, while Evan and Vernon were going around in khaki caps. In other respects, however, he was riding loose to his moorings, and was only steadied by the friendship of his fellow-pupil, George Christopher Carter.

[1] Now demolished.

We have noted Eric's admission that he was easily led; but every intelligent person likes to be led, and one proof of his intelligence is the people he chooses to lead him. In this respect Eric had shown remarkable judgment. The Prebendary, the art master, the assistant organist, and now George Carter – he sat at the feet of them all in devoted discipleship and with lasting profit to himself. Carter would accompany him on his lunch hour visits to the Abbey, and Eric would lean on Carter's moral and intellectual integrity. He had 'all the virtues and all the gifts'.[1] He seemed to Eric perfect, as his sister Cicely had been perfect. He taught him that architecture was not a matter of style, but a matter of building. It was only incidentally a matter of plans, and the plans that came down from Mr Caroe quickly seemed irrelevant and sentimental with their expensive recipes for sham Gothic and unnecessary ornament. The idea that good architecture depended on the way you lived and prayed – on your beliefs about God and man – was a revolutionary idea in the 1890s; but Eric and Carter were not the only revolutionaries in Mr Caroe's office.

Eric had, of course, been to London before. During visits to his relations on Blackheath he had been taken to see the sights. He had been fascinated by St Paul's Cathedral – not only by the solemn music and ordered ceremonial, but by the whispering gallery and the foggy mist in the dome. At Westminster Abbey he had admired the stress of the vaulting and the simple tracery of the windows, the work of architects who had not yet become too clever. That, he would discover, was the trouble about all making – the overweening cleverness of the makers. But for the time being he had seen London through a mist of romanticism; and every young provincial has seen it so. Its architecture – to adapt the *mot* of Whitman – had been what you did to a building when you looked at it. In 1899, however, Eric looked at it with different eyes. He might be reacting against the complacencies of Chichester, but he was equally sensitive to the shabby and suburban sprawl of London. On his occasional free day he would make sketches of St Paul's as well as the Abbey. One of these (of St

[1] *Autobiography*, 1940.

Paul's seen from Fleet Street) was acquired by H. E. Seccombe in exchange for the reproduction of a drawing by Rossetti of Mrs William Morris. Eric would go back a long way behind Rossetti and William Morris, but it is the whole point of his story that he walked – he was perhaps the last to walk – in the trail which they had blazed. Already we find him reading Ruskin in the Seccombe's garden.

It is a curious fact that the favourite joke among the apprentices in Mr Caroe's office was the Church of England. Of course the Church of England is quite used to being treated as a joke, and it has shown a remarkable capacity for surviving the laugh. Even someone who is not a member of that Church may be permitted to wonder whether the laugh is not occasionally on the other side. Be that as it may, Eric was quickly, and inevitably, caught up in the fashionable agnostic current. He rejected, reasonably enough, the fundamentalist interpretation of the Bible to which many Christians of all denominations still clung. Instead of going to church on Good Friday he would pick the buttercups with his sister Angela. He was fascinated by H. G. Wells and hypnotized by *Omar Khayyám*. For several months on end he read *Sartor Resartus* at breakfast. He devoured the sixpenny tracts of the Rationalist Press Association and the rather more respectable brochures of the Fabian Society. He discovered *Unto This Last*, and *The Seven Lamps of Architecture*, which he possessed in a first edition. He called himself a Socialist and sported a flowing red tie and red socks. He had seen the ugliness of capitalist-industrialism and, although he had little experience of factory-hands, he deduced their degradation from the objects they were compelled to produce. He was less concerned with the indifference of the rich and the unhappiness of the poor than with the status of the workers; less concerned with how much money they got, or ought to get, than with the work they did or ought to do. With the political and economic means of their emancipation he was, at this time, hardly concerned at all. Although he had never heard of Péguy, what he was reaching after was the *cité harmonieuse*.

He had immediately to decide whether the profession of architect was one that he could honestly pursue – and he concluded that it was not. The only kind of buildings he wanted to put up were functional buildings in brick or stone, and there was no market for functional buildings in 1900. Even if there had been, their erection would have depended on servile and irresponsible labour. How far the labour that goes towards the erection of a modern building is in fact servile and irresponsible is a very complicated question, but it is a question that Eric cheerfully begged. Rather than be a designer at his desk he would prefer to be a workman at his bench. Cost what it might, he would begin his revolution at home. He would dignify his own status, even if he could not dignify other people's. And so, with the encouragement of George Carter, he gave the lectures on architecture a miss, and went instead to the Westminster Technical Institute to learn about masonry, and to the LCC Central School of Arts and Crafts in Upper Regent Street to learn about lettering.

After a few months he was cutting letters in stone. The first of these inscriptions[1] was doubtless inspired by a wall tablet in Westminster Abbey: 'IANE LISTER dear childe died Oct. 7 1688.' Eric's inscription simply read: JANE LISTER A DEAR CHILD. It was unsigned, but on the top right-hand corner was noted: 'My first inscpt.' This was followed in 1901 by a stone tablet in Chichester Cathedral in memory of Percy Joseph Hiscock, and foundation stones for the cloister of Charterhouse School at Godalming and for St Michael's Church, Edmonton. Early in 1902 he was recommended to a Mr J. D. Batten who wanted an inscription for his father's tombstone in Brookwood Cemetery, Surrey. This took him three months' work in the evening, and he was paid £5 for his labour. Then Batten recommended him to John Tweed, an eminent architect, who commissioned an inscription for the outside wall of Holy Trinity Church, Sloane Street. This was in memory of Admiral Sir George Ommaney Willes, GCB (1823–1901), and it recorded the gift of gates and railings erected by his widow. From now on Eric was never out of a job.

But the Central School brought him something more valuable than these two commissions. On the evening of September 21, 1899, he

[1] Now in the possession of Mrs René Hague.

be touched which were essential to the safety of the cross; and where a carved stone had to be replaced, it was better to cut a new one to a contemporary (but not a conflicting) design. There was also a proposal to remove the bell-cote; but although the workmanship of this was inferior to that of the cross itself, Eric viewed with dismay the 'quasi-Gothic' erection which had been designed to replace it. The most interesting point about this letter of 1901 is that it might just as well have been written in 1940. Both the principle and the style are fixed.

From January 1, 1902, Eric began to keep a diary – a habit which he continued until his death. It recorded his doings rather than his thoughts, although occasionally the thought breaks in. In the early London years his minutest expenses are put down; even when he 'spends a penny' he says so. We find him reading anything that comes to his hand from William Morris and *Wilhelm Meister* – 'what can be finer than *Wilhelm Meister?*' – to Marcus Aurelius, Selborne's *Natural History*, *As You Like It*, Walter Pater, and *The Prisoner of Zenda*. He listens to Wagner at the Queen's Hall, and Gounod at St Paul's Cathedral. He sees *The Importance of Being Earnest* at the St James's. He pays 3d to go up the Monument, and 1s to ascend the campanile of Westminster Cathedral or to purchase a cigar. He goes to the National Gallery and, more often, to the British Museum. Then, in the spring of 1902, came an unexpected stroke of luck. In April Edward Johnston wrote to his fiancée from his rooms at 16 Old Buildings, Lincoln's Inn:

I have been thinking about a plan to let a deserving young architect have the other half of my bedroom. It will make a considerable change in my régime, tho' it will not affect expenses at present one way or the other. I hope Mr Gill will earn more money presently, and then he will be able materially to reduce my rent. He is the stone-mason who is cutting the tombstone for Mr Batten. I hope the plan will be good.[1]

A month later Eric moved in, and Johnston writes again:

Gill came on Saturday and has quite settled in. He improves on acquaint-

[1] Quoted in *Edward Johnston*, 1959.

ance and I think we shall get on very well together. . . . Gill has been reading *Literature and Dogma*, and reading a few lines to me now and again. We have had a number of pretty warm arguments on the matter. I object to destroyers of creeds who have no equivalent ready to offer for the shelter they have pulled down. I object to the appeal to 'science' combined with unscientific statement. I object to rhetoric displacing logic . . . but I will not say more till I have read the book.[1]

Evidently Johnston had been putting on the brakes.

[1] Quoted in *Edward Johnston*, 1959.

4

In the early hours of October 25, 1902, Eric set off on his bicycle and rode to Chichester. He arrived at 9 a.m. The entry in his diary for that day contains the single word 'sweetheart'. This was Ethel Mary Moore, daughter to the Beadle of Chichester Cathedral. Mr Moore was also a prosperous nurseryman, a profession that might have been deduced from the scent of lavender that hung about his four-poster beds. The Moores were better off than the Gills, and Ethel – or Ettie, as she was known to Eric – helped him with small sums of money, which he would repay as he was able to. Sometimes she came to London and he would take her out; more often he bicycled, or went by train, to Chichester. He bought her small presents of books or gloves or chocolates; and on June 22, 1903, he bought her an engagement ring. She rode him on the curb until they were married, and Eric's temperament felt the strain. On an expedition to Arundel and Burpham in December we find the entry: 'O cruel, cruel: O Ethel forgive me.'

Fortunately he continued to be busy. The controversy over the Chichester Market Cross dragged on until January 26, 1903. A certain Mr Frith Bailey wrote to the local *Observer* suggesting its removal on the grounds that it was holding up the traffic. Mr Bailey cited as a precedent the removal of Temple Bar and the Marble Arch.[1] Eric, abetted by George Carter, replied anonymously to this proposal. Why not erect the cross in Chichester's Jubilee Park and convert it into a bandstand? If it were not big enough for this, why not surmount it with a 'cast iron glass and bric-à-brac canopy, supported on atrocious cast iron columns'? Or if this were not feasible, why not transplant it to the cathedral yard, where visiting photographers

---

[1] Author's note: In the second instance he was incorrect. The Marble Arch was isolated, but not disturbed, in accordance with a plan conceived by my father and accepted by the Office of Works.

could include the cross and the cathedral in a single snapshot? Eric's previous intervention had been welcomed by a prominent local architect, Edward Prior, and after this happy essay in sarcasm the two men became acquainted. Prior wrote to the *Observer* in support, and Eric, forsaking his anonymity, sent him a letter of thanks. Prior invited him to tea and offered him the job of cutting some inscriptions on the new Medical School at Cambridge. It was the moment of decision. If he were to accept the work at Cambridge, he could not continue in the architect's office. Without consulting anyone, and without even a personal interview with Mr Caroe – for it is always easier to do these things by letter – he set off to Cambridge. Caroe magnanimously gave him his articles and a certificate of three years' work, with a promise of future commissions for lettering, as opportunity occurred.

Another commission came to him through Prior: the inscription on the church gate at Great Warley, near Ingatestone in Essex. 'I will strengthen thee, yea, I will help thee.' Meanwhile he was giving private lessons, and on at least one occasion taking Edward Johnston's class. On September 17 (1903), Johnston returned from Scotland with his newly married wife. Many years later, on the occasion of Mrs Johnston's death, Eric told Johnston what this marriage of his master had meant to him.

I was so moved, excited, all of a tremble, that I stood in the middle of the street outside what was then the Central School . . . so that I might see you through the window of the room where the writing class was. I was so overwhelmingly in love with my girl, and with you. Your marriage was a type of all heavenly fruitions and consummations. I had to look at you from a distance, in secret, before I dared approach. . . . I only want you to know, as I think you have not known before, that, as I think, your marriage meant more to me than to anyone else in the whole world except to you and your wife. (April 1936)[1]

Shortly before his marriage Johnston had moved to Gray's Inn, where Eric often called on him. 'Gill shall have the sofa and Rooke the camp bed,' Johnston had told his fiancée. 'Gill is now preparing

[1] Quoted in *Edward Johnston*, 1959.

Dearest, just a morning greeting to my Love +
I want to ask you dear what size writing
would look best for me to write the
psalms in. I thought about as large as
this or do you think dearest a little larger
would look better? And shall I write them

in italics or like this? We have been to the

Cathedral this afternoon + The service was
"Walmsley in D minor" please excuse this
writing dear Love I am merely amusing
myself as you will observe

+ Eric + Ethel +
+   +

Letter in red and black ink, to Ethel Mary Gill.

dinner, a large tongue, toast, nice butter, etc., etc. I am going to take this to Euston, where the late fee letters are collected, and as Gill likes engines, etc., he's coming with me.' Old hobbies die hard.

A week or two after Johnston's return, Eric attended the life class, and for the first time exulted at the sight of a naked woman. 'This is a privilege I am not yet oblivious of,' he wrote in his diary. In June he was still drilling with the Queen's Westminsters and being inspected by Lord Roberts, and in November he was shooting at Bisley. In December he was in Paris, lettering the signboard of W. H. Smith's shop in the Rue de Rivoli, paying two francs to an interpreter and one to go up the Eiffel Tower; and in the spring of 1904 he was moving to 13 Battersea Bridge Buildings.

On August 6 he was married to Ethel Moore by his father, assisted by Dr Codrington and the Reverend Spencer Walker, in the Sub-deanery Church at Chichester; and now for the first time there appears in his diary a particular 'hieroglyph' which always means the same thing. He took his bride back to their rooms in Battersea with £15 in the Bank, 'a bed, a table, some chairs, and a few knives and forks'[1] and the top hat he was married in. One feels pretty sure that the combined persuasions of Moores and Gills had enforced the latter conformity; and one suspects that this was the last occasion in his life when Eric could have been mistaken for a member of the upper middle classes. The blissful slumbers of the young couple were disturbed by a conflagration next door, where a timber yard had caught fire. The smoke poured into their bedroom, and the flames set the walls of it aglow. The next afternoon they paraded in Battersea Park with the other married couples and, as Eric was afterwards to write,[2] they lived happily ever afterwards.

In 1904 Eric received his first commission from Count Kessler. This was to produce drawn titles and headings for the *Grossherzog Wilhelm Ernst* edition of the German Classics published in twenty-one volumes by Insel Verlag, Leipzig (1905–11). Later on he was to engrave, on wood, decorated initial letters designed by Maillol for

[1] *Autobiography*, 1940.
[2] ibid.

GAUGUIN

. . . .

ZWEITER BAND
WELCHER DIE ERGÄNZUNGEN
ZU DEN VIER BÜCHERN DES ER-
STEN BANDES ENTHÄLT——————

Paucis natus est, qui populum aetatis suae cogitat.
Sen.

. . . .

HONORE DE

BALZAC's

MENSCHLICHE
KOMÖDIE
I BAND

Lettering for the Cranach Presse, Weimar, including a design for the
title page of a new German edition of Balzac.

Virgil's *Eclogues*. This was printed by Kessler's Cranach Presse at Weimar and published by Insel Verlag in 1926. In December Eric was inscribing the Ten Commandments on the eastern panels of Byefield Parish in Northamptonshire, for which Christopher Carter had built the chancel. His total earnings for 1904 amounted to £158 18s 11d, and he started the new year with a balance of £75 3s 5d. He could afford to think of buying further kettles, teapots, saucepans, chairs, plate racks, brooms, porridge saucepans and sink dishes; and a double bed – if he could find one in the Walworth Road. He was lettering more signboards for W. H. Smith & Son, at Southport, Leicester and Burnley. Indeed it was by these signboards up and down the country that Eric's work became most familiar to the British public. Like so much of his best work they bear no signature except the authority of perfect workmanship. At the same time he was giving classes in gilding at the Central School.

With all this activity the need for a studio became urgent. He acquired one in Upper Cheyne Row, but was forced to leave it because the noise of stone-cutting disturbed the painters at their neighbouring easels. The birth of his eldest daughter, Elizabeth, on June 1, reduced the amenities while it increased the population of the Battersea home, and by October he was already house hunting. A month later he had installed the family at 20 Black Lion Lane, Hammersmith, with a converted stable as a workshop. 'We shall have two bedrooms', he had written to his mother, '(one larger than the one we have), a larger sitting-room, quite a nice-sized entrance hall, a wider kitchen, a closet inside the flat instead of outside, and last but not least windows looking on to the south and west right over the river. So therefore all the morning and afternoon sun.'[1] Ethel had her own room upstairs, which you reached by a wooden loft staircase; and there she worked on her gold leaf, holding an agate stone to her abundant hair 'to get electricity'. Eric had carved the words – 'My love is like a red, red rose' – on an oblong mirror, and Ethel covered the frame with gold leaf. At other times she played on the rosewood piano while Eric played the flute. One gets the impression

[1] December 18, 1904.

of a house spick and span and sparsely furnished with its red curtains and rush mats and bare, stained boards.

At Hammersmith the Gills were more accessible to friends. Cobden-Sanderson would drop in at the workshop and the Sydney Cockerells to tea. The Johnstons also came regularly, and on July 26, 1905, Edward wrote Eric the following testimonial, which secured him a teachership at the Central School:

I have known Mr Gill for several years and have been much interested in his most valuable work. Mr Gill's work is made the more valuable by his sense of architectural fitness. I am glad to be able to testify to his knowledge of lettering – both theoretical and practical – to say that I consider him in every way fitted to conduct a class in inscription, cutting and monumental masonry.

In August Eric was appointed teacher of monumental masonry and lettering for stonemasons at the LCC Paddington Institute. He gave his classes twice a week, and was flattered that 100 students turned up for the first of them. He now regularly attended the meetings of the Fabian Society, where H. G. Wells would talk about the future and Bernard Shaw would talk about Darwin. Or he would go to a meeting of the ILP at which Cobden-Sanderson talked about H. G. Wells. Then there were the regular Saturday meetings of Edward Johnston's 'Society' at Lincoln's Inn. This consisted of four members, E. C. Laughton, Noel Rooke, Eric, and Johnston himself; and for a time Eric acted as Secretary. There was no lack, in these early days of the new century, of clever people putting the world to rights. It was at a meeting of the Fabian Society that Eric first met William Rothenstein, and at an At Home at the Cobden-Sandersons that he met the sister of William Morris. The new movement was reflected in the Vedrenne-Barker season at the Royal Court Theatre, where the young dramatists no doubt seemed as angry as they do today. The Gills went twice to *Major Barbara* – 'wonderful', exclaims Eric in his diary – and twice to *Captain Brassbound's Conversion*. They also saw William Poel's famous production of *Everyman* at the Coronet. They were in the swim.

The Society
(Name at present unknown)

Preliminary meeting: Sunday: 25 Feb. 1906. 4.P.M
　　　　　　　　　at 20 Black Lion Lane, Hammersmith, W.
Present: A.E.R.Gill, Edward Johnston, E.C.Laughton, Noel Rooke.

Aggenda: To discuss objects and methods of the Society.
　　　　The discussion took the form of two readings.
　　　　I. Chap III. Par. 7 of Wells' 'A Modern Utopia'
　　　　II 'The Arts & Crafts Movement' by T.J. Cobden Sanderson.
　　　　The former as representing a specific practical application.
　　　　The latter as representing 'Ideals'.
　　　　A.E.R.Gill was elected secretary.
　　　　Suggested by Ed. Johnston that for the present no subscription
　　　　should be asked, but that the Secretary's expenses should be
　　　　paid in equal shares by those members present.　　Agreed.
　　　　Suggested by Ed. Johnston that desirable members might be
　　　　roughly defined as: Those who are sincerely sympathetic, &
　　　　who have some definite line, and who have no axe to grind.
　　　　Agreed.
　　　　A.E.R.Gill gave a short account of the movements that had
　　　　led to the forming of the Society.
　　　　Meeting closed at 7.30.
　　　　Aggenda agreed to for next meeting on Mar. 11:
　　　　　　'The Aims of the Society' each member to come
　　　　　　prepared to speak.

Signed by order:　　　　　　　　A.E.R.Gill.

Minutes of the first meeting of 'The Society', February 1906.

They had not been able to afford a honeymoon, but in the spring of 1906 the Central School awarded Eric a prize of £20 for an inscription. With this he took Ethel on a Cook's Tour to Rome. It was a professional visit and he spent much of his time studying the ancient inscriptions with a letter cutter's and signwriter's job in mind. They went back several times to the Forum; thought Raphael's loggia in the Vatican a little pallid after the Sistine Chapel; walked along the Appian Way and admired the aqueducts; marvelled at San Clemente; had tea in the Pincio Gardens; went out to the Villa d'Este and missed the waterfall; and attended High Mass at St Peter's on Easter Sunday, but came away because the place was 'bung full' and they 'couldn't see a thing'.[1] Normally they should have seen the Pope – who is on these occasions literally head and shoulders above everyone else – but if they had, they would not perhaps have been very interested. Eric, when he came to make up his mind on the matter, was the least Roman of Roman Catholics; no man who counted so many ecclesiastics among his friends was in himself so little ecclesiastical.

The Gills already had a maid and now, in May 1906, Eric acquired an apprentice. Joseph Cribb came, and stayed with him for many years; the time would come when even an expert eye would have found it hard to distinguish between an inscription by Eric and an inscription by Cribb – and that was just as Eric would have wanted it. He was busy besides with noteheads for W. H. Smith at 186 Strand, and with a sign for their shop in Fetter Lane. He was now seeing a good deal of William Rothenstein, who was in general sympathy with his ideas. He did a Latin inscription for Rothenstein's portrait of George Edward Baker, the Bursar of Magdalen College, Oxford, and a lettering job for the New English Art Club came to him in the same way. He went to the meetings of the Art Workers Guild, listening to J. W. Mackail talk on William Morris, or Rothenstein on Hogarth. He lectured to their junior branch himself on inscriptions. At the same time he was feeling his hand at wood-engraving. It was a period of intense and varied activity, during which his Fabian associa-

[1] *Autobiography*, 1940.

tions grew closer. He heard Shaw speak on Socialism and Art, and was a member of the Special Committee set up to report on this subject. 'I am heart and soul for the Special Committee', he wrote in his diary. He also wrote a pamphlet in support of the Labour candidates at the Borough elections. There was a second visit to *Captain Brassbound*; he saw *You Can Never Tell* with Johnston, and *Man and Superman* with his sister Gladys, and heard Harley Granville-Barker read Gilbert Murray's translation of *The Trojan Women* at the Kensington Town Hall. In the evenings, when he was not otherwise occupied, he amused himself with photography; and sometimes, during the day, Edward Johnston read Plato to him and Ethel in the workshop. There was never a moment wasted.

The Gills had a few days of anxiety when Elizabeth – Betty, as she was known in the family – ran a temperature of 105, but this passed and Ethel gave birth to a second daughter, Petra, on August 18, 1906. It had been a good year, with an income of £553 11s 6d balancing an expenditure of £478 4s 4d. New friendships had been formed, notably with A. R. Orage to whom Eric was introduced by Johnston. Orage took him to a meeting of the Theosophical Society, where he was speaking on Human Consciousness. Other new influences were making themselves felt, and the most important of these was Nietzsche. Eric would read *Zarathustra* by the hour, and this was connected with the only cloud that ever darkened his domestic horizon. The wind of liberty was blowing pretty strongly through the circles in which he moved, and the wind of liberty is often a wind of change. He became strongly attracted to a girl he had met at the Fabian Society – she may have been a member of the Arts and Philosophical Group to which Eric also belonged, since she presented him with *Zarathustra* – and the attachment developed into a full-blown love affair. Ethel knew her too, and there was one occasion, humiliating for all parties, when she came to the girl's house at a time when Eric was there, and was unable to get in.

In February (1907) he was giving her writing lessons; and on March 7, after listening to William Rothenstein's lecture on Art and Religion, the three of them – husband, wife and mistress – sat up talking till 5 a.m. Eric and Ethel continued the conversation – not a pleasant one, presumably – till 6.15. The following day the girl came to supper, and as a result of this she and Eric decided to have no more to do with one another; Eric's diary has the following laconic entry: 'A.E.R.G. decides to fulfil all obligations to E.' The resolution was short-lived, for he saw the girl again the following day, and at the end of the month he was whisking her off to Chartres for the Easter week-end. It was in the glow, therefore, of a romantic liaison that Eric received the stunning revelation of what he was afterwards to describe as 'the holiest thing ever made in stone'. On their way back they heard the *Walküre* at the Paris Opera. Eric was a very temporary Wagnerian and thought the music, on the whole, 'of Titans, not of Dionysus'[1] – and on the following evening they were both listening to Orage on 'Nietzsche versus Socialism' at the Reform Club. But Eric had been stunned in more ways than one. When he said goodnight to his girl that evening it was goodbye to all that.

They remained friends, however, and it was not long before Ethel and the girl had 'made it up'. Two days later they were all three listening to a concert performance of *Tristan* at the Queen's Hall – rather a tactless choice in the circumstances. This was followed by a lecture on the Samurai Idea by H. G. Wells – not in his best form – and before the evening was out the girl was suggesting that if she could not be Eric's mistress, might she not be his apprentice – at least on a six months' trial? She came on May 1, and we find her with Eric and her fellow-apprentice, Joseph Cribb, sitting under Shaw while he was talking about 'The New Theology' – whatever Shaw may have meant by that. She also played a good game of tennis. But she gradually faded out of the picture; Eric had a great many other things on his mind, and he had Ethel very firmly in his heart.

He was now seeing a good deal of Orage, for whom he designed the type heading for *The New Age*. He also wrote an article for the paper on the relation between engineering and art. Here he admitted that engineering work was 'often work of extraordinary beauty in the living sense that beauty is power made visible'; but he denied

[1] Diary.

that the engineering workman was an artist – he was only 'an intelligent living tool' – because his work was not, and could not be, 'the expression of himself'. Eric did not claim, as yet, that all men should be artists; those claims must wait. The limitation of machines was not that they could not produce good buildings, but that they could not produce good ornament. Beauty was not entirely a matter of form – it was a matter of life – and life could not be imitated. If ornament were not to be sham ornament, the conditions of industry must be reorganized. Under existing conditions plain engineering was the only work that could be said even apparently to be done well. Here again Eric was saying already what he would go on saying to the end of his life. Put the Theosophical Society, and Nietzsche, and Chartres Cathedral in the balance against orthodox Fabian Socialism and free love, and you have an idea of the tensions in which he was now caught up.

He was happy and successful, but he was not yet decided. He was at once more radical and more conservative than most of the people with whom he associated. It was theology, not theosophy, which had made Chartres Cathedral. Dimly, as yet, Eric realized that what he wanted was a religious basis for the way of life in which he believed. It was all very well listening to Lowes Dickinson explaining in his perfect Cambridge accent what Plato meant by 'guardians'; but romantic Hellenism was never much in Eric's line, and he had not, in his whole composition, a grain of Attic salt. All these clever and politely revolutionary people were talking their heads off about all manner of important things. Eric was a great talker himself, but he was essentially a man of action – rarely quite at ease with artists, and never at home with aesthetes. It was pleasant enough when Will Rothenstein brought Lucien Pissarro to the workshop, but these men – for all their admiration for Eric – lived in a different world and were satisfied with aesthetic values which he had long deemed insufficient. Most of them were aesthetic materialists, agnostic even when they were high-minded. If Eric had ever been forced into materialism, his materialism would have been dialectical, not aesthetic; and although he now no longer went to church and still described himself as an agnostic, 'high-minded' is the last thing that anyone would have called him.

On June 9, 1907, he applied for the Principalship of Westminster Technical Institute, but his thoughts were far from Westminster, and he was probably relieved that the job did not fall into his lap. Five days later there is a momentous entry in his diary. 'To Ditchling with Ethel: went over three houses.' One of these had taken their immediate fancy – a pleasant, Georgian house in the main street. The dignified doorway had two windows on its right, as you looked at it, and one on its left. A flagged path, shaded by lime trees, led to an outbuilding. The house was called 'Sopers' and is so called to this day. Eric immediately made an offer through his solicitors, Christian & Cowell of Brighton, and this was evidently accepted, since he returned to Ditchling a week later to discuss the necessary repairs. The decision was not prompted by any desire to live in the country for the sake of the green fields and the green hills – though Eric and Ethel had loved and tramped the Downs since childhood. It was simply the desire for more elbow room than Hammersmith could afford for a growing family. They had no idea of founding a community; they merely wanted to bring up a family in decent surroundings. Eric was the reverse of Bohemian; he had his temptations and occasionally succumbed to them, but he wanted his life to be as tidy as his workshop. One might at first sight imagine him more at home with the robust temperament of a Sickert or an Augustus John – whom he hardly knew at all – than with Rothenstein's messianic high-mindedness. But then Rothenstein was genuinely concerned to relate art to daily living, whereas for Sickert and John, and many others, art had no purpose beyond itself. Eric was on the way to becoming something of a Messiah himself, and in certain respects his own temperament was timid rather than robust. The truth is that he had a more powerful mind than any of these men and a far more simple character. Unlike the majority of artists, he thought it normal for a man to get married if he were in love, and normal to have children once the woman he loved had become his wife. What Cobbett had called 'the great wen' was no place for children; inhuman in itself, it obviously frowned on humanity.

For a few months life in London went on as usual with *Don Juan in Hell* at the Royal Court, and Cecil Chesterton at the Fabian Society, and the Sidney Webbs At Home. But if Eric had wanted an example to illustrate the seemingly unbridgeable gulf between the powers that were and the powers that were becoming – between the Edwardian Establishment and the people of England who had not spoken yet – he found it in Whitehall on Sunday, July 19. In the afternoon he was one of a crowd of 4,000 to 5,000 people which had gathered in Trafalgar Square to protest against the Anglo-Russian *entente*. Eric was a political innocent and he knew nothing of the motives which had persuaded a Liberal Government to these *fiançailles de convenance*. Like most of his friends, he saw Russia as the last citadel of serfdom. There were speeches from Fisher Unwin, Aylmer Maude, Cecil Chesterton and others; and then the crowd were invited to march four abreast down Whitehall and pass a resolution outside the Foreign Office.

The demonstrators were assured by the police that if they proceeded in an orderly manner the would not be interfered with. With Cunninghame Graham at their head – the patrician mouthpiece of unpopular and romantic minorities – they had reached the corner of Downing Street when the police rushed out from the side streets and scattered them in confusion. There were no banners or flags, and no noise but the singing of the Red Flag and the Marseillaise, and the tramping of determined feet. Jack Williams had proposed 'Three groans for Grey'[1] before being hauled down from a window sill, and then, as the police set upon them despite the promises of Inspector Jarvis who had himself walked ahead of the procession, cries of 'Cossacks' were unleashed. It was the demonstrators who had kept the peace and the police who had broken it. Henceforward – with the memory of a policeman's grip on his neck – Eric would have his own ideas as to what was meant by the preservation of public order.

Later in the month he accompanied Sydney Cockerell to Bruges

---

[1] Sir Edward Grey was Secretary of State for Foreign Affairs.

for the Tournament and the Exposition of the Toison d'Or, and in the evening watched the torchlight procession. They saw the Memlings, and Michelangelo's *Virgin* in the church of Notre-Dame, and Van Eyck's *Adoration of the Lamb* in Ghent cathedral. Sydney Cockerell was already publishing his opinion that in Eric's 'own particular sphere of the designing and carving of monumental inscriptions he is admittedly without a rival in England'. At home, Eric's work continued to take him in all directions – to Ryde and Yarmouth in the Isle of Wight, to Goudhurst and Upton-on-Severn, and he could still afford the time to take Ethel for a four hours' row on the river with Joseph Cribb.

Henry Arthur Jones asked him to design a poster for *The Hypocrites* at the Duke of York's Theatre, and afterwards sent him tickets for the play at which he sat with Max Beerbohm. One hopes that he enjoyed it, although no one could have been more remote from Eric than the author of the play that he was watching or the man with whom he was watching it. More often than not he went to the theatre with Ethel, but Ethel was now seriously ill in the Chichester Infirmary. The next morning – August 29 – he received a telegram: 'Ethel worse, come immediately. Peritonitis. Operation 7 p.m. All well so far.' Her condition slowly improved during the week following, while Eric and Cribb were getting the house in order at Ditchling. Eric himself moved in on September 11, but on the 24th Ethel had a relapse and he was warned that a second operation would be necessary. This was successfully performed on the 29th and Eric was able to go to Bognor for his father's birthday dinner. On October 17 Ethel came out of hospital; on the 26th Eric met her with the children at Hassocks; and at 5 p.m. on the same afternoon they 'came together at last to Sopers'.[1]

[1] Diary.

PART TWO

Ditchling

1907-1924

I

When one speaks of Ditchling in connection with Eric Gill, one is thinking of a particular community engaged on an experiment in communal work which really had its home on Ditchling Common two miles to the north. Ditchling itself is a typically attractive Sussex village lying at the foot of the beacon which bears its name. There was, as we have seen, nothing dramatic or even abrupt in Eric's departure from London. It was, as it still is, quite usual for English writers and artists to live and work in the country. This is in marked contrast to the French tendency to collect in coteries, issue passionate manifestos, and form movements for this and that. The same tendency, it is true, was at work in London during the first decade of the century, but there were still deep differences in outlook between three such men as Bernard Shaw, H. G. Wells and G. K. Chesterton who nevertheless liked and admired one another. Eric himself, though he would shortly be caught up in a movement of his own, had taken from the new currents of thought as much as they had to give him. For some time to come he remained a close friend of Will Rothenstein and Roger Fry; Rothenstein's friendship, which was inspired by a sincere admiration, is shown by the following letter in reply to an illustrated postcard that Eric had sent him:

It is as though I went to the door to take in the milk and find Venus in person, without any clothes on, handing it to me. Damn you, sir, a few more P.C.s and you are the first artist in Europe. When, how, and where did you make the young sun god? He is a wonder – as witty as he is beautiful, as virile as he is short and tubby, and I love his bad temper. Send a card of him to B. Berenson. (August 30, 1910)

Later, Epstein would come into the picture. Yet it is worth remembering for anyone interested in the workings of what is called 'the artistic temperament' – the horrible phrase cannot easily be avoided – that Rothenstein quarrelled with Epstein and Fry, and became seriously estranged from Eric; and that Eric quarrelled with Epstein also. None of these men, with the exception of Epstein, were quarrelsome people in themselves; but they were either too serious or too sensitive to get on easily with those who disagreed with their ideas. It was fortunate for Eric's peace of mind that in all essential matters he stood on his own feet. He was, in fact, a particularly friendly person, who liked most people unless they gave him good reason to feel otherwise; but he did not cry over spilt friendships. They were the price of sincerity, and the incidental casualties of life.

He still kept on his workshop in Hammersmith – sleeping in a hammock when he had to spend the night there. He still went to the same lectures and meetings. But a note of criticism now creeps into his record of them. Wells is talking to the Fabians about his 'faith' – and Eric follows his note of this with a mark of interrogation. Chesterton is addressing the Fine Arts Guild on 'Democracy' – and Eric adds 'Oh Lor'!' More important and seminal was Ananda Coomaraswamy on Indian Art at the Art Workers Guild – 'a most splendid paper'.[1] Coomaraswamy was a Hindu from Madras, who had written a book on the art of Ceylon and was now making a profound study of Indian painting. Rothenstein had recently made his acquaintance and was also present at the lecture. No doubt he introduced him to Eric. It was Eric's good fortune throughout life to meet the right person at the right moment, and the list was already a long one. His friendship with Coomaraswamy ripened *pari passu* with their religious and philosophical inquiries. Whenever Eric was inclined to confuse art with usefulness, Coomaraswamy was there to emphasize its sacral foundations. The art of India, like the art of the European Middle Ages, reflected the communal beliefs of a civilization, not the individual vision of a particular man. But unlike the art of the Middle Ages, it was both contemplative and sensual. Eric would always insist that art must be allowed to express the life of the senses as well as the life of the spirit, and to do so without evasion. The romanticism from which he was now in headlong flight was a muddlement of both.

Diary.

All roads, from now on, led to Ajanta or Chartres, and in the meantime Coomaraswamy was yet another influence weaning Eric away from the hygienic aridities of Fabian Socialism. Shaw had not yet preached his biological millennium, but it might be as well to take a longer look into the past before putting one's money on so bright a horse as Wells' scientific Utopia. It was easier to do this from Ditchling than from Hammersmith, or even from Lincoln's Inn. The first impression one gets of those early Ditchling days is, quite literally, of a sortie into the open air. Eric was both a keen tennis player and a tireless walker. Before the year is out – with 'cold December's bareness everywhere' – we find him tramping over the hills to Brighton; walking to Plumpton with Max and Romney and back via Westmeston, or to Clayton by road and back along the tops; going up on to the Beacon in the dark and flashing a message with his bicycle lantern to Ethel as she sat in the window at Sopers. He is stretching his legs and filling his lungs, modestly content as the old year comes to an end with an income of £361 5s 1d against an expenditure of £349 14s 7½d. He never got into the red if he could help it.

Eric once said that he disapproved of nudist colonies because they induced frigidity, but where there was no risk of safety in numbers he was always ready to take off his clothes. As the weather warmed up in the spring of 1908 he was running about unashamedly on the Downs with E. C. Laughton, and a couple of months later they were applauding Isadora Duncan two nights in succession at the Duke of York's. Eric was not a *balletomane*, but although Isadora's autobiography had not yet been written, he may well have deduced it from her dancing. In certain respects they were kindred spirits. If Eric had an idea in his head, he would always push it as far as it would go; and it was only a short step from reacting against machines to reacting against modesty, from reacting against capitalism to reacting against clothes. Perhaps it was as well that when he called on the great dancer one morning Ethel should have kept him company.

Meanwhile he had moved his workshop to Sopers, with the following motto inscribed outside: 'Bad workmen quarrel with their tools, because good workmen do not use bad tools.' In London he stayed at Johnston's former lodgings in Lincoln's Inn which he now shared with his brother Max. Normally he was there from Tuesday afternoon till Friday. He was now seeing a great deal of Rothenstein, who both gave him advice and lent him money. It was already becoming clear that the Arts and Crafts Movement was a failure, and Eric told Rothenstein that he wished to avoid placing himself under its banner. 'I spend all my spare time', he wrote to his brother Romney, 'doing all I can to smash the arts and crafts "movement" – if you know what that is. If you don't – so much the better. Not being of an entirely negative turn of mind, I am endeavouring to persuade myself and other people that it would be desirable to see some modern furniture whose only novelty was good construction and let art take care of itself as it very well can.' (September 6, 1909.) He expressed much the same views in *The Socialist Review*, which was the organ of the Independent Labour Party.

At Ditchling Eric was at work on Count Kessler's edition of *Homer* – Kessler was doing his best to convert the Germans from the Gothic to the Roman script – and was also carving some small sculptures. These excited Kessler's admiration. He wrote:

There is a sort of rude, elementary force and humour in your work which is racy, of England, or even of the Anglo-Saxon swordsmen and seabears that came over with Hengist and Horsa. I have rarely seen anything so thoroughly *personal* and *national*. This, and the way everything is evolved out of the tool and material, makes your work quite unique. (October 26, 1910)

It therefore occurred to Kessler that Eric would benefit by working for a time under Aristide Maillol in his studio at Marly-le-Roi. Like most sculptors, Maillol modelled in clay and employed carvers to convert his clay models into marble or stone, which was done with a 'pointing' machine. Kessler thought that Eric could teach him about direct carving and learn from him about modelling:

I showed the photos to Maillol who liked them very well. He says they show great talent; but he rather deplores you do not work in *clay first*, as it is very difficult, or rather, impossible to *correct* mistakes in stone.[1]

Eric himself was only interested in carving directly from the stone, and while he agreed that he could learn a great deal from Maillol, he wondered what would happen to his work in England if he transferred himself bag and baggage to Marly. Kessler, however, had found him a house and was preparing to sign a three years' lease on his behalf. At once flattered and dispirited, Eric went to Paris and met Maillol with Kessler acting as interpreter. He was further depressed by the thought of deserting Sopers for a French suburban villa. On returning to Paris he went to the Grand Hotel where Kessler had booked him a luxurious suite of rooms, for which Kessler was naturally to pay. Presently the manager came knocking on the door and explained that obviously the Count had not intended to reserve him such elaborate accommodation, and that he had better leave his bag at the reception desk and come back when more suitable arrangements had been made. This was the last straw. After a lonely and indifferent dinner Eric fetched his bag, still leaving the management under the impression that he would return for the night; took a taxi to the Gare St Lazare; and caught the night boat to Newhaven. A letter dispatched to Kessler before he left Paris announced his departure, and a further letter explained it. Apart from the loss of his English connections, Eric questioned the whole purpose of the proposed apprenticeship. Technically, he would learn nothing from Maillol, because Maillol was primarily a modeller; and artistically he would learn nothing because Maillol and he were already in substantial agreement.

The similarity in our ideas, if I may so presume to speak, would be so seductive . . . that I should cease to oppose. And one *must* be in opposition. Maillol has a vision which I feel to be very largely my vision. Well then, if I am to achieve the expression of that vision, I must achieve it for myself, through my own struggles, in my own battle with life. I do hope I am making myself clear to you. Well then, if these things are so, it is obvious that what I need to learn is about tools and the uses of tools – the

[1] Quoted in a letter to William Rothenstein from *Letters of Eric Gill*, 1947.

chisel and hammer and what they are capable of doing. I cannot learn that from Maillol. Infinitely better would it be for me to go and apprentice myself to the most skilful and the most ordinary of monumental masons and learn to hack idiotic angels out of white marble. Then indeed I should be in opposition – and should find out what *I* meant and what *I* should do and say. Do you know I almost feel as if in that brief afternoon at Marly I got as much out of Maillol as I ever should get.[1]

Kessler understood Eric's reluctance to 'enter a world not only as foreign as France is to England but as foreign as paganism is to Christianity';[2] and Eric had the sàtisfaction of knowing that the management of the Grand Hotel had received a piece of Kessler's mind. As for Maillol, Eric always thought that 'in his own line of business' he was 'the greatest man in the world';[3] and when, many years later, one of his sculptures was slightly damaged on its way to an exhibition at the Tate, Eric was called in to repair it.

On February 1, 1910 – only a week or so after his return from Marly – Ethel gave birth to a third daughter, Joanna. This was intimately connected with Eric's new found interest in sculpture. Ethel's pregnancy had obliged him to what he described as 'comparative continence', and in order to have in one way what he could not have in another he had set about creating for himself a woman of stone. It is interesting (and rather surprising) to note that up to this time he had never made an erotic drawing or carving of any sort; and although he made plenty of them afterwards, he started in a big way. It is also interesting to note Eric's own opinion that 'no one would guess the fervours which conditioned its making'; for there was always a certain asceticism – a sort of diagrammatic cerebration – about his work in this kind. Carving a woman seemed to him not essentially different from carving an inscription. It was simply 'a new alphabet – the word was made flesh'. He showed the carving to Kessler who in turn showed it to Roger Fry. They were both encouraging. Eric himself did not think it as good as all that, and it was some time before he was able to reconcile the two opinions:

[1] *Letters of Eric Gill*, 1947.
[2] *Autobiography*, 1940.
[3] ibid.

I discovered that my inability to draw naturalistically was, instead of a drawback, no less than my salvation. It compelled me, quite against my will and without my knowledge, to concentrate upon something other than the superficial delights of fleshly appearance. It compelled me to consider the significance of things rather than their charm.[1]

From inscribing funeral monuments it was now a natural step to carving them. Eric's attitude to this side of his work is illustrated by a letter to Easton Gibb:

Broadly speaking there are two kinds of monument – there is first the mere headstone, i.e. a stone recording the name and date of the dead. This of course may take a thousand different forms and, in its material and the manner of its design, may record a great deal more than merely name and date but essentially it is simply an historical (in the ordinary sense of that word) record. On the other hand there is, secondly, that kind of monument which, though it may contain a record of names and dates, is directly and essentially an expression of the attitude of the living to the dead – an attitude of respect, love, admiration, fear or what not – or an expression of the attitude of man towards life and death.

Now of course it is obvious that in the generality of cases the former kind of monument is not only the more appropriate but also the only kind possible. People are seldom in the position either intellectually or financially to consider the monumental expression of philosophy but that being so there is all the more reason why, when a sculptor or maker of monuments finds himself brought in contact with a client of your calibre, sir, he should at least endeavour to persuade him to put up a monument which shall be more than a mere headstone.

Well, on thinking over the conversation I had with you on the subject, I remembered very clearly that you had expressed your dislike of the 'white marble angel holding a wreath', but knowing as I did the extraordinary beauty of the form of monument used by the Greeks (the 'stele') I was convinced that it was not the fact of sculpture which disgusted you but the vulgarity of the angel idea and the degraded quality of the workmanship in which that idea found expression. So I made the rough design which I enclose herewith.

May I explain its significance? The figure of the woman stands in what I hope is sufficiently obviously an attitude disconsolate and sorrowful. The subject of sorrow is also obvious for her arm is extended over a tablet

[1] *Autobiography*, 1940.

recording death. She is an ordinary person (not an angel). She represents the grief which is the common heritage of mankind. So far the theme is commonplace enough. But while grown ups grieve the work of the world must go on – must it not? Does it not seem, to any mourner, extra-ordinary that while there is sorrow anyone can be oblivious to it? Yet I have often seen children happy with their toys while their parents grieved for the loss of the beloved. Now does it not seem to you that man is a child? Does it not seem to you that man is a child in the sense that woman seldom is? What are men's employments but so many games of skill? – games which he plays with all the intentness and self-forgetfulness of a child – so I have made a child playing with bricks while grown ups mourn – with bricks because you, sir, are a builder of bridges. (May 6, 1910)

A great many other artists were working along the same lines as Eric in pencil or paint, and he did not presume to emulate them. But no one else was doing the same thing in stone, with one possible exception – and that was Epstein. Eric had admired Epstein's carv-ings in the Strand, and on April 20 (1910), they had tea together. Rothenstein, who had done a great deal for Epstein when he first came to London, fostered the friendship and was a kind of godfather to the plan which Eric and Epstein now had in mind. Eric described this to Rothenstein as 'a great scheme of doing some colossal figures together (as a contribution to the world), a sort of twentieth-century Stonehenge – and we have been looking out for a piece of land for the purchase'.[1] They found it, a plot of about six acres, hidden away in a valley with a house and farm buildings attached. Eric had first seen the house – Asham House – from Eddington Hill when he was walking over the Downs to Alfriston. It was empty and in need of repair, but it was ideal for their purpose.

Rothenstein was enthusiastic:

You shall get a fourteen years' lease, and when you have turned the potter's field into a Valhalla, the nation shall reluctantly buy the freehold. You are wonderful, and I believe quite irresistible, and your vision of a second Stonehenge is superb. You had better get people to order their tombs there in good time, and money will flow in perhaps in that way. You shall save a little corner for me, and you shall carve neatly on it – here lies one

[1] *Letters of Eric Gill*, 1947, September 25, 1910.

who loved more than he was loved – and Epstein shall carve Shaw nude, and you shall make Wells glitter in the light of the sun. (September 26, 1910)

Augustus John wanted a temple as well as a cemetery:

I got up this day feeling considerably younger so your grand idea works even on my debilitated physique. Do you know the architect? The Temple must be built. People will take to their heels at the sight of so stupendous a thing walking about in daylight, but they must be overtaken with giant strides. Some sacrifice will be necessary at the foundation – all great buildings begin with the accompaniment of the shedding of blood.

On September 10 the Epsteins came for the weekend; Eric and Epstein photographed each other, and the Gill children, in the nude; and visited Asham House together. The next day Eric was off to Portland to inspect the quarries, and went on to study the original Stonehenge on Salisbury Plain. On October 12 they had an interview with the owner of Asham House. This must have been promising, since on the following day they were off to Wirksworth in Derbyshire to examine the quarries of Hoptonwood stone.

Our great scheme (Eric wrote again to Rothenstein) is alas! hanging fire just at present. The owners want such a devil of a price for the place and we are now running round risking all our friendships by asking for money. I very much fear we shan't pull it off. . . . (October 15, 1910)

The project was still afloat in November, when Augustus John joined them for a further visit, but it was afterwards abandoned. The owners had at first agreed to a fourteen-year lease at £50 per annum, but then decided to sell. Eric and Epstein would themselves have preferred to buy the property outright, but £3,500 was more than they could afford or reasonably hope to raise.

One result of this association was to bring Eric, willy-nilly, back into the artistic current of the day. 'Ditchling' was still a far cry from Ditchling. In July Eric had spent a week with Rothenstein and other friends at Vattetot, near Dieppe. He walked to Etiques along the shore and to Etretat along the cliffs that Monet had painted. Rothenstein gives us the fuller picture:

He was delighted with the barns, the carts, the flails still in use, and the reaping hooks; he played charmingly on the penny whistle, and astonished the visitors at Etretat, whenever we went there, with his sandals, his red beard, and his hatless head.[1]

Rothenstein does not mention that Eric was less delighted with the company, and seems to have left abruptly. Involved as he was with this society and its excessively aesthetic preoccupations, Eric still felt – or a strong part of him felt – that he did not belong to it. He was devoted to Rothenstein, and had recently sat to him for a portrait drawing; but while Rothenstein was himself feeling his isolation among his fellow-painters of the NEAC and, like Eric, was closer to Epstein and Fry than to anyone else, he lacked Eric's personal intransigence and intellectual granite. He was a man of the world – or wanted to be a man of the world – even when the world was giving him the cold shoulder.

The friendship with Roger Fry ripened quickly, and Eric sent to Rothenstein (who was on a visit to India) his impressions of the Post-Impressionist Exhibition which Fry had organized at the Grafton Galleries. He would suggest many years later that 'perhaps the chief reason why the people who visited the Grafton Gallery in 1910 thought Post-Impressionist pictures were ugly was because they thought the painters were playing cricket when really they were playing football'.

All the critics are tearing one another's eyes over it and the sheep and the goats are inextricably mixed up. John says 'it's a bloody show' and Lady Ottoline[2] says 'oh charming'; Fry says 'what rhythm' and MacColl says 'what rot'. As a matter of fact those who like it show their pluck, and those who don't show either great intelligence or else great stupidity. The show quite obviously represents a reaction and a transition and so if, like Fry, you are a factor in that reaction and transition then you like the

[1] *Men and Memories*: Vol. 2, 1932.
[2] Lady Ottoline Morrell.

show. If, like MacColl and Robert Ross, you are too inseparably connected with the things reacted against and the generation from which it is a transition, then you don't like it! If, on the other hand, you are like me and John and McEvoy and Epstein, then, feeling yourself beyond the reaction and beyond the transition, you have a right to feel superior to Mr Henri Matisse (who is typical of the show – though Gauguin makes the biggest splash and Van Gogh the maddest) and can say you don't like it. But have you seen Mr Matisse's sculpture?[1] (December 5, 1910)

Eric himself had a garden statue in the exhibition which Mark Gertler described to Rothenstein as 'inspiringly beautiful. Really splendid. I wish you would tell him so. I could have wept for joy. When I went out the world seemed full of pleasure and joy, and I was happy all that night. I should so love to meet him.' Gertler went on to admire the statue's 'enchanting purity of line' and 'astonishing technique'. It held its own beside Matisse's *Pose de Nu*, Vlaminck's *Rouen*, Flandrin's *Paysage*, and Picasso's *Nature Morte*. But Eric had matters of greater significance than 'significant form' upon his mind just then, and in the same letter he took Rothenstein into his confidence:

There is one thing more I must tell you as it is the most important of all, and yet I don't know how to begin. I almost think I shall have to wait till you come back and yet I don't want to do that because I owe it to you to tell you. The fact is it is really too splendid if it's true, and so splendid that I hesitate to write about it. I will just hint it to you – there is a possibility that religion is about to spring up again in England. A religion is so splendid and all-embracing that the hierarchy to which it will give birth, uniting within itself the artist and the priest, will supplant and utterly destroy our present commercial age.

In due course this wide-eyed optimism would receive its rebuff from the least expected quarters; but it is not difficult to trace the pedigree of Eric's convictions and the influences which fostered them. First, there had been the revelation of Chartres; then Coomaraswamy had opened his eyes to the sacred civilizations of the East, and Rothenstein was even at that moment exploring their treasures; and lastly there was Epstein ready to raise a new temple, even if it were only to

[1] *Letters of Eric Gill*, 1947.

the unknown deities of a twentieth-century Stonehenge. Only Fry was content to worship no higher than Cézanne. Eric assured Rothenstein in a further letter that he and Epstein were both agreed that 'the best route to Heaven was via Elephanta, Ellera and Ajanta' – and Rothenstein now knew better than either of them what these names conveyed of contemplation and holiness, not to mention 'significant form'. Moreover Eric had become very friendly with the Cornfords, Francis and Frances, staying with them at Cambridge and lettering the name of their house, Conduit Head. He made a pot for them and in thanking him for it Cornford wondered 'whether to use it as a hipbath or plant a Deodar in it'.[1] Francis Cornford was a profound student of Greek philosophy and religion, and Eric would talk with him by the hour.

The Cornfords were already close friends of Rothenstein, who had in fact introduced them to Eric; and on Rothenstein's return from India in April (1911) Eric wrote to him again, suggesting that in company with Epstein they should 'form the nucleus of a larger and finer co-operation than any that existed, or had existed, since the decline of the Roman Church' (April 20, 1911). What exactly the co-operation was supposed to achieve is not clear; and probably Eric was not clear about it himself. Rothenstein evidently brought his head down from the clouds (where it did not usually reside), and a scheme was set on foot, with John, McEvoy, and Neville Lytton, to take a house and sell their work independent of the dealers. This was altogether more practicable than the 'co-operation' Eric had proposed to Rothenstein; but the owner would not sell, and Eric concluded that John would prove 'quite unmanageable'.[2] His assumption that the Roman Church was in decline is worth noting in view of developments that were much closer than he suspected.

Any such scheme would certainly have failed from the sheer flimsiness of its syncretism, but the personal relationship as well as the professional co-operation of these more or less kindred spirits was now to be put to the test. Eric may not have been heart and soul with

[1] Letter to Eric Gill, May 23, 1912.
[2] Letter to William Rothenstein, July 22, 1911.

the Post-Impressionists, ardently as he admired Cézanne; but he was still on excellent terms with Roger Fry. He carved a statue of Cupid for Fry's garden at Guildford, and was a frequent visitor there. An article by a Modernist in the *Nineteenth Century* had provoked a long talk on religion. 'I've thought heaps about our talk,' Fry wrote. 'The great question is – can we be religious?' Fry was then thinking of giving up his art criticism in *The Nation*, but Eric had persuaded him – at least for the time being – that there were some things even more important than art.

What a queer world it is, but you have made it very exciting and more full of hope for the future than I had dreamt say ten years ago. Then I was mainly interested in myself, a comparatively dull subject. Now I suppose it's what you call God. (December 4, 1910)

Eric had made him a carving of a pair of lovers, and Fry writes:

The last thing is the best of all. I find it strangely beautiful and noble. I think it is wonderful that you have gone so straight – not influenced in the least by all the associated ideas, mostly impertinent, that have gathered round the act in the turbid course of human life. This is real religious art. (February 15, 1911)

Fry wanted Eric to do away with the gilding on the necklace of the woman:

It is a false note, I think – the thing was finer before. I believe it side-tracks the idea – starts people off on the pornographic side of the thing – that's there right enough and should be, but it ought to be altogether noble in its animation. The more I look at them the more I like it. You have to me at all events said all you wanted, and it ought to be put up in a public place. It can't be till we're much more civilized in the real sense.

Fry confessed his doubts as to whether he could put up the statue where totally inartistic people would see it on their way to his sister's philanthropic meetings. 'It will mean at the worst that I shall keep *my* statue in *your* garden.'[1]

When Eric exhibited his sculpture at the Chenil Gallery in January

[1] June 23, 1911.

1911, Fry described his work, in *The Nation*,[1] as 'an astonishing phenomenon, for here is certainly a sculptor, one to whom the language of plastic imagery is instinctive and natural. And he proves it all the more conclusively by reason of his complete ignorance of the knowledge, and his innocence of the appliance of the sculptor's atélier.' Fry went on to emphasize that Eric was essentially a stone-cutter; and 'the exquisite quality and finish of his surfaces bear witness to this no less than the perfection of those incised inscriptions for which he has long been celebrated'. Eric's long apprenticeship in a formal and abstract art had 'given him what the efforts of the modern artist at representation do not always provide, a sense of scale, a power of co-ordination and rhythm which are the first essentials of great artistic expression'. Any suspicion that Edward Johnston was 'bound upon a mission of futile antiquarian revivalism' was allayed by these 'living, powerful images of Mr Gill's'; they showed 'the immense advantages of the craftsman's training of the Middle Ages over the studio training of our own days'. And if the contemporary craftsman 'happened to be a man with a burning desire to express himself, neither ignorance of anatomy nor unfamiliarity with the figure' would stop him for long. As examples of Eric's 'religious faith in the value and significance of life' Fry singled out a figure of Christ 'not crucified, but stretched in voluntary self-immolation upon the Cross', and 'a maenad, in all the insolent splendour, not indeed of her beauty, but of her unquenchable will to live'.[2] The critic recognized that while beauty might not be the central aim of Eric's work, it was the inevitable accompaniment of such impassioned expression as was his. The *Manchester Guardian* admired his two statuettes of a Mother and Child 'where the dumb love of the mother as she holds and gazes at the child in her arms leaves her no other expression of her heart's fullness, but to give the babe her breast'.[3]

Fry was not alone, however, in thinking that the erotic bias of Eric's carving was restricting his reputation. Rothenstein had written earlier:

[1] January 28, 1911.
[2] Both sculptures are now in the Tate Gallery.
[3] February 1911.

Of all the people I know you are the one it is most possible to make public use of. Your mood at present and for some little time has, however, been a personal one. Some day you will have expressed it and have more general ones to express. Given that society will accept nothing that has erotic or sexual significance, it is clear that anyone who is occupied with that side of life can expect no patrons. . . . At least I have faith in you, though I think you bring – I suppose we all do – more difficulties on yourself than you need. (September 8, 1911)

Now Roger Fry had long been one of Will Rothenstein's most constant and discriminating admirers; he thought him head and shoulders above the other painters who normally exhibited with the New English Art Club. But Rothenstein was resistant to Post-Impressionism, and this ultimately caused a breach with Fry which embittered Rothenstein until the end of his life. The rift began soon after Rothenstein's return from India, and he was offended because Eric had not taken his side. Rothenstein was far too sensitive for the *mafia* of artistic politics, and the following letter to Eric justifies the epitaph which he had, half playfully, composed for the Sussex Stonehenge:

I have not the smallest grievance against you or the minutest resentment. But I spent a day or two with John, who had a cold, at Rottingdean, and where a week or two ago I would have come out at once to see you. Something kept me from coming when I had the chance, that is all. I shall always admire your work and like you, but the particular quality I always thought would be present has gone, as it went from my relations with others, and I must wait until it quite naturally comes back again. I have not the charm which keeps for some people their friends' entire devotion and I am settling down to life much more quietly and reasonably now that I quite fully realize it. I believe I can be just as friendly and yet keep my peace of mind better on a less affectionate basis. (April 25, 1911)

Eric described this letter in his diary as 'W.R. chucking me over'. He composed more than one exasperated reply, drafts of which remained among his papers, but he did not post them, and sent instead the following short note:

I have torn up both your last letters and also three long replies to the same.

I have spent about 4 hours at the job and now give it up. The door of this house is open wide. I'm not sure that I understand men. But I'm quite certain I don't understand artists (except when they're clergymen). As for the 'ending': I think it's a case of ending or mending. I should wish for the latter, but I don't want a mere patch up. (May 4, 1911)

In fact, the friendship was quickly mended; but at the same time Eric quarrelled with Epstein, who also blamed him for the failure of the 'co-operative society'. Epstein thought Eric had tried to rope too many people in. Eric replied with a letter which Epstein regarded as so abusive and impertinent that it might have been written at the *Six Bells* – a public house which they frequented in Chelsea. There was a further dispute about their respective financial obligations over a carving they had worked on together; and the fruitful relationship ended 'not with a bang, but a whimper' when Eric complained that Epstein had left his tools behind in the Ditchling studio.

2

Apart from these fracas Eric had spent a busy year. In April he gave up his rooms in Lincoln's Inn and brought the furniture down to Ditchling; if he wanted to spend the night in London, he stayed with his sister Gladys. He was at work on a 'child' for the Cornfords and had been working on a 'woman and child' for Epstein, who had spent Christmas at Ditchling. In Cambridge he stayed with the Cornfords and met Lowes Dickinson at dinner with them. He was carving an altar stone, commemorating Francis Thompson, for Wilfrid Meynell, and a Madonna for Roger Fry; and he was lecturing on 'Politics: Male and Female' for the Liberal Christian League at Burgess Hill. One would like to know what exactly was meant by the title of the lecture and the name of the audience before which it was given. But when he spoke on 'The Artist as Flunkey' we know just what he meant, although he was convinced – no doubt rightly – that no one understood him at the time.

On May 8 he saw his first aeroplane, flying from Brighton to Burgess Hill, and on the 13th he watched the Flying Race from Shoreham to Black Rock – 'a splendid sight'.[1] It was perfectly natural that a man who had begun by admiring railway engines – and never stopped admiring them – should have admired aeroplanes as well. We grossly oversimplify Eric's philosophy of making if we imagine that he disapproved of machines. He did not even disapprove of commerce as a means to an end, only as an end in itself. He had tried to make these distinctions clear in an article for *The Highway* (October 1910). Commerce, he had argued, was laudable in so far as it was an end to the purpose for which man existed – 'the production of fine works and fine men'. The time was coming when he would extend the definition, but this was as far as he could take it then – and so far was so good. He was challenged by a Mr Goodman, and did not deny that

[1] Diary.

commerce was 'one of the most potent civilizing powers humanity has yet developed'. But he distinguished between commerce and commercialism: money making was the essence not of the first but of the second. Eric had conceived his article as the Preface to an Unwritten Book; this would be concerned 'with the products of a people rather than with the conditions of its being'. His opponent had supported machinery because it relieved the drudgery of the workers; Eric admired machinery because it was capable of producing good works. He would not spend five minutes, he said, trying to reduce drudgery. If drudgery produced the kind of works that were made 'in the year 2000 B.C. in Egypt, or 400 B.C. in India and Greece, or A.D. 1300 in England' then so much the better for drudgery. Eric did not say this in so many words, but he implied it. His definition of commerce was the pure milk of Ruskin, who had said much the same thing;

all healthily-minded people like making money – ought to like it, and enjoy the sensation of winning it; but the main object of their life is not money; it is something better than money.

Or again,

the wealth of nations, as of men, consists in substance, not in ciphers; and . . . the real good of all work, and of all commerce, depends on the final intrinsic worth of the thing you make, or get by it.

There was nothing here with which any Fabian would disagree, but Eric was leaving the Fabians behind him.

On June 15 he was making a flag for the Coronation of George V, and on the day of the Coronation, June 22, he saw the lighting of the fires on Ditchling Beacon – 'a grand sight in wind and mist'[1] – and the torchlight procession. In the following month he went on a four days' walking tour with Ethel along the Downs. It was a very warm summer and August 9 was the hottest day of the century – 96° in the shade at Ditchling. There was bathing on the Common or at Burgess Hill, and in the sea at Cuckmerehaven. Perhaps Ethel had been over-

[1] Diary.

exerting herself, for later in August she had a miscarriage; and it may have been during these summer months, if it had not been earlier, that Eric was at work carving the 'Woman' of which he speaks in his *Autobiography*. For Eric stone carving was '*conceiving things in stone and conceiving them as made by carving*. They are not only born but conceived in stone; they are of stone in their inmost being as well as their outermost existence.'[1] Ethel recovered quickly, but she was not able to have any more children. Her father died in November of the same year.

Work continued as usual. Eric went to see the mural decorations at the Borough Polytechnic, which had been executed under the direction of Roger Fry, and thought them 'very interesting and in many ways admirable but terribly stylistic and wilful; E.G. take warning'.[2] Fry had written to him: 'I think we shall be on the same side in coming years, but I doubt if I shall ever get your full approval – well that's as it should be. I am inevitably *vieux jeu* and my chief use is to give your generation a better chance than mine had'; and again, 'Do you know it frightened me when I found out one day how really naïve you were. I was afraid that when you began to find out facts you would think they had some value altogether of their own, but this makes me think you're safe.' (February 23, 1912)

On April 18, 1912, Augustus John wrote to Eric:

Have you got further with your idea of a religion? It seems to me there never was or ever can be other than one – fundamentally – those of the ancients and of the Medieval Church. They all seem to tally in their esoteric significance, and to agree in the glorification of man and of God conceived as the Greater man. Have you studied the Cabbala?

Eric may not have studied the Cabbala, but he had got a good deal further with his idea. He was already feeling himself to be a Catholic. It went back to Browning's *Bishop Blougram's Apology* which a friend had put into his hand when he was in Caroe's office. Given the temper of the Ecclesiastical Commissioners' apprentices, it was

[1] *Autobiography*, 1940.
[2] Diary.

probably intended as an anti-clerical broadside, but it had just the opposite effect. Eric began to see beyond Blougram to the thing he represented – universal and proceeding 'confidently in her doctrine of God'. The Church spoke with the authority that Eric was looking for; the question remained – had she a title for it? And here is where Eric stood clean apart from his progressive contemporaries. Where they were looking for authority to the State or the individual, he was looking for an authority which would dictate to both. He had already discussed the matter with Rothenstein:

. . . It matters little whether I personally (or you) like the Church or need it – because, whether I like it or not, the Church is desirable and necessary. I can quite understand people neither liking nor feeling need of the Church but if I am right in thinking that all the ills of modern 'industrialism' are the result of the loss of religion and the powerlessness of religious organizations then I think we are in duty bound to join the Church in any ways possible and we are in a bad way if it's not possible.

The fact is I think the Church should rule the world like a government. If there were no Church it would be necessary to make one. If I am going to live in England under the English government, I want to be a naturalized English citizen and not an outsider. If I am going to submit to the Church's vision of the significance of the universe – and you admit that the Catholic Faith is such that such submission is possible – then I want to be a member of the Church and not an outsider.

The desirability or necessity of submission is a temperamental matter.

The desirability or necessity of membership is a political matter.

(e.g. If I believed in Socialism I should not only call myself a Socialist – I'd join a Socialist Society.) (January 21, 1912)[1]

His discontent with the Church of England had been expressed three months before in a letter to his brother Romney, who was a missionary in Papua:

We live in the middle of a chaos and at present the only forces making for order are purely materialistic – therefore doomed. England will never obtain salvation by Act of Parliament. What are the churches doing? may be asked. So far as I can see they are confining themselves to district visiting and such like. Otherwise they take their cue from the politicians.

[1] *Letters of Eric Gill*, 1947.

You will find parsons who are Tariff Reformers and those who are the other thing. There are Socialist parsons and Tory and Radical ditto. There are parsons who support the House of Lords and there are those who don't – but, so far as I can make out, there is not a parson in the land who realizes that it is the politician's business to take his cue from the Church and not vice versa. You will agree that this is the inevitable result of the Reformation – whereat the Church became subordinate to the State and hence these tears – but what's to be done now? (October 26, 1911)

Instinctively, Eric was now putting a halo round the head of a Mother and Child; and drawing a picture of the slaughter of the Holy Innocents. At the end of January (1912) he was attending Mass with his brother Max at St George's Retreat on Ditchling Common. Three days later he was at the Caxton Hall listening to a discussion between Chesterton and Bishop Gore on Christian Social Obligations. Above all, he was talking; talking to all and sundry; talking all the time. He knew no Catholics except the Meynells – his work on the Francis Thompson altar tomb had brought them together – so he now wrote to Everard Meynell putting his position plainly. He had been to school with Everard's brother-in-law, Percy Lucas, who still kept one of his locomotive drawings. There could not have been a happier introduction.

I understand that you are a Catholic – will you forgive me therefore for my presumption in writing – and, if so, you are the only Catholic with whom I have had personal dealings.

My father is a Church of England parson and so, until I was old enough to read Huxley and H. G. Wells and Co., I was a protestant. Since the age of 17 or thereabouts I've wandered among the 'new arts' and the 'new religion', and new politics too, and have been as enthusiastic as could be expected. But I've got through the Arts and Crafts. I've got through the Socialisms and I've got through the new theologies. At the same time there is something in them all which is right. They are all revolts against the present devilish state of England. It seems to me from what I can learn and also guess that the Roman Church is the right answer to modern England and also to Morris and also to Wells and Shaw and also to the Campbellites and Besantites and Anglicans and all the rest. But how can I find out? I know no Catholics to speak to. I don't want to bother you to convert me – even if I were worth it – but can you of your charity just tell me to whom such a one as I can apply for information, instruction, and enlightenment? I hope you won't think it a bother. (January 18, 1912)

Everard Meynell replied with excruciating preciosity:

To me, born in it, the Church is like the presence of mountains on the horizon: over them, your letter shows me, I have made no intelligible tracks – guidance never having been asked. From the heart I bear witness though with dogged thought and word, to the sense (often neglected or abused) of her shelter, of her scope. Perhaps she contains Morris and most schools and arts: rebels and rebellions that 'fondly thought to err' have not seldom found themselves in her embrace. Socialism must be half hers, since her sacraments and mysteries are the daily bread, share and share alike of rich and poor. England you find hideous; evil makes her and all countries so, but for the elucidation of the inscrutable presence of evil you will not seek in Catholicism, although to Paris and to Poverty the Church provides the clue. She values the suffering from which may grow obedience, renunciation, humility. But I shall not for several reasons, of which my incompetence is chief, attempt a statement; nor can I even, by return of post at least, guide your inquiries. For myself, I go for instruction (not specific reading of the law) to Francis Thompson and Patmore (the Odes). It was Cardinal Manning, I think, who said that he would not cross the road to make a convert – his meaning probably being that if converts *are* to be made, they make themselves. But for all that, I am writing to my father, who knows such things, to get from him the name of a responsible adviser.

Eric acknowledged this letter on January 21:

It was very good of you to write to your father about me and I look forward to going to see him soon. I dare say I can quite easily get over to Pulborough. I quite understand your quotation from Cardinal Manning and quite agree with him. Converts must make themselves: but, even so, there comes a time when the 'convert' feels he can't go further without further knowledge – knowledge only to be obtained from those already initiated and you see there's no Catholic church in this neighbourhood that I know of, to which one would naturally go.

It was evidently on Wilfrid Meynell's advice that on the day following

5. Sopers, Ditchling, the house occupied by Eric and Mary Gill from 1907 to 1913.

6. Capel-y-ffin.

7. Tea at Pigotts. Left to right: Hugo Yardley, Clemency Geddes, Eric Gill, Dr P. J. Flood, D.D., Chaplain at Pigotts, Joanna Hague, Ethel Mary Gill (photo Tunbridge Ltd).

the Caxton Hall meeting he went to see Father King, the priest in charge of St Ethelreda's, Ely Place. He spent the weekend with Wilfrid Meynell at Greatham, walking and talking all day. He even walked back to Ditchling in the snow, probably talking to himself. The next weekend he was at Cambridge, still talking about religion with the Cornfords, Lowes Dickinson and Maynard Keynes – the two weekends must have provided a pretty contrast in conversation. There were further meetings with the Meynells, and he sat up with Edward Johnston, talking again, till 5 a.m. All through April he was going regularly to Mass and carving a Madonna for Ethel's birthday.

Meanwhile he had been invited by Dom Bruno Destries, O.S.B., of Mont César, near Louvain, to send a carving to an exhibition of religious art in Brussels. He replied that he was not a Catholic and that he did not wish any work of his to appear under false pretences. On this point Dom Bruno reassured him and went on to say:

I am interested specially in your situation because I am myself a convert. For years I have been an artist living without any other religion than the religion of beauty. I have still religious feelings for everything that is beautiful, but that has now quite a different meaning of course for me, and since I entered the Benedictine Order – about twelve years ago – I have lived of course much more happy than I have ever been when I was supposed to be free and independent. (March 22, 1912)

The statue of the Blessed Virgin which Eric proposed to send was too heavy for transport, but Dom Bruno suggested that, notwithstanding, he should spend a few days at the Abbey of Mont César. Thinking that the visit might help to resolve his doubts or clarify his convictions, Eric decided to go. It was a strange, and in some respects a disquieting, experience. Eric knew little French and less Latin. He sat by himself in the middle of the refectory with the monks ranged along the wall on either side. He had only a faint idea of what was happening, and knew no way of expressing either his spiritual or material needs. The guest master knew no English, and having to go away one afternoon left him in charge of a Father Anselm who knew none either. With the help of a dictionary, however, they got down to brass tacks.

Eric announced that he could accept the philosophical and meta-physical basis of Catholicism easily enough, but that he could only admit the historical basis as symbolical – to which the Benedictine gently objected: 'Pas symbolique, pas symbolique.' Eric replied that the miracles didn't matter to him, and that anyway they were a bore. The monk answered that, boring or not, they were 'pas symbolique'. Then a lay brother came in with a cup of tea, and Eric who never liked losing an argument – even when he was arguing his way to his salvation – went on and on insisting that the Resurrection didn't matter; and Father Anselm continued to repeat 'pas symbolique, pas symbolique'. The words were still echoing in Eric's ears as he listened to the B Minor Mass in St Gudule with Dom Bruno, and again as the Belgian coast receded in the wake of the channel packet. There came an echo, too, from *Captain Brassbound's Conversion* – 'what an escape, what an escape'; and, as if in answer to his irrational fears and obstinate doubts, an echo of the Plainchant he had heard at Mont César: 'When I first, all unprepared and innocent, heard: *Deus in adjutorium* . . . I knew, infallibly, that God existed and was a living God – just as I knew him in the answering smile of a child or in the living words of Christ.'[1]

These echoes died away with the emotion they had excited, and Eric was stranded between his reasonings and the implacable 'pas symbolique' of Father Anselm. He was never at any time historically minded. The civilizations of the past haunted him with the perfection of their works, and the hints they threw across the centuries of the reality he was seeking. The facts of history interested him not at all. The personality and teaching of Jesus claimed his allegiance; he was content to assume that Jesus could have risen from the dead if He had wanted to – unless perhaps He had found it a bore. The evidence for the Resurrection which has convinced so many sceptics left him unmoved rather than unpersuaded. Indeed, he was no longer a sceptic; he was a believer who wanted the confirmation of the Church

[1] *Autobiography*, 1940.

in which he already believed. The panoply of Catholicism impressed him very little; it was simply a proof that the Church was made up of body and spirit – 'both real and both good' like man himself – and like man, not invariably attractive. There was more to the Church than Bishop Blougram, but the Church was only the more convincing because Bishop Blougram had worn its tonsure.

And so Eric continued to go regularly to Mass and set himself a stern course of reading – Chesterton's *Orthodoxy* and Francis Cornford's *Philosophy's Foundations in Religion*. In his Fabian days he had made little of Chesterton, but now he began 'to revere and love him, as a writer and a holy man, beyond all his contemporaries'.[1] And indeed there was no other writer of that day to whom the virtue of holiness could be ascribed without absurdity. Eric knew no Catholics beside the Meynells, and the monks of Mont César. This was fortunate; as time went on he would find them far more shocking than Bishop Blougram. So he now wrote, probably on Dom Bruno's advice, to Abbot Ford, the Prior of Ealing, who replied offering to come down to Ditchling:

You must not in this life expect to *know* what is hidden and can only be reached by faith. We see these things now only through a glass darkly. That is the supreme trial of life. If we had knowledge, we should not need faith. Whatever people (science) may pretend everyone knows that he is in the dark in regard to the things that matter. Those that have any light only know enough to understand their ignorance better than others – and know that their knowledge is not an ignorance but a faith. You will say that this is mysticism, but I suppose that the mystics are those who are nearest to knowledge about the hidden world. We must remain content to see darkly. (June 13, 1912)

Fry had been right in his judgment that Eric was naïve, and Ford in suspecting that he was inordinately curious. The Abbot came down to Ditchling on June 19 and Eric 'liked him very much' – perhaps because he said that 'ideas were more important than morals'.[2]

[1] *Autobiography.*
[2] Diary.

Meanwhile, on July 31 – the Feast of St Ignatius – Dom Bruno wrote again more sternly:

I believe . . . you are quite wrong not to do and to have done already what I advised (you) to do without delay – that is – to confess yourself after two or three days very simple instruction. God does not want people to be so clever about the understanding of His mysteries. You will know them as far as one can know them – after having shown your goodwill by practising. But as long as you will remain a 'dilettante', and to kneel only from time to time, and to sign yourself with the blessed water – it will never go. You will remain always at the same point.

With Pius X's encouragement of frequent Communion for the very young in mind, Dom Bruno went on:

A lot of these good little children – wiser and more clever than you, dear Eric – go now every day to Communion. . . . Please, dear Eric, do not postpone any more. You would be so happy if the Confession and first Communion were done. Go together and with Madame Gill to the Father Abbot at Ealing. It will be quite a new life for you and all your family – but you must not waste time, examining always a state of mind which has been more than enough examined. 'Be quick: look sharp' – as say the boys in the London streets, if my memory is right.

Eric took this importunity to heart. He had already paid a second visit to Father King at Ely Place, and on August 15 he called on Abbot Ford, but found him away. In the previous week he had met Wyndham Lewis with Roger Fry at Guildford; Fry was 'very argumentative and antagonistic to Catholicism'.[1] Meanwhile Eric was busy carving acrobats, demons, phalluses, and dolls. He was reading *Piers Plowman*, while Vespers at Westminster Cathedral revived memories of Mont César. On September 22 Joseph Cribb left for Paris to cut the inscription on Epstein's monument to Oscar Wilde, and on the same day Eric wrote to Abbot Ford asking for instruction. Early the next month they met at Downside. Ford was in the position of a Harley Street specialist who finds out what is wrong with you and sends you back to your local G.P. Moreover, Dom Bruno had been altogether too optimistic in imagining that Eric could be re-

[1] Diary.

ceived into the Church with 'two or three days very simple instruction'. Eric paid a further visit to the Abbot in November, but for his
formal instruction he went to Canon Connelly at Brighton, while
Ethel received hers at a convent. They went over together once a
week. Canon Connelly, Eric observed later, told him 'a lot of
things that sounded jolly odd', but he took them on the chin.

Otherwise the course of life was not disturbed. Ethel posed for a
new statuette – perhaps the 'Woman holding herself and looking
down' – and Eric started work on a marble phallus, and on a 'Mother
and Child' in bronze. He spent a weekend with the Cornfords, his
faith surviving an argument with Bertrand Russell. Christmas was
spent happily – though it was too wet to go to Mass – with a doll's
house for Joanna, a doll for Petra, and a stamp book for Betty. Various
villagers came in to see the tree, and on December 29 Eric showed
his pictures through a kaleidoscope to an audience of twenty-five
people. One of these was of the *Trinity* – which was asking rather a
lot of Ditchling in the Christmas holidays. Edward Marsh brought
Rupert Brooke to lunch in January – 'atheistical beggars'[1] Eric
thought them, although Brooke commissioned the statue of a
Mother and Child. There was an evening at Coomaraswamy's at
which Coomaraswamy's mistress sang some beautiful Indian songs;
and a meeting with Henry James – 'the novelist' Eric adds in his
diary – arranged by Roger Fry. Eric watched the Varsity Rugger
match at Twickenham, and attended a debate between Belloc and
Shaw at the Queen's Hall. He thought Belloc 'first-rate', but Shaw
'vague, feeble, and a mere debater and rhetorician'. He would not
have thought so once. He was also at work on his designs for the new
Great Seal, and in his spare time he was reading St Thomas Aquinas.
At last, on his birthday – February 22, 1913 – he and Ethel were
received into the Catholic Church by Canon Connelly. In the evening
Leonard and Virginia Woolf came for the weekend, and after Eric and
Ethel had made their first Communion the next morning they spent
all day walking with their guests along the Downs. Faith and agnosticism – each in its purest form – can rarely have mixed so easily.

[1] Diary.

3

One thing lacking at Sopers was the companionship of the Edward Johnstons. The Gills missed the Boat Race parties at Hammersmith in the room with the old-fashioned chintz curtains – large gay flowers on a white ground – and the mirror over the mantelpiece which had been their own present to the house. It was a special joy, therefore, when the Johnstons settled at Ditchling, in October 1912, in a red brick villa on the outskirts of the village. Johnston tried to interest Eric in a scheme for designing a new alphabet of block letters. McKnight Kauffer would design for posters and Holden for architecture, and the style should carry the clear signature of the twentieth century. For some reason, however, Eric dropped out of the scheme, but the two friends were now neighbours once more, and it was in the back bedroom of his house at Ditchling that Johnston designed his own block letter alphabet.

Betty, Petra and Joanna were all baptized on March 1, and Ethel took the name of Mary. For some time Eric would refer to her as 'Mary Ethel', but in the course of time she became simply 'Mary', and it was as 'Mary' that she was known to their friends. From now on she will be known only as Mary here. Eric made two rosaries for the children and a silver crucifix for himself. In March he spent a weekend at Royston with the Raverats and Stanley Spencer, discussing a plan to illustrate the Gospels. A deadlock was reached over the text to be used, Eric maintaining that he could not now work on the Authorized Version – though why he should have had such a scruple it is difficult to see. He seems, however, to have overcome it – or some sensible person overcame it for him – for he was shortly afterwards exchanging views on the subject with Wilfrid Meynell and hard at work on his preliminary drawings. He was now trying the 'plank' method of woodcutting, rather than cutting on the end grain as one does with boxwood. In April he was staying with the Rothen-

steins in Gloucestershire, and shortly afterwards the statue he had
made for William excited an eloquent admiration:

The lady looked like the divine mother of all the world when I saw her in
the red wax, but now that you have coloured her in some mysterious
way she has become the Virgin Mary unmistakably suckling the Christ. . . .
You have painted her most beautifully, and she reigns over my desk above
me, my Chinese ivory mother facing her from the other end of the room.
(May 17, 1913)

Eric's youngest sister, Angela, had sat as a model for this statue –
though she was only 14 years old at the time.

Before the arrival of the Johnstons in Ditchling (October 1912),
the Gills had begun to look for a new home in the neighbourhood. A
house, with two acres of land, was up for sale on the western fringe
of Ditchling Common, and this property they acquired. Although
the move was consistent with Eric's theories about life and living,
it was not in itself theoretical. The Gills simply wanted to own a
house and such land as would allow them to produce their own milk,
butter, pigs, poultry and eggs, and to make those things, like bread and
clothes, that could be made at home. They were confident in the
superiority of their own produce to that of modern commerce. No
custard powder was allowed; custard must be made with eggs.
There was, however, an intimate connection in Eric's mind between
Communion on Sunday morning and custard for Sunday lunch. The
motive behind the move was none the less religious for being the
gratification of a natural appetite. There was no idea of founding a
community; all they wanted was to make a home.

On August 30 the contract was signed and £52 10s deposit
paid down. A loan was raised through a broker in Burgess Hill; the
purchase was completed on October 27 when Eric went home with
the keys; and by November 13 they were moving in from Sopers.
Hopkins Crank stood a few feet back from the main road as it
crossed the Common. When Eric had made the necessary alterations
and additions, it enclosed three sides of a quadrangle. On the right,
as you faced it from the road, was a square two-storeyed house with a

gabled roof. The greater part of this was occupied by a large living-room, with a gallery, and staircase leading up to it at the southern end. There was a hole in the floor of the gallery big enough to keep a hip bath in position, and the water for this was heated from the bread oven underneath. The rest of the cooking was done on the open fire. The unsuspecting visitor sitting in the inglenook would occasionally feel the maggots dropping on his head from the cured hams suspended above him. A door connected the living-room with the kitchen, and an annexe led from this to the converted stables, an office, and a wooden shed which Eric had brought from Sopers. It was not long before a nine-gallon barrel of ale indicated a new degree of self-sufficiency, and it was good-bye to the *North Star* and the *Sand Rock*. The move had been complicated by Mary's illness. She had had a second miscarriage in September and was in bed for some days after they were established at the Crank.

The Catholic Church is slow to count its converts before they are hatched, but once they are out of the shell it is quick to make use of them. Very soon Eric was invited to submit designs for the Stations of the Cross in Westminster Cathedral. On August 16 he met the architect to the cathedral, John Marshall, and immediately set to work on preliminary drawings. At the same time he was com-missioned to carve a font for the Catholic Church at Pickering in the North Riding of Yorkshire. The font is octagonal, standing on four slender fluted pillars. Four of the panels represent the Baptism of Jesus, and Jesus in Joseph's workshop with the tools of his trade. The others show designs of foliated stone. It is not one of his best works – the detail is rather crowded – but it austerely rebukes the repellent statuary surrounding it. Since he described the Parish Priest as a 'darling',[1] perhaps later incumbents must bear the blame for this grotesque contrast. Indeed the interior of the church at Pickering is a ghastly reminder of how the English Catholics are still content to desecrate their churches, and of Eric's patient, and largely ineffectual, protest. In the naïveté of his unrelenting logic he ex-pected his co-religionists to apply as he did the principles they held

[1] Diary.

in common. With few exceptions they did not fail to disappoint him.

He was now beginning to make their acquaintance. A liturgical controversy with Adrian Fortescue brought him down to Letchworth and earned him a night's lodging at the Garden City Hotel. Ecclestiastics came to call. He listened to Robert Hugh Benson lecture on Miracles at the Caxton Hall; went over to Belgium with Mary; talked with Dom Bruno; and heard, once again, the Plainchant at Mont César. Later he visited Quarr Abbey in the Isle of Wight, then the home of the French Benedictines from Solesmes who rendered the Chant with fastidious perfection. He studied early vestments from manuscripts in the British Museum for his illustrations to the Four Gospels, but decided that the proposed woodcuts were too elaborate a project and that he must confine himself to a smaller book with initials and frontispiece. Working on the prints of a woodcut of the Blessed Trinity taught him that a dabber was better than a roller for inking the blocks.

There were still the necessary visits to London with excursions – although these were rarer now – into the world of the artists and the connoisseurs; a glimpse of Epstein at the Café Royal – 'but he did not see me'[1]; a glance at Epstein's exhibition – 'quite mad on sex'[2]; even attendance at one of Lady Ottoline Morrell's At Homes. Eric held an exhibition of his work at the Goupil Gallery in January (1914), where his monumental 'Woman' (*Mulier*), carved from Portland stone, won the admiration of Lewis Hind, writing in the *Daily Chronicle*:

It dominates the gallery. It is easier to say what this austere mother of men is not than what she is. She is not the dainty nymph that we see at the Royal Academy. This woman has no allure, no shop-window charm; she is monumental, a type, a symbol of sex with no secret but motherhood, deep-breasted, broad-hipped, eternal, a figure for reverence, not for love. The carving is severe, in broad planes. Certainly she would look more in place in the forecourt of some ancient temple than in the sculpture room of the Royal Academy. With the other exhibits one also has the feeling of

[1] Diary.
[2] ibid.

being swept back to the remote past – that sketch for a statue, that 'Gravestone' beautifully unbeautiful with haunting effects of light and shade: that 'Crucifix' might have been carved by an early Gothic crafts-man, but he could not have given to his work such precision. What are the memories that stir in me as I look at these statues, so regardless of the individual, so regardful of the type, so far from actuality, so near to humanity? That monumental figure of a 'Woman', details submerged in the archaic mass, moves me more than the most perfect modern represen-tation of any particular woman. What are the memories that stir – not the perfect art of Greece at her highest, but the peering, brooding art, perfect, too, in its single-hearted converse of an infinity that cannot be measured, of Assyria and Egypt. (January 28, 1914)

On April 1, Eric brought his completed designs for the Westminster Stations to John Marshall, and a week later he was given the com-mission to carry them out. 'The work is mine,' he exclaims exult-antly. 'Deo Gratias.'[1] He saw Cardinal Bourne after Easter, and received the confirmatory agreement. The work in prospect, and now in progress, would seal Eric's reputation as a sculptor, and give him a position, not always comfortable, in the community he had joined. In the meantime he could afford to buy a pony and lay out a tennis court.

These were official contacts and acquaintances; more personal ones were quick to follow. After a visit to Pickering in June, Eric went on to Edinburgh in answer to an invitation from André Raffalovitch. Raffalovitch was a wealthy Jew of Russian origin, and the lifelong friend of Father (later Canon) John Gray, Rector of St Peter's, Edinburgh. Gray himself had been a minor literary figure of the 'nineties; a volume of his poems with an inscription to Oscar Wilde proves him to have been the prototype of Dorian Gray. His destiny, however, had been more fortunate. After his conversion to Catholicism, he had been ordained priest from the English College at Valladolid. He was a poet of distinction and, in the words of one dis-criminating critic, his nouvelle, Park, has the 'dryness of a patrician wine'.[2] He lived at the Presbytery, where no letter went un-

[1] Diary.
[2] Walter Shewring.

answered by return of post, no beggar was turned away, and where every parochial duty was performed with ascetic thoroughness. He allied the courtesy of the drawing-room to the charity and wisdom of the confessional. Raffalovitch lived at a house near by, renowned for its elegant hospitality. Not a day passed without Gray and Raffalovitch calling on each other or otherwise communicating if either were away.

It was into this atmosphere of rarefied personal relationship and rather precious taste that Eric was now introduced. He met Father Gray at dinner and walked with him in the afternoon. He listened to Mrs Kennedy Fraser and her daughter sing Hebridean songs. He heard High Mass on the Feast of Saints Peter and Paul sung to the music of Orlando di Lassus in the church designed by Hew Lorimer against the background of a reredos painted by Frank Brangwyn; listened to a sermon by Father Vincent McNabb; and made a portrait drawing of Raffalovitch who sent him back to London in a first-class sleeper with the promise of a cheque for £280. Of this £100 was a gift and the rest was to be repaid in kind. Raffalovitch wrote to him afterwards, referring to a –

roominess of mind through which I could move without knocking against misunderstanding. It is a rare treat for me to find a roomy spacious mind. I expect mine is more like a curio shop where one can pick up some bargains if one can stand the things one does not want. One dear friend of mine is like a bare room with no furniture but a settee and an ashtray. (July 1, 1914)

He gave Eric further commissions for a bookplate, and statues of St Sebastian and an acrobat.

The outbreak of war on August 4 left the Gills relatively undisturbed. They watched the BEF embarking at Newhaven; fixed the curtain over their skylight; and helped to organize a committee for the relief of reservists' wives. Eric's younger twin brothers, Evan and Vernon Gill, arrived in England with the first Canadian contingent, both in the 1st Battery of the 1st Brigade, Field Artillery. Eric himself enrolled in the Home Defence Brigade, scoring 71 out of 100 at the miniature range at Burgess Hill. He was not concerned with the issues of the war; innocent of politics in general, he was particularly innocent of foreign affairs. He was conventionally patriotic, and prepared to do what was asked of him, but for the moment he saw no obligation to leave a wife and three children with no visible means of subsistence. He was 32 years old, and there was no demand as yet for married men. People were still expecting the BEF to be in Berlin by Christmas.

It seems, nevertheless, surprising that so immense a catastrophe should have interested an intelligent man so little. The easy answer is that Eric's was a one-track mind, but this is not quite true. His mind had several tracks, but he was not easily diverted from them. He was certainly more interested in ideas than events – and war is a supreme event, the tragic consequence of events which have begotten it. Of these Eric knew nothing, and cared less. He had travelled little; was a poor linguist; and had no feeling for Europe as the cradle of a civilization which he disliked the more he looked at it. He may have been reading Chesterton – *The Flying Inn* – but Chesterton's romantic militancy left him unmoved, although he went to hear Belloc lecture at Hove on the military prospects. It was like him to be more interested in how the war might be won than in what it was about. For the time being he was content to read Newman and Dostoievsky to himself, and Balzac to Mary in the evenings; to slaughter his first pig, and to shoot his first rabbit. In fact it was Black Sam the butcher who did the slaughtering; Eric looked on and supplied the beer.

Later, as the war's protracted agony grew plain, he took his military duties – light as they were – more seriously. We find him drilling and skirmishing on the Common with Johnston and some wounded soldiers, shooting with a new rifle, and winning 4d for a top score of 75 per cent. This was later improved to 92 per cent at the 25-yards. In July 1915 he was in camp on Lewes Racecourse, mounting guard all night and taking part in manoeuvres on the Downs. Mr Gill had now been appointed Vicar of West Wittering, and Eric went over for the wedding of his brother Max to Muriel Bennett. His younger brother Kenneth was also there, on sick leave after being wounded in France; he was later awarded the MC for gallantry and good service. With four brothers at the front, the war was never so far away as it looked from Ditchling Common when Eric, Johnston and Hilary Pepler sat down to the first of many meetings devoted to the study of medieval Latin on that late September evening of 1915.

This is the place to bring Hilary Pepler into a story where he was to count for so much. Pepler came of a Quaker family; his father was partner in a firm of brewers in Eastbourne. Hilary had been educated at Bootham School, York; and, after a short spell in the tea trade, had taken up a post with a firm of wholesale grocers in Cannon Street. With £250 inherited from his grandfather, he set up as a pewterer, employing a staff of eight men, and then sold the business to an American competitor. While he was in London he made friends with the children of Wilfrid and Alice Meynell, since he shared rooms with a relative of theirs from the Quaker branch of the family. After his marriage in 1904 he took to land surveying and spent a year at Tunbridge Wells learning his way about it, later returning to London to take up social work with William Beveridge and others. He was the organizer appointed by the LCC to supervise the provision of meals for children while they were attending school. At this time he was living at Hammersmith Terrace, where he became close friends with Edward Johnston and made the acquaintance of the Gills. Although he did not see much of them at first, Eric gave him some lessons in stone carving; as he admitted later, he was himself a rolling stone.

He stood, without success, as a Socialist candidate for the Hammersmith Borough Council – Eric may well have assisted his campaign – and then devoted his energies to adult education. In 1914 he visited penal institutions in Vienna and Budapest. There was a suggestion that he should enter the Home Office, but owing to the outbreak of war this idea came to nothing. In 1907, however, he had founded the Hampshire House Club for working men. This was a manor house of some architectural pretentions, situated in Hammersmith between Kelmscott House and some adjacent slums. Pepler had enlisted the help of Chesterton, Belloc and William Rothenstein, and during the summers of 1912–14 he organized holidays for the members of his Club at the seaside. His friendship with Johnston brought him to

Ditchling. A Londoner by temperament, he wanted nevertheless to earn his living in the country, and it occurred to him that a hand printing press, not dependent on electricity, would afford him a convenient means of doing so. So in 1915 he settled at Sopers as soon as the Gills had vacated it, and set up his press in a shed conveniently near by. The two men had much in common – many of the same ideas and a charismatic power to propagate them – but where Eric was a professional to his finger-tips, Pepler was a happy amateur. He had tried his hands at too many things to be quite an expert in any one of them. Also – and this would be important later on – he had a reasonable private income.

With the slaughter of pigs, the storing of apples, the baking of bread, and the mutual Latin tutorials, something like an outline of what came to be known as 'Ditchling' now begins to be discernible. Notice, however, that of the three men who gathered on that September evening only Eric was a Catholic, and Johnston was never to become one. He stands, therefore, a little outside the story – though his influence was seminal, and he had arrived at a religious view of life long before Eric himself. All Eric – and others – had to do was to enter the Church from the point to which Johnston had led them, or at which they had simultaneously arrived. Johnston's casual jottings demonstrate the debt:

Three questions every honest and practical man must ask of things, What, How, and Why? What is this thing? How is it done? Why should it be done? Why should one, why ought one, why must one? Why is it good, proper, beautiful, civilized, progressive? To man an answer is necessary, and he has found one in the idea of God.

Things are His will.

If we think that Material Creation has purpose or can be fulfilled with purpose, then all material objects – including our bodies – are 'Tools' – the flesh is a *sine qua non* for the spirit of man – an opportunity rather than an obstacle.

The Truth – its other names are goodness and beauty, the Way and the Life, the Light (of the World), the Word, and many more.

It is that against which we sin.[1]

[1] *Edward Johnston, 1959.*

4

Eric worked steadily at his Westminster Stations when other jobs did not keep him at home or take him about the country. He carved them not in their devotional or chronological order, but as this or that milestone along the Via Dolorosa appealed to his imagination. He began, therefore, with the Xth Station in which Jesus is shown stripped of His garments. The result did not altogether please him. The IInd followed where Jesus receives the Cross, and the XIIIth – perhaps the best of all – where He is laid in the arms of the Blessed Virgin. Then Eric went back to the Ist where Jesus is condemned to death. These had all been fixed by June 1915. The laying of the Cross upon Simon of Cyrene, and the meetings with the Blessed Virgin and Veronica came afterwards. The second fall of Jesus, the mourning of the women of Jerusalem, and the third fall followed in their usual order; then the death of Jesus, the entombment, and the nailing to the Cross.

The whole work was finished on March 11, 1918, and canonically 'erected' on the afternoon of Good Friday. A small tablet was placed underneath the XIVth Station after Eric's death, with his initials and dates. Later, when both he and his widow were beyond reach of protest, the inscriptions underneath the carvings were coloured in red. Evidently the ecclesiastical authorities – whose Philistine impertinence, as we shall later see, knew no bounds – thought the effect would be prettier. They were matched by the *dévote* who, passing Eric at work, observed: 'I don't call that a pretty carving.' 'No,' he replied, 'it is not a pretty subject.'

The Westminster Stations are the most considerable work that Eric undertook for the Church which he had joined, and they must be judged not on their merits alone but in relation to the cathedral they adorned. Now, well as he knew the cathedral, Eric was very far from approving of it:

I hold that Westminster Cathedral is as disgraceful a piece of sham stylistic building as any Pugin Gothic. It was endurable because brick and concrete construction happens to be a suitable method for industrial building. The outside of the building is absurd. The inside will soon be equally so. As to Brompton Oratory the same applies. It is a fine spacious and well-proportioned church but architecturally it is sheer nonsense. The virtue of medieval building was that it represents the builders as much as those who paid for it. Both Brompton Oratory and Westminster represent the snobbery of those who paid. (Letter to a priest, undated)

Those who believe (with the present writer) that the interior decoration of Westminster is an expensive and anachronistic folly should remember, notwithstanding, that the general idea of this was envisaged in Bentley's original design; that it was not unreasonable to suppose, before the impoverishment resulting from two world wars, that the money could be found to pay for it; and that the pale expanse of London brick, so well adapted to the fine proportions of the place, would hardly have conveyed the same impression of aesthetic honesty in the first decades of the century as it does today. Nevertheless, the effect of Eric's Stations will clearly not be the same against a background of marble as they were against a background of brick. The sculpture will disagree with the setting very much as the sculptor himself disagreed with it, long before the work was completed and could be judged as a whole.

Both setting and sculpture had their critics; P. G. Konody in *The Observer* complained that the Stations were 'neo-primitive' and 'affected' and that, instead of assimilating the severity of an archaic style, Eric had merely adopted its incidental ugliness. A correspondent, signing himself 'Fidelis', accused the sculptor of 'harking back to the first or second childhood of art' and of assuming 'the infirmities of infancy or decrepitude – or at times the rigor mortis itself'. Another correspondent – 'Catholicus' – came to Eric's support. He pointed out that Bentley had left no more than rough indications as to the interior decoration of the cathedral, and that these had become a 'hidden and potent Deposit of Faith' upon which the present architect could draw to justify any work he chose to put in

8. Portrait of Eric Gill by David Jones, 1930.

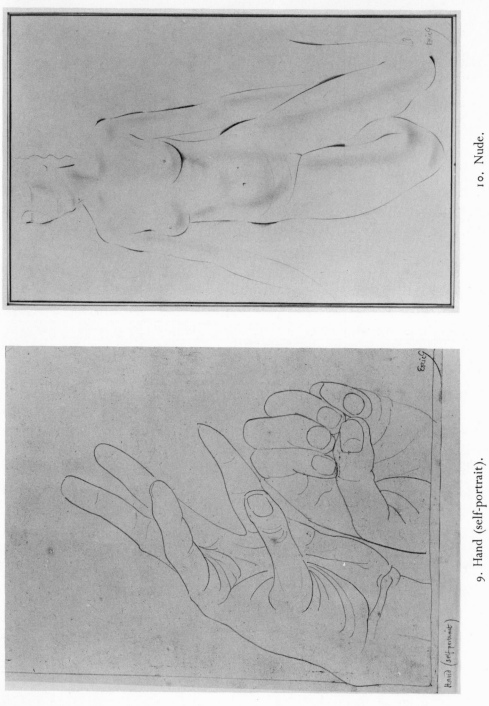

9. Hand (self-portrait).

10. Nude.

hand and which he alone had seen. Bentley himself was profoundly dissatisfied with the work carried out under his supervision before his death, particularly with the Chapel of the Holy Souls. Great architect as he was, his own work in decoration was 'poor, tawdry and mortiferously derivative'. Where the cathedral was concerned, he had probably doubted his own capacity; his ideal – or so 'Catholicus' believed – was a Master of Decorations with a school of workers under him. Where they were to come from was another matter. The result of leaving the completion of the work in the hands of anonymous and incompetent authorities had been 'an unchecked series of disasters', including 'a trail of shamrocks in mother o' pearl' on the altar of St Patrick. Against these frivolities Eric's Stations stood out 'on a plane apart from any other work in the Cathedral'. (October 17, 1915)

Eric replied to these, and other, criticisms in an interview with a representative of *The Observer*. It had been said that certain touches of colour – blue lining and red borders to the tunics of the Roman soldiers, green grass in the 'Deposition' – far from giving life to the cold surface had just the opposite effect. He explained that the patches of colour were purely experimental, and in fact they were afterwards erased. If it were objected that his work was out of keeping with Bentley's design, he answered that it was not necessary to follow a great engineer's work in decoration simply because he was a great engineer. The original intention had been to carry out the Stations by the method known as *opus sectile* – in which pieces of tile were glazed and burned in colours. The method had been tried in one of the chapels with unfortunate results; it was a method, anyway, that required large kilns and plant – 'it is factory work and to any real craftsmanship it is death'.

Although the method of low relief was preferred because it was the only kind of carving that could be done in the circumstances, and the only kind believed to have been used in a Byzantine building, Eric questioned whether the cathedral was a Byzantine building at all. It was a fine building 'covered with quasi-Byzantine ornament', which was a weakness rather than a strength. Eric denied that he was working in any particular bygone style. 'I am working in the only style in which I can work. I am not a learned antiquarian who can work in any style at choice.' At the same time he advised the public, through the *Westminster Cathedral Chronicle*,[1] how they should regard the Stations. If there were no crowd depicted, it was because 'we ourselves are the crowd'. The costumes were purposely unhistorical and the expression on the faces deliberately impassive. He described the treatment as 'diagrammatic' – analogous to plain language in print and Plainchant in music; 'a sentence without adjectives'.[1] The Stations should be regarded like the beads of a Rosary; they were designed to excite piety, not emotion, and the Catholic following the Way of the Cross from one to another must say his own *Hail Mary* and make his own appropriate meditation. For some reason, which is not very clear, Eric signed this article under a pseudonym, E. Rowton.

Since no work of Eric's in stone is better than the Westminster Stations, it may be useful to examine in more extensive detail how he looked upon his work as a stone carver. Here a correspondence with Jacques Raverat is to the point. In an introduction to Coomaraswamy's *Visvakarma* – a book containing 100 reproductions of Indian sculpture – Eric had opposed Indian and classical canons of aesthetics to the detriment of the latter. Raverat wrote in correction:

I am not nearly so disposed to agree with a good deal of what you say as I should have been a year or two ago. I have lately come to a great admiration for 'classic art', i.e. Phidias and Praxiteles among the Greeks; Raphael and Poussin, for example, in Western Europe. I never used to understand them before and I think now they are as much misunderstood by their enemies as by their admirers of the Victorian era. In the same way I can now – I flatter myself – appreciate the succession of 'styles' in a great cathedral like Chartres. I think it is a mistake to oppose primitive and classical work. One is the fulfilment of the other's promise. Of course it has *not* that romantic element of promise, and of indefiniteness in the future. But it is not necessarily less religious; only less ecclesiastical perhaps. It is less emotional but far more intellectual; if understood, as I

[1] March 1918.

think, rightly, less sensual and much more abstract. It is the art of the manhood of a nation. It is difficult to write about beauty without feeling self-conscious – after all the cant and tommy rot that critics talk – but I do think that just beauty of composition and beauty of form is deeply religious; perhaps just because it is so useless, so gratuitous, a truly unselfish offering of the best we can conceive (being earthly) to God; and perhaps, too, most directly proceeding *from* God. Doubtless it must have roots in good workmanship; but yet it is different from that. We *must be* CATHOLIC. The Church – your Church – embraced the Evangelists and St Jerome; St Francis and St Dominic; the hermit and the giver of alms. Should not that be our aim too? (Mind you, it *did* reject the Heretics, and so must we; but short of Heresy, we cannot and must not damn this to enthrone that, else would our world be one of Prussian-like uniformity and stagnation.) To return, shall we say, to Phidias; what I mean is that a really beautiful – and beautifully carved – body does *not* fill me with all sorts of unlawful lusts or any kind of sensual emotion. It fills me with an intellectual joy not so very different as one may derive from Euclid or Thomas Aquinas – at the wonderfulness and perfection of design. The sixth-century Greek work, for instance, does on the contrary stir in me depths of primitive blind passion, orphic, or dionysiac or whatever you like to call it: all too human and sometimes not a little diabolic, perhaps. Much early work does seem to me rather diabolic than divine in its inspiration. Certainly all the Assyrian work and very much of the Indian. Some of the Chinese, but not most (and by the way, I think the Chinese far nearer to us Europeans than the Indians). And a good many of the Byzantine mosaics. (February 15, 1915)

Many of Eric's friends would use these arguments against him as time went by, and the only answer he could make to Raverat was disconcertingly pragmatic. He was becoming the prisoner of his *parti pris*.

I do not think I disagree with you at all (i.e. I do not disagree with what you say at all) – in theory. I suppose my Preface to the Indian sculpture was special pleading to some extent. But I think it is essential that you should 'take sides' in this world, and just as in the 'political' sphere, admitting all sorts of things in theory, the question is: are you on the side of the poor or on that of the rich? – upon which side does your heart beat, not your head? So in this other matter, attempting to steer a course not of contemplation but of action – and a course potent, almost pregnant, for the future, the question is: are you on the side of the children or of the grown-ups? I am just a letter cutter who has taken to 'sculpture' and so far all things wonderful are 'primitive', elementary, clear, symmetrical, hieratic, ordered, smooth, serene, young, playful . . . other things are admirable, not beloved. The Catholic Church is like a mother to whom all her children are dear, but her children are not their mother and must fight among themselves. However, my words are not convincing – even to myself – it is not a matter of words. All I know is that the only kind of work I can do or can wish to do is of some sort more allied to that of children (whether bad kids or good) than to that of the more obviously grown-up old masters. Anyway I know what side I'm on – tho' I know nothing about orphic or dionysiac emotions – they sound like the discoveries of Miss Jane Harrison (not that I've read her). And, in brief, I think it would be a good thing if all art education were done away (with), and all men became workmen and made *things* – oblivious of the past and remembering that beauty is an 'accident' and the gift of God as well. (February 28, 1915)

This letter throws up into clear relief the limitations of Eric's polemic, which was much more subjective than he would have cared to admit. The rich and the poor had nothing to do with comparative aesthetic values, and to deny that these values existed made non-sense of the history of art. Eric might have preferred that art should have no history, but the history of art was a fact of life as plain as the history of man, and a part of it; it invited analysis rather than ana-thema. Nor was Eric's own sculpture nearly as primitive as he liked to imagine; much of it was highly sophisticated; and the best of it – like the Westminster Stations of which Raverat was a warm admirer – combined simplicity of feeling with a classical strength and grace. The whole bent of Eric's mind disposed him to an art which, in some way or other, belonged to daily living; he was fighting the Renaissance in art as he would presently be fighting it in economics. On the one hand, he wrote to William Rothenstein, were –

Giotto, etc., Persian rugs, bricks and iron girders, tools, steam engines, Folksong, Plainchant, Calligraphy, Toys (not some few modern ones tho'), animals, men and women physically regarded, Hair, Lines, String, plaited straw, Beer, and so on. On the other are Velasquez, Rembrandt, etc. No, this second list is too difficult – what I wish to convey is that such things as I name in the first list and such things as young children's drawings and the works of savages are themselves actually a part of nature and in no sense outside her – while, on the other hand, the work of Rembrandt and most moderns (the modern contribution to the Renaissance) is not a part of nature but is apart from nature – is in fact an appreciation and a criticism of nature – reviewing of nature as of something to be loved or hated. . . . (October 15, 1916)[1]

Eric admitted that this post-Raphaelite conception of art might be a 'higher' thing than his own more utilitarian conception of 'making', but he never arrived at a philosophy of the imagination which would justify its claims to be so. This failure did not impoverish his own work, because he was not a great imaginative sculptor, but it limited his appreciation of other people's. An artist can admire Houdin or Donatello without thinking himself bound to copy them, but instead of looking Eric looked away.

His own later sculpture, like his later woodcuts, was spoilt not by simplicity but by affectation, as if he were repeating a formula, or as if he did not quite believe in what he was doing. When he was carving for capitalist employers, this was certainly the case; he was working to earn his daily bread. But the Westminster Stations were an expression – he would perhaps have preferred to say a statement – of what he believed in most profoundly. Moreover they served a devotional as well as a decorative purpose; they were designed to be a focus of prayer. Other work executed about the same time had a similar inspiration and effect. On the recommendation of Raffa-lovitch, he carved a Mother and Child for François Mauriac who thanked him for it five years later when the English Channel was open for the passage of *objets d'art*:

The strange and delicious little queen of the Orient that you have sent me has crossed the sea without trouble. Nothing has tarnished the brilliance of her red veil, her blue tunic, and the fragile foot peeping out of its socket has not been broken, as we might have feared. You will allow me to add your own name to that of our mutual friend when I invoke the

[1] *Letters of Eric Gill.*

Virgin Mother before the simple and lively effigy that you have carved. This is the only way I have of discharging my debt to you.[1]

Eric never met François Mauriac nor, so far as I know, read any of his books. Two temperaments more opposed could hardly be imagined within the household of the Faith.

In a searching essay[2] David Jones has arrived at what I believe is a just estimate of Eric Gill as a sculptor. He pointed out that in a world devoid of culture Eric worked 'as though a culture of some sort existed or, at all events . . . as though one should, and could, *make* such a culture exist'. Because of the man he was, his carvings sometimes looked like the products of a culture that was living and authentic. They stood apart from the academics and the eclectics – although the future might label them as 'early twentieth-century eclecticism'. They excited a similar distrust to that aroused by people who admired the painting of Picasso without agreeing with his politics. 'Poor Gill,' it might be said, 'he was a superb stone-cutter – had great possibilities – pity about this Roman Catholic thing.' Roman Catholicism was certainly extraneous to the many good artists who 'made a god of art' because they could find nothing better to worship, and Eric always suffered from being judged by standards not his own. Yet it was the 'Roman Catholic thing' which inspired the Westminster Stations, and the hard, practical experience of a monumental mason, carving, as no other sculptor was then carving, directly on the stone, which gave the inspiration plastic effect. It may be true, as David Jones suggests, that the Stations are not profound works of sculpture; but they are at the very least 'adequate and right and perhaps the only live things in that building', and they owed their excellence to Eric's 'simple and workmanlike approach'. They remained 'appropriate, unworrying', and 'curiously unidiosyncratic considering the severe personal convention'; and having regard to the existing divorce between the arts and civilization they constituted 'a unique achievement'.

[1] Author's translation.
[2] *Blackfriars*, February 1941.

5

The versatility of Eric Gill – or, more exactly, his conviction that 'it all hangs together' – was shown by a piece of work only revealed to the public when his achievement in typographical lettering was exhibited at the Monotype House in 1958. Among the items was a copy of *The Ship Painter's Handbook* by George S. Welch in the 1900 edition. The margins of this useful but specialized publication were covered with revisions by Eric in red ink. At the same time that he was occupied with the Westminster Stations, he was approached by the publisher of the book, James Hogg, asking him to edit and revise it for a new edition. Eric agreed and proposed the modest fee of £10. Later, however, he wrote: 'I quite understand the position and if you think £5 5s is the figure the book will stand I will do the work for that sum with pleasure, and will put it in hand at once. . . . I gather from what you say that there is no question of giving offence to the original author by my meddling.' Eric spent 103 working hours on the revision. Chapter 13 was re-written and its crude line-blocks redrawn; as Beatrice Warde has pointed out, it offers 'a very early expression of Gill's lettering philosophy, and its example of a "block letter" (which at that time he thought should carry minimum-weight serifs) offers any modern type-founder a dignified version of the neglected style that the Trade calls "engravers" Gothic'.[1] Men will go on painting ships to the end of time, but few of them who buy the current edition from Messrs Brown, Son and Ferguson, Ltd. of Glasgow realize the extent to which Eric is helping them with the clarity of print and expression.

It was in 1908 that Hilary Pepler had first received a card of Christmas greeting from Eric and Mary Gill – simple lettering framed by two panels of sculptor's tools – and Eric had done relatively little wood-engraving until Pepler set up his hand press in January

[1] 'The Diuturnity of Eric Gill', *The Penrose Annual*: Vol. 53, 1959.

1916 at Sopers. This was where Pepler had lived before moving to the Common. The sum total of Pepler's equipment was a Stanhope of 1790, a folio Albion and two founts of Caslon Old Face type. He obtained his hand-made paper from the firm which had supplied William Morris at the Kelmscott Press, and it was on this that Eric illustrated Pepler's *Devil's Devices*. We owe to Pepler a picture of him at work which at first was almost as casual as a game:

The first thing which struck me as an observer of Gill at work was the sureness and steadiness of his hand at minute detail; the assurance and swiftness of a sweep of line is one thing (and here he was a past master) but the hairs on an eyelash another – and he liked to play about with hairs and rays which can hardly be distinguished with a magnifying glass (and easily tended to be filled with ink in printing). Then he was always obliging. When I wanted a tail piece to end a chapter or an initial letter with which to begin one, he would tumble to the point at once, probably improve upon my suggestion, supply the block ready for the press within an hour, and come in to see it printed that same afternoon.[1]

Perhaps it was the casual nature of these printing experiments that gave its name to the 'occasional magazine' which now began to give Ditchling a special significance in the eyes of those who were in sympathy with ideas held in common by Eric, Pepler and Johnston. The first number of *The Game* was published in October 1916. Its Prologue was taken from the opening chapter of St John's Gospel in the Vulgate text: *In principio erat verbum*. The most fundamental of all beginnings was followed by an epigraph in English:

A man having seen the glory of God must thereafter
work for the glory of God, the things which he makes
will work *for the glory of God*.

Like everything that Pepler touched, *The Game* was frolicsome as well as fundamental. Its purpose was to print views 'about things in general which we regarded, as all men regard games, of supreme importance. In the strict sense of the word it was not with any idea of

[1] *A Letter from Sussex*: Cherryburn Press and the Society of Typographic Arts, Chicago, 1950.

propaganda; it was more a corporate letter-writing to others who were willing to play with us.'[1] Johnston himself inscribed by hand a text on the first Christmas number – a kind of joint Christmas card; and only enough copies of this were printed to satisfy the exact needs of a small number of subscribers. For the October number Eric contributed a triangular variation on the theme of the Devil's tails, and a serious essay on The Control of Industry which was afterwards published, slightly abridged, in the *Architectural Review* (April 1926). For the Christmas number he did one of his most beautiful woodcuts, the animals – horse, donkey, cock and cat – silhouetted against the light that shone in darkness, and inside the Blessed Virgin reclining on the straw with St Joseph sitting meditative and apart. It was on January 20, 1916, that Eric walked over to Ditchling village, saw Pepler's press, and did his first piece of printing. A week later he was at work on a wood-engraving for Pepler's edition of Cobbett's *Cottage Economy*. Cobbett and St Thomas Aquinas were the law and the prophets for what was now developing into 'Ditchling'.

Eric took regular instruction in serving Mass from a priest at Westminster Cathedral, and was soon composing the text for a book on the subject which Pepler was preparing to print. He served Mass at the cathedral whenever he had the chance, and it was on one of these occasions that he met Belloc for the first time. At home he started the practice of reading the *martyrologium* before dinner, while the girls read the Epistle and Gospel. In March 1917 he took Pepler on the first of many visits to Hawkesyard Priory (near Rugely in Staffordshire) where the English province of the English Dominicans had their house of theological studies. Father Vincent McNabb was the Prior, and it would be hard to over-estimate his influence upon both Eric and Pepler. Pepler and he argued to and fro round the fire in the Common Room, and Eric lectured to the students on Art and Beauty. 'The chief feature of the lecture', wrote one who heard it, 'was the humility of the lecturer. He never hesitated about saying "I don't know".'[2] Asked for a definition of the Beautiful, Eric drew

---

[1] *The Hand Press* by H. D. C. Pepler, 1934.
[2] *Father Vincent McNabb* by Ferdinand Valentine, O.P., 1955.

a sketch of himself and Pepler in Brother Ferdinand Valentine's autograph album, and Pepler added the following verse:

> Lives of great men all remind us
> We are winkles in the slime
> Ready to be picked and salted
> Bolted down before our time.
> Life as Gill and Pepler lead it
> Leaving much to be desired
> Is a Beacon or a Footprint
> For the muddled or the tired.
> Life as Gill and Pepler lead it
> Would not do for you and me
> But the seed we sow – they need it
> Only to set others free.

Pepler went away with his last objections shattered, and on October 4 he returned with Eric to begin a Retreat under Father Vincent's direction. The next evening Eric made his confession to Father Vincent, and afterwards the three men discussed the project of forming a religious order of artists. On the afternoon of October 6 Hilary Pepler was received into the Church by Father Vincent, and at the end of the Retreat he and Eric received the Papal Blessing. It is difficult to pinpoint a day on which 'Ditchling' was conceived; but it was born at Hawkesyard on October 6, 1917, and it was baptized by Vincent McNabb. At Ditchling, when he went there, Father Vincent met something more than an illustration of his social theories; in the words of his biographer, he 'met Nazareth', and in his own words, spoken many years later, 'I loved Ditchling with a love surpassing that of women'.

The friendship of Eric no less than the persuasions of Father Vincent had brought Pepler into the Church; this was a case where Eric seems to have exerted influence rather than submitted to it. Mrs Pepler was slow to follow; indeed she regretted not only her husband's conversion to Catholicism but his conversion to country life with the separation it brought from London friends and interests. 'Ditchling' was essentially a masculine conception of the good life;

the men did not conspicuously dig, but the women were still expected to spin – in the intervals of producing children, baking bread, and curing hams. Pepler and Eric were both in flight from Fabian feminism, and *Man and Superman* at the Royal Court must have seemed a remote and regrettable heresy. As a matter of fact, one of their Ditchling neighbours – Ethel Mairet – was celebrated for her spinning, and her husband, Philip, was a musician of some parts. He was also a student of philosophy and had played Polonius at the Old Vic. Eric himself had learnt to play the flute, and evenings at the Crank were tuneful, even if they were not loud, with song. The brewing of beer was ardently discussed as well as professionally practised. 'You wouldn't believe what thundering good stuff "home brew" is – knocks the pub stuff off the earth. At present we're trying malting 'cause the brewers, taking fright at the thought of "home brew", have got the Govt. to stop the sale of malt. But we can get or grow the barley so we'll beat 'em yet.'[1]

The war dragged on, and inevitably pacifism was opposed to 'the honour of arms' in the conversations for which all these busy people seemed to have unlimited time. Pepler's Quaker background would have given him an instinctive sympathy for the pacifist point of view, although he was disqualified for military service on medical grounds and pacifism was not a Catholic hobby-horse during the First World War. Belloc and Chesterton had seen to that. As the casualty lists mounted, Eric came to be in demand for war memorials. His first important work of this kind was the village cross at Bryantspuddle in Dorset. When the stone had been carved it was placed on a horse-drawn lorry which Eric and Pepler drove across the south of England. We find Eric 'somewhat put out of action by a kick from one of the horses';[2] cooking kippers at an open fire in a farmyard; sleeping in a barn; and bathing under a bridge on the Hants and Dorset borders. The journey took them six days, and at the end of it there was talk and music with his brother Max at Tonerspuddle. On the way home they slept in the trolley, now emptied of its sculpture. One of their

[1] Letter to Geoffrey Keynes, September 27, 1917, published in *Letters of Eric Gill*, 1947.
[2] Diary.

halts was at Fareham, which moved Eric to the following limerick:

> There was a young lady at Fareham
> Who thought of a new way to wear 'em.
> She said 'I'll use paste
> And not strings round the waist
> And then they can't possibly tear 'em.'

They finished the journey by train, sending on a man with the trolley.

The Bryantspuddle Cross has a figure of Christ with a sword and a stigmatized hand raised in blessing. Underneath the following words from Juliana of Norwich are inscribed:

> It is sooth that sin was cause of all this pain.
> But all shall be well, and all shall be well, and all
> manner of thing shall be well.

Under that again is a ram with its head turned back and foot holding a cross with a pennon; and below it is a massive figure of the Blessed Virgin, seated, and holding out her breast for the Infant Christ. Thomas Hardy and his wife were among those who came over to see the Cross before its dedication by the Bishop of Salisbury on November 12, 1918 – just twenty-four hours after the signing of the Armistice. Other notable work by Eric in the West Country was the memorial inscription to Raymond Asquith on the south wall of the church at Mells, and his lettering on the War Memorial in the same village:

> We died in a strange land facing the dark cloud of war,
> and this stone is raised to us in the home of our delight.

From Mells it was an easy step to Downside where Pepler joined Eric for a discussion on Plainchant with Dom Shebbeare. They were considering the publication of a Plainchant Hymn Book, and with this evidently in mind went on to Stanbrook Abbey in Worcestershire. Here they met Dame Laurentia – perhaps she asked them when Bernard Shaw was coming into the Church – and later examined the Worcester Antiphonal. Almost any Sung Mass was a musical purgatory for Eric; 'Oh, Lor', what muck for music!' he exclaims after trying to say his prayers in St Mary Magdalene's at Brighton. In

October (1917) he was at the Parkminster Charterhouse with Pepler to discuss the printing of Plainchant with one of the monks. In the evenings Johnston and Mairet joined them for the singing of Plainchant hymns, and very soon the children were being taught 'Nunc Sancti Nobis Spiritus' from a large manuscript which Eric had drawn up as a result of these consultations.

Another important war memorial was conceived about this time, although it was not executed until later. In 1916 Eric had submitted a design for a monument to commemorate the employees of the LCC. This envisaged a colossal work in bronze, describing the expulsion of the money-changers from the Temple. The LCC evidently failed to see any connection between war and usury – indeed they would not have been alone in failing to do so – and the design was rejected. A photograph of it, however, appeared in *Land and Water*, and Michael Sadler, then Vice-Chancellor of Leeds University, was taken with the idea of erecting such a monument somewhere in the University precincts. Eric received the formal commission to execute it on September 13, 1917; met Sadler in London shortly afterwards; and went up to Leeds to examine possible sites.

You see (he wrote to Geoffrey Keynes), I'm thinking of making it a pretty straight thing – modern dress as much as poss, Leeds manufacturers, their wives and servants, don't you see. . . . Here is the sermon given into my hands, so to say. I didn't invent the notion – I got it from the Gospels if you'll believe it! I'm only the aesthetic instrument of the moralists and philosophers. But there's no need to apologize, is there? Even as artist I may well be enthusiastic quite apart from the fact that, as 'citizen of this great country' and member of Christ's Bride, I rather like the job, the revolutionary job of turning out the money-changers.[1]

It was hardly surprising, as we shall presently see, that the Leeds manufacturers saw the matter in a rather different light.

Since it was impossible for Mary to have any more children, the Gills now decided to adopt a boy from the Infants Home at Haywards Heath. Gordian Gill joined the family after Christmas, an event which inspired Eric's carving of the 'Foster Father' – and on

[1] *Letters of Eric Gill*, September 27, 1917.

February 5 (1918) Eric resumed the lessons which were all the schooling they were allowed. There were visits from Father Vincent; further visits to Parkminster; and an evening with Belloc at Kings Land where Father Vincent was also staying. In these early days Eric and Belloc would have agreed about a good many things, and particularly about Father Vincent. Eric was captivated by the single-mindedness – some would have said the fanaticism – of this extraordinary man, and his admiration survived eventual disagreement. Both were captivated by his sanctity.

On April 5 Eric's diary has the following significant entry: 'Westminster Cathedral Station of the Cross IX all day, without interruptions. Desmond Chute came to see me in morn 12.0 and I talked with him till nearly 3.' This conversation was the overture to the longest, closest and most creative friendship of Eric's life.

Desmond Macready Chute was descended from the famous Victorian actor-manager, and his father had owned the Theatre Royal, Bristol. After an education at Downside he was now studying sculpture at the Slade. He had no introduction to Eric beyond an admiration for his work and an interest in his ideas. He was delicate in health, refined and ascetic in appearance. On the following day he lunched with Eric, Mary and Pepler, and a week later came down to Ditchling for the weekend. He was never to forget his impression of that first visit.

Hopkins Crank was at that time a neat square toy of a house on the western fringe of the Common, an untouched Georgian squatter's cottage, preceded by a porch and diminutive fenced garden. Here amid sweetwilliam, honesty and marigolds there grew two rose-bushes of the kind which, on stems furry with prickles, bears amid many deep-grooved leaves large flat single blooms, white or magenta. These stand out in my recollection as the only flower I ever saw Eric pluck. 'There's a rose for you!'

His taste was satisfied, his mind moved by its 'heraldic quality' (always a favourite word of his and never more so than at this time).

The trim sash-windows, the 'stone colour' paint led naturally up to the wooden latches, the scrubbed refectory table, the Dutch brass chandelier, the pewter mugs and dishes, the wooden platters and, somewhat less naturally, to the Omega Workshop plates. Occasional drawbacks were not unknown, as when once during grace the logs collapsed in the open fireplace and the whole family's midday meal went up in an odour of burnt sacrifice. . . . Having arrived at dusk, I was not prepared for the morning view out of my bedroom facing south: pigeons circling around a dovecote in the midst of a yard lined with workshops; on the right the stonemasons, on the left, next to a large wain in a shed, a big black shop where Eric stone-carved, whence there jutted out at right angles a lower red-roofed shop in which he drew and engraved. An opening between this and a similar shed marked *Joseph Cribb* led the eye through a meadow to the top of Bulls' Brow and thence across the hidden Weald to the Downs and open sky. Quince, apple and medlar bloomed in the orchard behind the house. Grey in the shadow of the workshops, sudden as a monolith on Easter Island, stood Gill's first colossal carved figure – MULIER.[1]

It was on this occasion – or perhaps later on during the same summer of 1918 – that Desmond Chute heard Father Vincent McNabb ask the question: 'I wonder how many people have spent five minutes today thinking about the Incarnation?' The Rosary had just been said in the living-room, where Compline was now nightly sung. Chute described how –

At one end two candles burned beside a crucifix on the mantleshelf, at the other a stone niche flush with the whitewashed wall enshrined a small figure of Our Lady suckling the Divine Child; lights and shadows flickered round their feet from a wick floating in a bowl hollowed out of the same stone. Between these two focal points of light, members of the families and of the workshops, guests and friends, stood on either side of the refectory table so as to form two choirs. Eric acted as cantor or maybe one of the girls; more often Betty whose voice was as plumb in the middle of the note, as English-sweet as her father's.

From now on Chute was a regular visitor to Ditchling until he finally settled there. He drew Eric's portrait, and Eric set him to work on stone-carving and took him to the Wirksworth quarries in Derbyshire. On their way home they stopped at Hawkesyard, walking there from Lichfield and narrowly escaping arrest as German prisoners of war. It was the Feast of Corpus Christi with soldiers from the

[1] *Blackfriars*, December 1950.

camp at Rugeley escorting the Blessed Sacrament in procession, and in the evening arguments about Beauty and Truth in the Fathers' Common Room till midnight. But all this life which centred around the new friends and the old religion was now threatened with interruption.

Anyone reading Eric's diaries might be excused for supposing that he had not noticed the Great War. Yet he had four brothers serving with the Forces, and when all allowance has been made for the claims of Ditchling it remains astonishing that so vast an event should have preoccupied him so little. His own call-up had been deferred to enable him to finish the Westminster Stations, but on May 10 – the Stations being now completed – he appeared before a local tribunal at Lewes. He pleaded exemption on the grounds of family responsibilities which no one could gainsay, and the case was postponed until he had been medically examined. He was passed Grade I for physical fitness and the exemption was withdrawn, but in answer to his appeal it was extended until September 12. The whole summer, therefore, was spent in tidying up his affairs and arranging for a competent apprentice to deal with such work as might come in. Foch had launched his triumphant offensive in July; American manpower was tipping the scales decisively in favour of the Allies; and it was clear to anyone who read the newspapers that the war could not go on for very much longer. But at Ditchling the Daily Missal was more important than the *Daily Mail*, and eternity more topical than *The Times*.

Pepler had now moved to Halletts, a house built for him near The Oaks where the Johnstons lived, about a quarter-mile from the Crank and on the southern fringe of the Common. The press (by this time St Dominic's Press) was in a near-by reconditioned farm building. Here there was a private chapel where visiting priests were able to say Mass and where Compline was recited daily. This was blessed by Father Vincent on July 27, and on the 29th he received Eric and Mary Gill, Hilary Pepler and Desmond Chute as novices of the Third Order of St Dominic. Mass was sung for the first time at Ditchling on the Feast of St Clare. Meanwhile Hopkins Crank was

11. Eric Gill at work on Prospero and Ariel, on Broadcasting House, 1931 (photo BBC).

12. The Sleeping Christ, 1925 (photo City Art Gallery, Manchester).

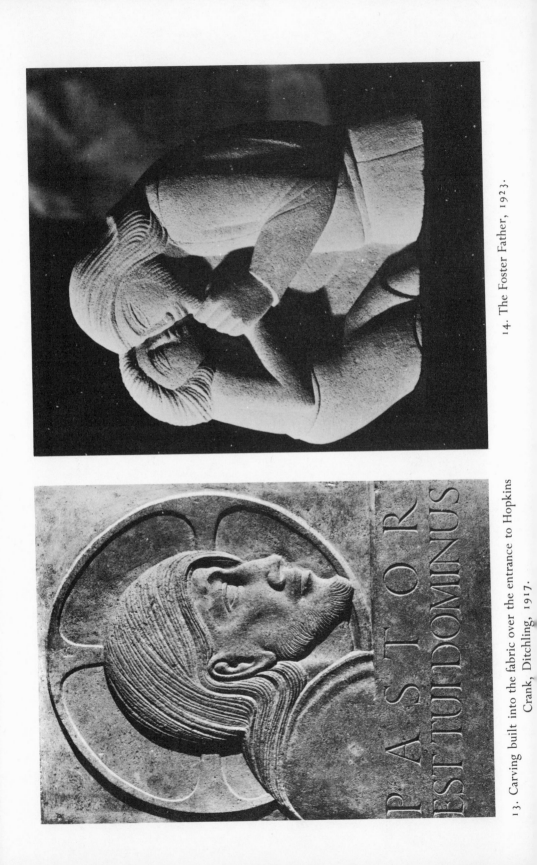

14. The Foster Father, 1923.

13. Carving built into the fabric over the entrance to Hopkins Crank, Ditchling, 1917.

solemnly consecrated to the Sacred Heart; and the tertiary novices held their first unofficial 'chapter'. All these last days before Eric went off to the Army were marked by a high seriousness which extended to the smallest material details of daily life. Realizing that he has a balance of £200 in the bank and a further £50 in the Post Office Savings, he observes in his diary, 'This is a sufficiently remarkable experience and one for which we should thank God and stand in great fear.' The tone is suddenly familiar; but is it Eric speaking, or the Assistant Curate to the Countess of Huntingdon's Connexion?

6

In a letter to his younger brother Cecil, written two years before he was himself called up, Eric had recorded the following conversation between himself and Mary at the breakfast table:

He: Listen to this: 'In the army he (the soldier) has work which seems to him worth doing for its own sake: whereas at home his work is often only worth doing for the wages sake. When he comes back are we going to find him work that will be worth doing for its own sake?' The devil of that is in the assumption that 'we' are to *find* good work for 'him', and that it is not in his power to *demand* good work or to refuse to do bad work.

She: Yes, but what about all those, surely there are *some*, who *have* to have work found for them?

He: Some? There are thousands, millions . . . just fodder for the slave market! But that's what I deplore. I am addressing the fodder. . . .

Whether he did address them just then, we may take leave to doubt. For Eric soldiering was a job like any other and deserved to be done well, however much you might wish to be doing something else. He did not, in any case, have to do it for long. Moreover he now fully shared the war aims as these were set out, week by week, in the *New Witness* by G. K. Chesterton and others, including Father Vincent McNabb. He did not realize how little Mr Lloyd George cared for the restoration of Poland or the dismemberment of Germany into its constituent states; nor how dear to the Masonic heart of M. Clemenceau was the disintegration of the Austro-Hungarian empire. Eric himself knew nothing about these matters, but he was content to take the word of those who did. On September 14 he went to the RAF recruiting depot in London and asked for a job as a draughtsman. Having passed a further medical examination, he was put in charge of a sergeant who missed the train to Blandford; so he was forced to spend the weekend in a Church Army Hostel, reading Clutton-Brock's *Studies in Christianity*. They reached Blandford on the Monday, where Eric failed a test on making and tracing a motor-engine. He did not know much about motor-cars, and was immediately given lessons in driving. The next day he was among those paraded to hear a lecture on 'Morale and cultivating an offensive spirit'; this depressed him a good deal.

The lecturer showed no knowledge of the former, but certainly cultivated the latter to perfection. He was utterly and damnably offensive. It gave me the hump like anything, but I am cultivating a submissive spirit and hope to win in the end. Our Lady and St Dominic are always at hand, and Our dear Lord is most darling.[1]

The following day he admits to breaking down 'horribly' at the thought of Mary and the children, and the next morning he is in hospital with a temperature of 102·6. This was an opportunity to finish Blosius' *Mirror for Monks* and to read St Paul's *Epistle to the Romans*. He was visited by his brother Max, and on coming out of hospital a week later, now suffering from diarrhoea, he was treated to a lecture on cleanliness. He described this as 'most obscene and irregular',[2] and reported the speaker to the Catholic Chaplain who gave the man a frightening piece of his mind. In the middle of October Eric was posted to Hurst Park, near London, and made further moves to be transferred as a draughtsman to the Admiralty. On the 22nd his brother Kenneth was killed in France – 'a life just thrown away, but perhaps the throw was caught by God'[3] – and on November 12, the day following the signing of the Armistice, he was back at Ditchling singing a Te Deum with Pepler. On the 30th he obtained his provisional discharge at Blandford, and was later instructed by the Admiralty to go home and do his own work until called upon. He was not called upon – and that was the end of his soldiering.

'I am in the army', he had written to Desmond Chute, 'for religious as much as patriotic reasons and make it my practice to

[1] Diary.　　[2] ibid.　　[3] ibid.

render unto Caesar what is his without complaint or subterfuge'[1] – he had refused to go to London when leave was stopped; and again, on November 29 –

I am very grateful for all the blessings of this life, I only wish you and Hilary had been with me to share it – but then it would have been so much less of an exile as to have lost much of the value it has been for me. But how short a time is three months (and barely that) when you think of the many who have borne it for three years. But I would have borne it for three years, if necessary and I think I would have continued to praise God.

The intensity of Eric's religious faith in these early days expressed itself in an idiom which may embarrass the unsympathetic reader. It was the idiom of the intensely private life – or at least the idiom of an extremely restricted circle. The circle was to widen again as time went by, and the idiom would be correspondingly modified. But in 1918 life was really one long conversation with Hilary Pepler, Desmond Chute and Vincent McNabb. They really did all believe that industrial capitalism would collapse under the weight of its own iniquity. We can only get Eric straight in our minds if we think of him first as a missionary and secondly as a stonemason. Evangelism was in his blood. A grandfather and great uncle had been missionaries in the South Seas, two of his brothers were missionaries in New Guinea, and a sister was a missionary in India. So it is less surprising to find Eric going about with a penny Catechism in his pocket ready for the first inquirer, or leaving Pepler's pamphlets where a casual eye might see them. One of these – *Does the Catholic Church protect Work People?* – had been compiled from the Papal Encyclical, *Rerum Novarum*, by Father Vincent. The Catholic Social Guild had refused to publish it without a commentary, and Father Vincent had refused to water it down.

What then, it may be asked, was the basis of the contemplative life upon which all this activity and polemic were founded? Eric's intuition, which never conflicted with his logic, suggested that the

[1] November 18, 1918.

rise of capitalism at the time of the Reformation – he would have agreed with Tawney, of course, in connecting the one with the other – had been reflected by a change in spirituality to match the change in economics. He put, therefore, a number of questions to a monk of the Parkminster Charterhouse, where a way of life and prayer had been established long before the Reformation was thought of. Was there, he inquired, any marked change of direction observable in writers on mysticism and the contemplative life since the Reformation? The answer (given in writing) was that of course such a change was discernible, and it was due principally to the Jesuits who were the spearhead of the Church in a period of crisis. The Jesuits had divided the spiritual life into two distinct compartments – one for ordinary folk who were to content themselves with discursive meditation to a set plan, the other for extraordinary folk who might be led to God by extraordinary ways about which the less said the better. This ideal had been enjoined on all members of the Society, and with certain exceptions – notably Père Grou in modern times – it had been invariably followed. The monk summarized the difference as:

the difference between the individual handiwork of a craftsman, who really made his own tools and used them in producing the articles of his craft, often enough from his own designs and the modern, uniform, correct to an inch-in-fractions article as turned out by machinery from a factory. Or the difference between the soaring vault of a Gothic church lost in the gloom as it goes up and the flat, gay, gilt-coppered roof of a Renaissance church.

This, it need hardly be emphasized, was grist to Eric's mill. He went on to ask whether the difference was fundamental, or whether it was no more than a difference of approach. The monk replied that the difference was indeed fundamental, and that it stemmed from the ancient Thomist and Molinist debate concerning predestination and free-will – the Thomist laying greater stress on God's action aiding and attracting the soul, the Molinist emphasizing human liberty and responsibility in the pursuit of holiness. Hence the 'minutely introspective character' of Post-Reformaton spirituality 'with its multiplied methods of self-examination, particular examination of pre-dominant faults, and discursive meditation'. The Molinist method might be described as exercising the powers of the soul in such a way as to draw down the Spirit of God upon us; the older method as waiting in peace for the Spirit of God to draw us up to Him. The first method, pushed to an extreme, would lead to a sterile activism, the second to an enervating quietism. But there was no doubt which method had prevailed during the later centuries of the Church, and no doubt either which method Eric found the more congenial.

He next went on to ask whether there was an analogy between men shaking hands as a sign of friendship and the soul coming to God. The monk reminded him that the shaking of hands was not a necessary sign of friendship – it might signify no more than casual acquaintance – but if the question implied that 'spiritual exercises' had once been the fruit of Union rather than a preparation for it, then – if one wanted to revert to older methods – it would be legitimate to dis-pense with them until one had achieved union with God. He put the matter in the form of a parable:

John Smith's earliest recollection was of a certain sunshiny day when he was taken to a Coronation Fete in the local park; he remembered some-thing of the tea and the buns; but the tangible memory of it all was a 'Coronation Mug' with bright-hued portraits of their Majesties in all the glory of Coronation garb. He was fascinated by it; and the dream of child-hood was to go to London to see the King in his golden crown. As he grew older, a good deal of the glamour wore off his day-dreams, but a curious and out-of-date reverence for kingship as such kept its place in his youthful mind. So, when he reached the age of discretion he 'sold all he had' and left his Father's house and set out for London. As he was a perfect stranger there he sought counsel of one Ignatius Farm, who had been recommended to him as knowing all about everything in London. Presently to him he unfolded his wondrous plans. He wanted to get to know the King in person; no more and no less; to get inside Buckingham Palace; to become, perhaps, one of the royal family. Now Ignatius Farm (who dwelt near a mews)[1] thought that he had met that kind of case before. 'My dear good fellow,' he said, 'do please be practical; that sort

1 The Jesuit Church in Farm Street adjoins a mews.

of thing may have been all very well for the middle ages; but all that is past and gone now. If you really have such reverence for the person and office of the King, and wish to know everything about him, read the *Court Circular*, which tells you of his movements; but better still, if you wish to serve him, join the army, where you may have a chance of doing something of practical use in his service.' Poor John Smith was disheartened, he crossed Green Park and looked wistfully at the windows of the Palace. It seemed so easy to get in. Just then a dear old gentleman, evidently of Italian origin (indeed his name proved to be Benedict Cassino) spoke to him and asked him what he was doing there. After John had told him all his hopes and fears, the old man said: 'Cheer up; of course you can get inside, even if it is only as a fourth-class royal shoe-black. But you must catch his Majesty's eye.' 'How can I do that?' said John. 'It is a long task for many; it just depends. But you will have to stand here all day long, admiring the beauties of the Victoria Memorial and the front of the Palace. The King will come out, and you must take off your hat and bow; that's all. He may notice you the first day, or it may be weeks, yes, years, before he will turn your way. But he will if you only stand here long enough.'

Thus it was that John Smith began his long vigil before the Palace. The very first day, out came his Majesty punctually at eleven o'clock and on foot. Off went John's hat, and his back was bent nearly double. True, the King did not look like the pictures; it is true that the morning coat was immaculate and that the gloss on the hat was as if it had been japaned; but what was that to an ermine-turned scarlet cloak and a golden crown? But never mind, it was HE! And it looked to John, who was standing quite alone, as if he acknowledged his salute! There was something to go on with. It were tiresome (as it was to John) to follow him all the weeks he was there but he never failed; always he was there when the King came out and always he showed the same respectful salute. It must be said that one day, tired of waiting he went forward a few paces to speak to his Majesty but he had scarcely moved when two well-dressed gentlemen came from nowhere, as he afterwards said (it is possible they were from Scotland Yard) and told him to be off. But skipping the rest THE day at last arrived. Out came the King just as usual, John bowed and lifted his hat just as usual, and then the unusual thing occurred. His Majesty stopped in his walk, and coming up to John, said: 'Good day, John Smith,' as he held out his hand and shook John warmly by the hand. 'I have watched you these many months and have at last found someone whom I can trust as a faithful servant. I want you to come right away now, into the Palace; there is a very small job waiting for you and it shall be the beginning of great things if you are equally faithful inside as you were outside.'

All the world knows how John Smith rose from one position to another until at length, after an incredible series of events, he was made heir to the Kingdom! And he used to say 'it was all that waiting, waiting outside in the rain, the wind and the heat and with the jeers of the by-passers, and contrary to the advice of so many who told me to get at "something useful", that brought me to where I am now on the steps of the throne'.

It was a fallacy, the monk concluded, to imagine that the ancient spiritual writers did not employ methods of spiritual exercise; but they did not tabulate, dissect and discuss – 'just as a composer, who presents his symphony for the first time, does not distribute amongst the audience copies of his themes; he gives the result.' The time-honoured advice to men who wanted to preach was equally applicable to men who wanted to pray: 'Begin low, and go slow, rise high and take fire.' But also 'aim high'.

Union is the normal term of the spiritual life but many are held back by the fancy that Union necessarily means Rapts, Revelations and Ecstasy, and alas! still more fail because they will not wait long enough in front of the Palace waiting for the King to take them by the hand.

It was not until 1922 that Eric, through the mediation of Dr Flood from Glasgow, entered into this vital correspondence; but his mind was moving in the same direction when he received the habit of a Dominican Tertiary from Father Vincent on January 19, 1919. For Father Vincent walked manifestly, and even dramatically, in the ancient ways which these Tertiaries were trying to recover; ways leading back to a spirituality even older than St Dominic. Once again, in the person of a Carthusian monk, Eric was to find a man able to point out to him what, in essence, he knew already.

7

The clothing of Eric and Pepler as Dominican Tertiaries did not take place at Ditchling, but at Hawkesyard; and it had an unexpected witness. Eric had been corresponding for some time with Stanley Spencer, whose recent letters had shown the need for 'hard tack'[1] in the way of theology. He therefore invited him to come with them to Hawkesyard, where Father Vincent might be trusted to harden the muscles of his mind. Spencer met them at Euston, having decided not to come after all, but they finally persuaded him. He jumped into the train 'just as he was, with his hands in his pockets and no luggage at all. What will be the upshot of it God only knows – but he is in a curious mixed state of pride, prejudice, humility and reverence.'[2] In the event he had long arguments with the Fathers, which he described as 'the hell of a time'.

Eric and Pepler were themselves in a mixed state of humility and pride when they took their places in choir for early Mattins. They went on from Hawkesyard to Bradford where they stayed with Father John O'Connor, who was liable to give one Marsala for breakfast and cigars immediately afterwards; to Leeds where Eric inspected the site for the proposed monument; to Edinburgh where they stayed with Father John Gray and André Raffalovitch; and to Glasgow where they lectured for Dr Flood's Catholic Institute against the background of an immense oil cloth crucifix. They spoke in public on Revolution or Servility and the Grammar of Industry, and in private argued about Art and Education.

Eric's commissions for War Memorials were now taking up a good deal of his time. He gave his views on this matter with some force in a letter to *The Burlington Magazine*. Sir Frederic Kenyon's report to the Imperial War Graves Commission had recommended that the

[1] Letter to Desmond Chute, January 11, 1919.
[2] Letter to Desmond Chute, January 20, 1919.

memorials to those buried in France or elsewhere should be placed in the hands of architects. Eric argued that while it might be desirable for the architects to give their advice, they could not give leadership because the making, either of central monuments or headstones, was not an architect's job but a sculptor's or a stonemason's. The business of the War Graves Commission was to decide what form the memorials should take, having regard solely to the sentiments of the nation and the funds at its disposal. If it were decided to place a headstone upon every known grave, then it should ascertain the number of headstones required and summon a representative body of headstone-makers – preferably from small firms – to discover how they could best be produced. The result would at least reflect the 'national culture, or lack of culture' and not merely 'the ideas of a few individual architects'. The idea that half a million headstones should be made according to the taste of a few architects was worthy of 'the Prussian or the Ptolemy'; and it was not made any better by the notion that the proposed memorials, in their mechanical and monotonous similarity, would commemorate 'the sense of comrade-ship and common service' and 'the spirit of discipline and order'.

Eric thought it appalling hypocrisy to erect crosses and altars to the dead, under the pretence that 'we are a Christian empire', and then, 'under the cloak of culture', deny 'to the mourners even the un-fettered choice of words' and to the workman a responsibility to which, as a Christian, he was entitled. Eric maintained that, provided certain regimental particulars were inscribed upon the stone, the relatives should decide the wording and that here 'the sentimental versifier or the crank' were risks that in justice should be run. He also claimed that 'an ordinary small monumental mason could, without turning his shop into a factory, easily and without hurrying, supply, say, 600 small headstones in three years at the cost of a few pounds each (say between £3 10s and £5)'. The work should be so distributed that the stones commemorating the men of a particular locality should be made in that locality. This variety would be worth the resulting difference in quality; and to Sir Frederic Kenyon's argument that the headstones would look like a regiment on parade

Eric replied that soldiers on parade were not 'all of one size and shape and colour and kind'. A crowd in Trafalgar Square was an impressive sight; but if it were composed of tailors' dummies the effect, though it might be architectural, would be less impressive. Moreover the repetition of 'feebly artistic lettering, made with the acid process' would never have been considered if the Government had not been anxious to save money and spare skill.

Needless to say, Eric's protest went unheeded, and he was left to make his own memorials, as and when they were called for. The tablet to Rupert Brooke in the chapel of Rugby School was unveiled by Sir Ian Hamilton in 1919. It consisted of a white marble slab bearing a portrait of Rupert Brooke sculptured by Havard Thomas from his photograph. Underneath Eric had inscribed his name, the dates of his birth and death, and the sonnet: 'If I should die think only this of me.' The letters of the poem were coloured. Brooke had been a warm admirer of Eric's work; at the Post-Impressionist exhibition he thought Matisse commonplace by comparison. He had given a Madonna and Child to the young woman he was so unhappily in love with, and bequeathed a green jade ornament to Cathleen Nesbitt.

At Chirk, near Wrexham, Eric had carved the bas-relief of a soldier on guard with his right hand holding a rifle and left hand up-raised, wearing his tin helmet and great coat. 'Soldier on the look-out – the most typical attitude representing the war of entrenchment,' he explained to Lord Howard de Walden who had commissioned the monument. It stood 15 feet high and seventy names in English and Welsh were inscribed on the four sides of the base. At Bisham, near Marlowe, he carved a wayside crucifix with pent roof and on the base inscribed the quotation from *Henry V*: 'Here was a royal fellow-ship of death.' The cross at South Harting, near Petersfield, had panels of St George and the Dragon, the miraculous draught of fishes, and St Richard of Chichester. St Michael as well as St George appeared on the cross at Trumpington, near Cambridge, with other panels representing the Blessed Virgin and Child beside the manger, and a foot-slogging soldier – suggested by David Jones.

Meanwhile, at Ditchling, Eric and Pepler bought a piece of land, Spoil Bank, on the other side of the railway line opposite the Crank. This was subsequently blessed by Father Vincent, and there was an idea to build a chapel and erect some huts upon it. This came to nothing, and a large wooden Calvary, which Eric had carved, was put up there instead. The effect of this, when seen from a distance, was obtained by the abnormal length of the body and by the taut strain upon the arms. The figure was merely a carved board, painted in the soft tones of flesh with a blue loin-cloth, and the eyelids were half-open. Over the sunken head the words: *Jesus Nazarenus Rex Judaeorum* – were inscribed. It stood on a solid base of brickwork, and was probably the most dramatic image of the Crucifixion to be seen anywhere in England. People travelling to Eastbourne or New-haven did not expect this sermon on the way. A further piece of land, known as Fragbarrow and adjoining Halletts and the Crank, was also secured and this was chosen as the site for the chapel and the disused Army huts which Eric had found at Southwick. The first of these – or part of it – was used for recreation; it was opened to cele-brate Joseph Cribb's release from the Army on August 29.

Visitors continued to call or to stay throughout the summer; Father Francis Burdett (brother of Osbert, the historian of the 'nineties) talking about Art and Religion till 4 a.m.; and Lord Alfred Douglas. Already there were rather too many of them and Eric's dreams of escape from the modern world did not stop short at Ditchling. On October 13, 1919, he set out from Hawkesyard with Pepler to cross the Irish Channel from Holyhead. Ireland was seeth-ing with revolt, but Eric's political sympathies were hardly engaged in this – not because he was wanting in sympathy for the Irish, but because he was a quite unpolitical person. Indeed he was annoyed by references to the inferiority of the English language which he read during a rough crossing. Nationalism of any kind was foreign to his nature. But he acquired an Irish dictionary in Dublin, and he was impressed by the foreign aspect of the city, and by the wooden crucifix in the left aisle of the Dominican church – 'all the paint gone from the knees downwards, gone by innumerable kissings and strokings of men, women and children'.[1] On October 15 they attended the High Mass for St Teresa in the church of the Carmelites, and found it a 'wonderful sight . . . deliciously, innocently worldly . . . real devotion and real ugliness and real beauty, all mixed up and transfigured' – despite the 'excruciating singing'. From Dublin they went on to Galway, with a battleship and destroyers in the bay and soldiers and sailors in the town, and no evidence of mutual hostility. Indeed the only anti-Englishman they met was an Englishman who had become an Irishman, and refused to talk English except as a concession to a foreign language. Conversation was carried on in French and Gaelic, with occasional lapses into English for Eric's benefit. This endearing character lived in a small villa, generally reminiscent of North Oxford, except when he was in gaol.

So far Eric had not discovered the civilization he was looking for – a Christian civilization untouched by industrial capitalism – but he found it in the Claddagh where the cleanliness was a *splendor ordinis*, and the men went out to fish, the children went barefoot, and the women wove and spun. The place seemed to him 'one in the eye for persons, like Lecky, with notions of the perfection of modern sanitary science and art'; and so did the Aran Islands to which they sailed on October 18. The little steamer was met by coracles – canvas over laths and tarred, with no keels, and the oars loosely fastened to the row-locks. In one boat there was 'a woman sitting . . . perfectly still and solemn in her shawl. They lifted her aboard just as if she were an image, no words said, like some goddess being taken from one place of worship to another.' They spent only the inside of a day on the islands, but Eric might have been a happier man if he could have stayed there for the rest of his life.

Back in Dublin they arranged an exhibition of prints and books at the Mansion House, and found the Liberty Hall men wedded to ideas of collectivist organization on trade union lines. They had little sense of individual ownership and responsibility, although here the Catholic principle of personal responsibility was clearly involved.

[1] All the quotations relating to this visit are taken from 'A Diary in Ireland', *The Game*, Vol. III, No. 2. Reprinted in *In a Strange Land*, 1944.

Countess Markieviez, just released from gaol, joined them for lunch – very garrulous about the Easter Rising. Where all these Irishmen were concerned with their political rights, Eric and Pepler were concerned with their economic rights. Dr Flood was also in Dublin, pointing out that while the state might, with the consent of the citizens, nationalize the land, such action would be inexpedient, even if it were not wrong, because ownership was the condition of liberty. Eric himself, at this time, was a far more convinced Distributist than he afterwards became; and Pepler always remained one. Ireland was, in fact, a largely Distributist country without saying so in so many words, and Flood was preaching to the proletarians of Dublin a sermon that would have sounded redundant to the peasants of Donegal. Where 'Church Decoration' was in question Eric reminded his audience that art could not be done by proxy. Middle class dilettantes could only tell people how churches should be decorated because the decorators had been deprived of their responsibility. They would not tell priests how to preach sermons, because the priests had preserved their responsibility. The decoration of churches – and Heaven knows, Ireland had need of it – was a matter of right and rational economics, not of good taste.

Eric and Pepler visited Maynooth, 'a great place. Pugin at his best – except the chapel, but even that would have been good if left plain.' They found little evidence of puritanism either in the dinner or the conversation. Later there was an interesting meeting with Arthur Griffith, who warmly resented – in common with most other Irish Nationalists – the hostility of the English Catholics to Sinn Fein. The false report that Cardinal Bourne had refused the Last Sacraments to Roger Casement was widely believed. Eric did his best to convince Griffith that political power was useless without economic power, but Griffith could only remark to a friend on the way home: 'How stupid the English are, see how little even intelligent ones like these understand!' In fact, Eric was a typical, though he was not in the least a representative, Englishman; no one was less qualified to understand the motive energy of Sinn Fein. He viewed the situation through the opposite end of the telescope. For all the intransigence

of his ideas, he was pacific where the Irish were quarrelsome, doctrinaire where they were empirical, and empirical where they were
doctrinaire. The one thing they passionately cared about – the
assertion of independent nationality – was the one thing he took
negligently for granted. Moreover, the hospitality of Maynooth was
deceptive. Beneath the genial appearances of Irish life there was a
rancorous puritanism which would have revolted Eric – and revolted
against him – if he had ever met it at close quarters. Perhaps, after all,
it was fortunate that he never did so.

There is no suggestion that at this time he and Pepler seriously in-
vestigated the possibility of settling in Ireland; but a year later, in
December 1920, they heard a report that Crappa Island off the coast
of Galway was for sale. They made inquiries and the idea of moving
there was seriously debated. Eventually, for one reason or another,
it was dropped. Ditchling was still very much in the making, but the
dream of a Ditchling over the mountains, if not over the sea, was to
haunt Eric as the years went by. When the political and economic
chatter of Dublin had died away, there remained the picture of a dis-
possessed proletariat at prayer, and the shawled woman carried like
an idol into the coracle that spun round like a top in the water.

Life at Ditchling went on as usual. The four Tertiaries were
professed on January 1, 1920, and from now on they held monthly
chapter meetings; but the Bishop of Southwark refused permission
for regular Mass in the Oratory which now stood beside the three
huts on Fragbarrow field. The Little Office of Our Lady was recited
daily, and the Rosary every evening. Prime and Terce were said at
6 a.m. followed by meditation; Sext and None at 12; Vespers at
4 p.m.; and Compline followed the Rosary at 6. On May 20, 1921,
decreed by the Bishops as a day of penitence, Eric and Desmond
Chute took the discipline.

But the Ditchling community included others beside the Tertiaries, and it had its own secular concerns. Its financial affairs were
complicated. It was not a trading association; each member earned
his living independently. The land had been purchased by Pepler
who erected his workshop upon it at his own cost. Another work-

shop was built at the expense of another member. Two wooden cottages were put up with money borrowed on the personal security of two others. When the Chapel was built money was borrowed upon the security of the title deeds, and other friends lent money for general purposes. The only income was the rents from the cottages and workshops, the monthly subscriptions from the members, and gifts from friends. In 1921, therefore, it was decided to put the affairs of the community on a more organized basis. First of all the Tertiaries formed themselves into the Guild of St Joseph and St Dominic. This was described by Eric as a craft Guild, but not as primarily a craft Guild.

It is primarily a religious fraternity for those who make things with their hands. . . . The love of God means that work must be done according to an absolute standard of form; the love of our neighbour means that work must be done to an absolute standard of serviceableness. Good quality is there-fore twofold: work must be good in itself and good for use. . . . The Guild holds that the principle of individual human responsibility being a fundamental of Catholic doctrine, and this principle involving the principle of ownership, workmen should own their tools, their workshops and the product of their work.[1]

At the same time a small private company – the Spoil Bank Associa-tion – was formed to own and administer the property which the community had acquired. There was no share capital and the liability of the members (seven in number) was limited to the amount guaranteed by them if the company should wind up. The SPA was formally inaugurated in October 1921.

In the discussions which led up to this arrangement a prominent part was played by a Catholic neighbour, Commander Herbert Shove, who had served with distinction as a submarine officer in the Royal Navy and been awarded the DSO. With his beard and burly physique, he had the appearance and spoke the idiom of the quarter-deck. He more properly belongs to a later chapter of Ditchling, when he had taken up metal work, and was a familiar figure on the Common with his shabby clothes and felt hat, playing melodies on a pipe of his own

[1] *The Game*, September 1921.

15. Mankind, 1927-28 (The Tate Gallery).

16. Alphabet stone cut by Eric Gill in 1939 for Graham Carey.

manufacture. But in 1920 he was already in the picture, ardently Catholic and Distributist.

Another new arrival had greater significance. On January 29, 1921, David Jones was brought down to Ditchling by a friend. After serving with the Welch Fusiliers during the war, he had spent some years at the Westminster Art School and was still looking for his bearings. He felt the lack of any tradition to which an artist could reasonably belong, and he had heard that Eric had some pretty clear ideas about what might be done in the contemporary, and confused, situation. Jones was curious, but nothing more; he had accepted the invitation of his friend as he might have accepted any other invitation to visit an eminent and unusual man. It was a very wet day, and he found Eric in his workshop. Eric went on working and presently said: 'You don't have a very clear idea of the direction you're going in, do you?' Jones agreed that he did not. Then Eric took a piece of paper and drew a roughly triangular figure with the corners not meeting, followed by a second in which they nearly met but not quite, and finally a third where they met perfectly.

'Which of those do you think is a triangle?' he asked. Jones replied that he did not know, but that he liked one of them better than the others.

'It's not a question of being better,' said Eric; 'the other two aren't triangles at all.'

David Jones did not, either then or later, agree with everything that Eric said; what struck him was the clear method of his exposition. It was like talking to Socrates. He recognized the genius of a teacher, irrespective of the rightness of his teaching; and the gentle integrity of a man who knew exactly where he was going. And so, instead of being a student in an art school, he thought it might be better to be apprentice to a master – and of Eric's mastery in his own field there could be no doubt whatever. One might question his ideas, or the length to which he pushed them, but his technical ability was beyond dispute.

Of all Eric's pupils or disciples David Jones was the only one gifted with creative genius. He had this in a far higher degree than

Eric himself; and he had the power of genius to assimilate without imitation. His imagination, first as a painter and wood-engraver and then as a writer, moved in a world of myth to which he wedded the world of his experience when time had enabled him to digest it. He had no idea, when he arrived, of coming to work and live at Ditchling, but the sense of life lived according to a rational order and of work produced in accordance with it decided him to stay. The Ditchling experiment might prove to be an impracticable *impasse*, and the most important work of David Jones stands outside it – work accomplished when he was standing on his own feet – but its effect upon him remained considerable. He stayed at Ditchling for the best part of four years, learning wood-engraving from Desmond Chute and living with one of the families in the settlement. But he was never a member of the Guild, and stood apart from the dis-agreements which persuaded Eric to sever his own connection with it. What he gained from Ditchling was less an influence than a friend; not so much the imprint of Eric's mind – greatly as he admired it – as the friction of that mind with his own. He was never to be quite as close to Eric as Desmond Chute, but then Eric was at one with Chute as he was at one with no one else, with the exception of his own wife. This little distance of growing disagreement did nothing to impair their friendship; it merely enabled David Jones to become the most discerning critic of Eric's work. Looking back over the years, he wrote to Desmond Chute:

It is then thirty years since we sat in that red brick house of yours in the summer at Ditchling and you began to teach me wood engraving! What a wonderful phase of one's life that Ditchling period was! When I think what I owe directly to Eric and then add what I owe *indirectly* to him it amounts to an enormous debt. What an inimitable man he was. There was a late fifteenth-century Welsh poet who wrote a couplet which being translated runs: 'it was difficult for me to part with one whose like did not live.' I think any of us who knew Eric must feel like that about him.[1]

In 1920 the Johnstons had moved into 'Anne of Cleves' house in Ditchling village, and the Peplers moved into the Johnstons' quarters

[1] December 29, 1952.

at Halletts. From now on, as the Guild took a more purposeful shape and the Tertiaries – with a group of Dominican Friars at their elbow – held strictly to their rules, Edward Johnston – always guarding his independence – drops away from the centre of the picture. With him were the Mairets, and Ethel Mairet's brother, Frederick Partriole, who made jewellery and was conspicuous in his shaggy Norwegian pull-over; Amy Sawyer, who was paralysed in one arm and wrote and produced plays in the village; Gerard Meynell, who ran *The Beacon*, and his wife; and a bricklayer – half French – who discussed philosophy with Johnston, as Mairet had discussed Soloviev with Eric. One would like to know what Father Vincent thought of Soloviev, if he had ever read him. He had read Maurice de la Taille's great book on the Eucharist and cautioned David Jones against infecting his mind with such heresy. Ditchling was hardening into two camps, still friendly to each other, under the rigid Dominican influence. When the railway strike was declared in 1921, Eric rejoiced that the rails in the cutting by the Crank were rusting; and when a guest arrived with a typewriter he observed: 'It's all right for you to use a writing machine because you are engaged on active work in the world; it would be wrong for me because I have left the world and am trying to lead the contemplative life in the desert.'

It was not quite a desert with the bells summoning to meals and the bellows helping to kindle the damp wood. For behind all these personalities – the rationalism of Eric, the versatile romanticism of Pepler, the refinement of Desmond Chute – there moved the self-effacing but essential figure of Mary Gill. She combined the practical sense of Martha and the sensibility of Mary. Sussex born and bred, and as incorrigibly English as Eric himself, it was she who made Ditchling work. Ditchling has been described as a masculine and paternalistic community in the sense that the men did most of the talking, and that the men had the big ideas. But the talk would have remained so much empty air, and the ideas have gone with the wind, if Mary Gill had not created the conditions in which they could assume a concrete shape. It was more than a matter of being a good manager and housewife, though she was all of these – with a Frenchwoman's flair for making a little go a long way; more even than knowing how to bring up a family in fairly unconventional circumstances. It was a matter of understanding in the concrete what Eric and others would lay down in the abstract. It was a matter of bringing these dry bones of rigid Dominican principle to spontaneous life, so that people who imagined Ditchling to be a fad discovered it to be a family. She was an entirely normal woman and she was able to give Eric the kind of love that he insatiably craved. If she had been different, Ditchling might have come to nothing, and Eric himself have come to grief.

Moreover, she met, in her quiet way, not only his body but his mind. He talked to her as he talked to anyone else, with his simple – his occasionally over-simple – assumption of intelligence in other people. A man does not read Conrad's *Victory* aloud to his wife, unless they have more than bed and board in common. Eric was very Victorian in his natural optimism, in his belief that a little good sense would put the world to rights, in his conviction that where there was a will there was a way. Mary Gill was Victorian also in her gentle demeanour, unruffled temper and happy acceptance of a constitution where the man and woman each had their reciprocal rights and duties; and like other Victorian wives she counted for more than superficially appeared. Ditchling was the imperfect realization of a dream, but there was nothing imperfect about the dream which Eric records in his *Autobiography*. He dreamt that he was walking in Heaven with Mary and the children, and they came upon Our Lord:

I said to Him 'This is Betty, and this is Petra, and this is Joanna, and this is Gordian,' and he shook hands with them all, and then I said, 'And this is Mary,' and He said: 'Oh, Mary and I are old friends.' It was a green open hillside with paths and brooks and a blowy sort of sky with downland clouds.[1]

The Game continued to appear at more or less monthly intervals until January 1923, and Eric was a frequent contributor. He attacked the factory system, not because it was incompatible with Christianity,

[1] *Autobiography.*

but because it was inconsistent with it. It robbed the workman of responsibility because it specified and sub-divided his work. The larger the output, the greater the sub-division. Profit sharing and combined management were no remedies because they ignored the real cause of discontent – which Eric admitted had not yet found expression. This was not the lack of money but the loss of responsibility. The factory fostered the war between masters and men, and the notion that leisure was preferable to work. It put a 'premium upon mechanical dexterity and a discount upon intellectual and spiritual ability'.[1] It flattered the consumer at the same time as it destroyed the personal relationship between him who buys and him who sells. It undermined the family by dragging both men and women into its coils, and promoted war by over-production and the consequent struggle for fresh markets. In a subsequent essay (Advent 1919) Eric applied these criticisms to art, distinguishing between the man who made with knowledge and the consumer, or the connoisseur, who only received with taste. Since the beautiful was the 'love of God visible in man's work', and since a man could not 'hire another to love God for him', the designer should also be the maker, and those who wanted beautiful things should 'win the right to make them for themselves and allow that right to others'.

A collection of Eric's essays was entitled *It All Goes Together*, and a good example of this integrity is the argument he wove around *The Song of Solomon*. This appeared serially in *The Game* during 1921, and it was reprinted as a whole in *Art Nonsense* (1929). With *The Song of Solomon* Eric was writing on his own ground. He had no personal experience of factories, but he had much experience of love and some experience of religion. He began by distinguishing between the sacred and the secular:

Those things we call religious which are ordained to God as their end. Those things we call secular which, though not irreligious, do not envisage God as their end immediately. Thus a church is called a religious building, and an inn we call secular. But an inn is not therefore irreligious.

[1] 'The Factory System and Christianity', *The Game*, Advent 1918. Reprinted in *In a Strange Land*, 1944; American edition, *It All Goes Together*, 1944.

Those things are irreligious which are ordained to mammon as their end.

In *The Song of Solomon* the physical love of man and woman was the symbol of God's love for man and of Christ's love for the Church, but the question still remained whether the author had intended the symbolism which the Church had placed upon his poem. How far was it a religious poem by interpretation, and how far by intrinsic quality? Eric answered that neither a lamb nor a man hanging on a cross were in themselves religious emblems; they only became so by interpretation. Nobody assumed that Christians worshipped sheep or doves, because they appeared on church banners. What determined the significance of a symbol was the place where it was put. A lamb was regarded in one way on a banner and quite differently on a cart. Eric went on to stress that the symbolism of *The Song of Solomon* was naked and heraldic because it was meant to be unequivocally clear; but it was not in the least naturalistic. *Venter ejus eburneus* was neither photographic nor obscure. Eric admitted that no verbal evidence suggested that the poem was intended to be a vision of Divine love; the intention had been ascribed to it by tradition, and confirmed by intuition. The poem was so beautiful that it could signify nothing less; 'no man could praise his mistress' body with such complete assurance, such appalling certitude unless his mistress were God himself'. This was surely pushing the argument too far; literature has other love poems as beautiful as the *Song of Solomon*. He could more safely have argued that by including the poem in the canon of authorized Scriptures the Church had affirmed the essential goodness of physical intercourse between man and woman, and had chosen this union as the symbol of the union between Christ and herself.

But, as Eric by now very well knew, many ecclesiastics affirmed nothing of the kind. His own parish priest was shocked by the article. Profligacy and puritanism each bred their opposites in a vicious circle of misunderstanding and fear. This essay may be read as Eric's first broadside in a battle against both. If modern society were profligate – or so he argued – it was because modern industrial conditions had made it so. Here he was riding his hobby-horse a shade too hard. A more intimate acquaintance with rural life might have convinced him that human passions ran as high in a hayfield as they did in a suburb or a slum; and sometimes they ran in a very odd direction. He was on surer ground when he maintained that wrong thinking always produced bad results, if not in one way then in another. The clergy who thundered against the artificial control of birth, and even the contemplatives who did their best not to think about birth at all, allowed their sentiment and their sensuality to run riot in repellent statuary and saccharine devotions. In the strictest sense of the word, it was time to return to the nakedness of the *Song of Songs*; to describe things, whether in word or image, by their proper names. Nakedness, he claimed, was not an occasion of sin; but 'the half-shown and the half-hidden – the blouse that is just low enough to show the hollow between the breasts – the wisp of drapery that covers but does not prevent thought or allay it'. When a man said 'I love the roundness of thighs' he might generally be understood to mean that he loved God, but when he said that he adored 'the hidden mystery in his mistress' eyes' and 'the gentleness of her gracious touch' he might generally be understood to mean that he loved lechery. This was going a little far; the reaction of a realist to romanticism. It was arbitrary to grant an exception to Dante and Beatrice because one admired scholasticism; or to excuse Rembrandt's interest in the anecdote because one admired Rembrandt; or Shakespeare's love for the Dark Lady because one had quite failed to grasp that Shakespeare's passion was compounded of love and hate.

For Eric the *Song of Solomon* was a religious poem by virtue of its intrinsic quality – and that was a judgment from which no one could reasonably dissent. The Church had canonized it, and displayed its charity in doing so. It had taken the optimistic view of a poem, as Eric himself generally took an optimistic view of people. But he got into trouble with a correspondent because he had described the Impressionists as the 'last idolaters', and then proceeded himself to canonize Cézanne. It was certainly true that the Impressionists had been concerned with appearances (though the appearances went far beyond representation), and that their successors were searching for a structure, and the truth that lay behind it. But it was surely no more idolatrous to describe poppies in a picture than passion in a poem. Eric had involved the Impressionists in his characteristic simplifications about the Renaissance, in which he justly saw a turning away from God to man – the transformation of a theocentric into a humanist culture. It did not occur to him that humanism was a necessary stage in man's discovery of himself. He saw the loss but he did not count the gain. Indeed he was not very interested in personality, and the reason why his eroticism – for all its careful definitions and theological warrant – was distasteful to many people was because it left the personal and psychological factor out of account. At least it did this in theory whatever it may have done in fact; and I think that the Jesuit priest who described it to me once as 'baptized animality' was not far out in his judgment. There was much of D. H. Lawrence in Eric's mental make-up. One is not all surprised that he both admired and illustrated *Lady Chatterley's Lover* and thought that Lawrence's essay[1] in explanation of the book should be made compulsory reading in the seminaries.

But on the question of marriage itself Eric was as orthodox as his severest critic could have wished. Where the nineteenth century had principally argued about faith, the twentieth century was arguing about morals. In 1921 a wife had to prove cruelty as well as adultery to obtain a divorce, whereas a husband needed to prove adultery alone. The feminists were naturally anxious that this inequality should be redressed. Eric, however, argued that the demand for greater equality was in fact a demand for greater facilities; he did not in any case believe that the sexes should be equal before the Government as they were equal before God. If a woman committed adultery, the damage was worse than if a man did the same thing. The demand for easier divorce was linked to the campaign for Birth Control. Eric attacked Dr Marie Stopes' *Wise Parenthood* in the *New Witness*; and he and Pepler attended one of her meetings in the Queen's Hall, where they sold fifty copies of an anti-contraceptive pamphlet. As he wrote to Desmond Chute afterwards, 'The platform was filled

[1] Apropos of *Lady Chatterley's Lover*.

with ladies and gentlemen in evening dress, Marie Stopes herself in the most diaphanous of low-neck dresses. Don't you think it very remarkable that such a subject should be discussed in such a get-up? Queen's Hall crowded and enthusiastically in favour of B.C.'[1] It was not, of course, remarkable at all.

In further articles in *The Game* Eric drew the deepest distinction between badly baked bread which might have to be bought if none other were available, and custard powder which served no other purpose than to spoil a good pudding.[2] It was characteristic that, while Eric would insist on custard being made with eggs, he would also insist on the children's shoes being made by Dowie & Marshall. He contrasted the Madonna of Cimabue and the Madonna of Sasso-ferrato – the one an image of absolute Beauty, the other of relative loveliness – the one beautiful because it proceeded from Truth and Goodness, the other attractive because it appealed only to taste. He labelled the Renaissance as the New Poverty, the Reformation as the New Obedience, and Industrialism as the New Chastity – because the first had canonized riches, the second had legitimized revolt, and the third had sterilized love. But the occasion of despair was also the occasion of hope:

It is exactly as though we were each one a Robinson Crusoe on his desert island. The ship that brought us is on the rocks and nothing is to be saved but the tool chest and the compass. So we can start life afresh, free from the shackles of traditions long since decayed and become frivolous.[3]

For Eric the world in which he found himself really was 'a strange land'; he had, to a greater degree than most of his contemporaries, the Christian sentiment of exile. As he looked around him he saw that thought was free and will was bound, and for this reason the art of writing – where a man was independent of collaboration – was the only art spontaneously to flourish. He admired the novels of Hardy, Conrad and Henry James, but he saw the pessimism of Hardy – who had 'discovered that the face of man is wrinkled, that

[1] June 6, 1921.
[2] October 1921; *Songs Without Clothes*, 1921; *Art Nonsense*, 1929.
[3] *The Game*, March 1922; *Art Nonsense*, 1929.

his eyes are full of tears' – as the result of the workship of man, which was only another aspect of the worship of Mammon. Having no God to look up to, writers of genius were forced to a deeper and ever deeper introspection; but here there was gain as well as loss. For Eric life was a matter of contemplation, where for others it was also a matter of discovery. It had been so for Augustine and Newman, neither of whom Eric knew very much about. For him the *Summa* had said the last word. But the last word is never said in the story of man's understanding of himself and of his situation. Teilhard de Chardin's 'point Omega' is the only full stop to which he can look forward without limiting the reach of his intelligence and diminishing the grandeur of his destiny. Progress, with its inevitable accompaniment of error, is a necessary option; its only alternative is decline.

The tidiness of Eric's workshop epitomized the tidiness of his mind; in neither was there anything left lying about. But life will not go into categories as books will go into drawers; Eric's categories were cages and people were constantly escaping from them. Here some observations of Father Martin d'Arcy, who loved Eric none the less for incidental disagreements, are very much to the point:

His metaphysic as laid out was probably correct but you have experience to discover that, though you can make abstract statements about man, you must be very careful to watch him in the concrete if your abstract statement isn't exactly right in all its details. All philosophy seems to me an attempt to make certain statements about life, about man, about nature, and so on. But all those are in our deficient language. It's like what Chesterton once said: you start by knowing your home, then you go all round the world till you discover what your home really is. Now it comes to the same thing in the end, but if you start off with what you've just learnt about home at the beginning and then decide what all humanity is like, you only make mistakes. I think Eric fell into the very nice fallacy of perfectionism. Many of us say that the present condition of life is a very accidental and unfortunate one. Round the corner is the true condition of human life, and if we could get round the corner out of our present troubles, everything would be perfect. But the new situation creates its own difficulties, shadows, problems instead – so we are always moving through a kind of warfare.[1]

1 In an interview for a *Profile of Eric Gill*, broadcast.

Some of Eric's best contributions to *The Game* were unsigned. Few people realized that he had the gift of verse, or that he had written his own *Song of Songs*; the following verses make no pretence to symbolism, and their romanticism is unashamed:

CAELUM ET TERRA TRANSIBUNT

What is it to the Sussex shore
    That Alfred's bones lie hidden there?
And how shall Egypt's parchéd sands
    Remember Cleopatra's hair?

No memory indelible of man's frail life
    Can earth in earthly prison set.
Even the pulsing of conjoinéd love
    Shall your own corpse forget.

But coals of fire shall still be piled
    On earth's unheeding land;
And men shall not forget the rounded hills
    Or leave deserted even desert sand.

And oh! my Lover, when your grave shall give
    His long embrace, and all your parts disdain
Love shall still keep our love imprisonéd
    And bless your breast whereon my breast has lain.[1]

The Game, March 1922.

8

Desmond Chute had not long been established at Ditchling before he felt a vocation to the contemplative life. Eric wanted him too much to feel able to give him impartial advice. He recommended him to take his problem to Father Vincent, who argued with Eric that he should serve a longer apprenticeship in the world – if 'the world' were not a misnomer for Ditchling – before cutting himself off from it. By the summer of 1921, however, Desmond had made up his mind, and on May 30 a Miserere was recited in the chapel, which had been completed and blessed earlier in the year. Eric had carved the piscina and the stone for the floor of the predella, and the crucifix hanging on the cross-beam, hewn from an oak plank. Desmond Chute had carved a Madonna and Child. It was here that he and Eric took the discipline for the last time before Desmond went off to offer himself to the Bishop of Clifton. Although he was proposing to enter the secular priesthood, he did his studies at the Albertinum in Fribourg, where the Dominicans were in charge of the Theological Faculty. The link with Ditchling was broken, but the link with St Dominic remained. With Desmond Chute's departure the best days of Ditchling had gone – 'will anything ever have the vigour and freshness of that first spout?'[1] – and for him, with his sensitive temperament and tendency to hypochondria, it had not proved a solution. 'There are three orders in our life (he wrote later) that of study, that of liturgy and that of asceticism, of the interior life; and these things are one. Imperfectly fused, they trouble the soul and impede progress in each separate order. Fused, I feel they would carry one through like a great river. But how to fuse them is the question.'

This was a question to which Ditchling had not provided the answer; and when Desmond left, his absence was felt not only as a

[1] Letter to Eric Gill, Whit-Sunday, 1925.

sadness but, increasingly as time went on, as a criticism also. Is it significant that Eric described the first meeting of the Tertiaries after Desmond had gone for his interview with the Bishop as 'a great failure'?[1] There was a farewell meeting with the Guild on September 29, and Desmond left for Fribourg immediately afterwards.

Eric and his daughter Betty kept him company. They spent two nights in Paris, staying at the Hotel Pas de Calais and assisting at High Mass in St Sulpice – 'very high and marvellous to us little Englanders'.[2] They admired the Italian Primitives in the Louvre; heard Benediction at the Sacré Coeur; and went to Notre Dame de Victoires for the blessing of the roses. On the following day they were at Chartres – 'more marvellous than ever and very different too for me since my first visit with L – – – and my second with Mary Ethel. Rubbed my rosary on N.D.de Pilar and visited N.D.de Sous Terre. Visited S.Pierre.'[3] They took the night train for Switzerland, and on October 4 were lunching beside the lake of Geneva at Ouchy. From there they proceeded to Gruyères, where Betty was to be left with a Swiss family. Eric found Gruyères 'the most perfect little town, there is nothing more to be said – God be praised for so good a thing'.[4] The next day they walked, all three of them, to des Marches; prayed before the shrine of the local Madonna – 'the darling';[5] and walked back by the river and the mountains. On the morrow Eric was climbing up to the col of the Dent de Broc, with its view of Mont Blanc, and coming home through the forest. In the village church at Gruyères they sang Plainchant according to the Solesmes mode, and there was dancing in the street on the occasion of the annual Fair. On October 10 Eric accompanied Desmond to Fribourg, where he was medically examined before entering the seminary. The right lung was pronounced 'delicate', and he was advised to live as much as possible in the open air. Eric said good-bye to Desmond; left Betty with her family; and returned home by way of Brussels, reading Garrigou-Lagrange on Luther.

Before long he was reading something much more to his purpose.

[1] Diary. [2] ibid. [3] ibid. [4] ibid. [5] ibid.

On April 23, 1922, we find the following entry in his diary: 'read with H.P. book on art and scholasticism (Maritain).' It is unlikely that he had ever heard of Jacques Maritain who was only just then becoming what T. S. Eliot later described as 'probably the most powerful force in contemporary French philosophy'. Converted to Catholicism under the influence of Léon Bloy, and in full reaction against Bergson, he was leading the neo-Thomist revival. With these philosophical battles Eric was not concerned, but the effect upon him of *Art et Scholastique* had the dramatic force of a revelation. For years to come it was to dominate all his thinking about the relation of Art to Prudence and of Art to Christianity. It clarified his own principles, and at the same time it enlarged them. Hitherto he had met only professional and ecclesiastical Thomists, whose concern with art was merely peripheral. There was no one of his acquaintance capable of discussing these matters with the experience and finesse of Maritain. Father Vincent McNabb would have been quite out of his depth with Satie and Rimbaud, Rouault and Stravinsky. But Maritain spoke from the heart of intellectual Paris, fully at home with its sophistries and its discoveries alike. He was educated – to say the least – in a way that Eric was not; a sophisticate who had got beyond sophistication; in a sense, even, a man of the world in a way that Eric never pretended to be; at any rate, a man who had never cut himself from the world in a way that Eric was attempting to do.

It was reassuring, therefore, to be told that if the artist was not to 'shatter his art or his soul, he must simply be, as artist, what art would have him be – a good workman'; that the builders (not architects, be it noted) of the great cathedrals 'thought very much less about making a work of beauty than turning out good work. They had the Faith, and as they were, so did they work. Their achievement revealed God's truth, but without *doing it on purpose*, and because it was not done on purpose.' Eric himself rarely tried to influence anybody, and when his influence was felt he often regretted it. One disciple burnt every painting or drawing he had made hitherto, except a few that his wife refused to part with. Of another Eric said: 'It is a pity he ever made my acquaintance. He did good honest work before his conversion, but he has never got anywhere since. His stuff is self-conscious and affected.'

So it was comforting to be told by Maritain that 'in every form of discipline and teaching the master merely gives assistance from outside to the principle of immanent activity within the pupil'. Certain distinctions were lapidary. 'The Man of Learning is an Intellectual demonstrating, the Artist is an Intellectual operating, the Prudent Man is an intelligent Man of Will acting well.' Maritain echoed the contrast which Eric was so fond of drawing between the Middle Ages when the artist 'did not work for society people and the dealers, but for the faithful commons; it was his mission to house their prayers, to instruct their minds, to rejoice their souls and eyes', and the Renaissance which was 'destined to drive the artist mad and make him the most miserable of men . . . by revealing to him his own grandeur and letting loose upon him the wild beast of Beauty which Faith kept enchanted and led after it obedient, with a gossamer thread for leash'. And Eric would have savoured the further contrast between the sacrifice of Prudence to Art in the Italian Renaissance when 'the *virtu* of the Humanists' had displaced the counsels of evangelical perfection, and the sacrifice of Art to Prudence in the nineteenth century, when 'right thinking circles inclined solely to respectability'.

These were clarifications of views which Eric already held, but Maritain's sympathies were wider just as his intelligence was more informed. Maritain could recognize 'the imaginative and verbal riches of romanticism' and see how 'the instinct of the heart, for all its intimate lack of poise and spiritual penury' still kept alive within it 'the concept of art'. He argued that from Bach to Beethoven and Wagner music had 'suffered a decline in quality, spirituality and purity', but no one of these composers was less necessary than the other. Rembrandt was a bad master, but 'would anyone refuse him his affection?' It was better that he should have 'played and won', even if painting was wounded by his victory. Eric, as he stood before the Primitives in the Louvre with Desmond Chute, would have felt with Maritain that their clumsiness was 'a sacred weakness revealing the subtle intellectuality of art'; and he would have agreed that in the sixteenth century 'deceit installed itself in painting'. But Maritain could also see that 'the great classics from Raphael to Greco, Claude Lorrain, and Watteau' had purified painting of the lie. Eric's appreciations were always at the mercy of a *parti pris* masquerading as an immutable principle; for Maritain novelty was necessary to art and, 'like nature', went 'in seasons'. It was of course no news to Eric that 'manual dexterity' was 'no part of art, but merely a material and extrinsic condition'; but Maritain drew a distinction between the Fine Arts and other kinds of making, of which Eric would still have been shy. They stood out 'in the *genus* art' as man stood out in the '*genus* animal'. They had 'a spiritual soul'.[1]

Art et Scholastique had an effect upon Eric's thinking about art similar to the effect of Parkminster on his thinking about prayer. Immediately he and Pepler invited Father John O'Connor to make a translation of the book, and on June 8 (1922) he was in Paris arranging for its publication with the director of *L'Art Catholique*. Eric himself worked with Father O'Connor on the translation and wrote an introduction to the book, which appeared in 1923 under the title of *The Philosophy of Art*. Five hundred copies only were printed, on hand-made paper, at St Dominic's Press; and on September 3 of the same year Maritain lunched with Eric in Paris. In a short notice the *Times Literary Supplement* condescendingly referred to this 'interesting little Roman Catholic book'. It may have been little in size, but it was large in scope; no other work of the French philosopher has been more seminal among English readers.

Eric paid a second visit to Fribourg with Mary in May 1922, and a third to Chartres with Pepler in 1923. He also went twice to Beauvais where 'the Lauda Sion was a hymn of all creation'.[2] But these were rare excursions. He was now engaged upon the work in stone which best represents the dominant preoccupation of his mind. This was the Leeds University War Memorial. Its erection was made possible by a gift of £2,000 to the Vice-Chancellor – a sum which

[1] All these quotations are from J. F. Scanlan's translation, Sheed & Ward, 1932.
[2] Diary.

covered both the making and the incidental costs of the work. Sir Michael Sadler had approached his Council warily, pointing out that Eric's design had already won a prize from the LCC, although it had not been adopted by them. The choice of subject, he rather speciously argued, signified 'the penalty which followed upon the covetous ambition of Germany in provoking the war'. Eric gave a more candid explanation in a pamphlet published by St Dominic's Press, which the burgesses of Leeds were highly unlikely to have read. The subject had been chosen because it represented the only occasion on which Our Lord is recorded to have used physical violence, and therefore commemorated 'the most just of all wars – the war of Justice against Cupidity – a war waged by Christ Himself'.

He had clothed the figures in modern dress because the point of the sculpture was 'ethical rather than historical or archaeological', and because the artist was better able to represent what he knows and sees around him than what he learns from books or museums. Thus Christ, though identified by a halo, was wearing a priest's alb to emphasize his priesthood, and thick boots to show that he was a priest in Leeds as well as in Jerusalem. The seven strands of His whip represented the Seven Deadly Sins, and the dog at His heels was the Hound of St Dominic, 'calling up the followers of Christ to continue the good work'. A woman and child sat at His feet, conscious that what was going on was neither their fault nor their funeral. At the opposite end of the group was a Fashionable Woman – 'probably the wife of the Pawnbroker who is following her'. She carried a vanity bag and wore 'two beautiful feathers in her hat and nice bobbed hair'. The Pawnbroker was followed by his Clerk, with the account books and 'L.S.D.' inscribed on one of them. He wore his hair rather long and was stumbling over a fallen stool. Next came a Politician, stuffing away a speech in his pocket, and a pair of nondescript Financiers. All the men, with the exception of the Clerk, wore frock coats, boots and spats. The spats seemed appropriate and avoided the horrific difficulty of carving shoelaces; but their straps were forgotten and were only put in at the last moment. Along the cornice was inscribed in Latin:

Go now you rich men, weep and howl in your miseries
which shall come upon you.
Your riches are putrid. (Epistle of St James v. 1)[1]

and in the panel above the Dog:

And when he had made as it were a little whip of cords,
he ejected all from the temple, and the money of the
money-changers he poured out and overthrew their
tables. And he said: do not make my Father's house
a house of commercialism.
(Gospel of St John ii. 15)[1]

Such was the design, and it exploded with predictable effect. Already, in 1920, Sir Michael Sadler had had his doubts. It had occurred to him that the place where the money-changers carried on their business must have been the outer court of the Temple, where visitors who had to pay their Temple dues in Jewish money could get the wherewithal to do so, and where they could herd the animals required for sacrifice. Why then should Our Lord have scourged these people out of court? Was not His whip designed for the driving of animals rather than men? Was it not the personality of Our Lord and the violence of His rebukes, and not the physical act of scourging, that drove the money-changers away? Sadler concluded:

Anyway, I am disconcerted by these doubts as to the analogy between this event in Our Lord's life and the mischievous Mammon-worship which was one of the fundamental causes of the war. Has any such thought crossed your mind? You won't for a moment take this as meaning that I have anything but the strongest possible desire that you should design our War Memorial. If it is not to be done by you, I would rather there was not one at all.[2]

Needless to say, no such thought had occurred to Eric, and on July 2, 1921, Sadler wrote again proposing a site:

[1] Eric Gill's translation.
[2] February 1920.

If I offer it as a War Memorial to the University, the philistines will be furious and spoil our game by their attacks. I propose to give it as a work of art to the University. We need have no inscription. The thing speaks for itself. The names of the fallen will be recorded elsewhere. Your work will stand alone, eloquent by its own meaning and beauty. If I ask for it to be put in the inner quadrangle of the University, the ungodly will raise difficulties. They will hate your meaning and find means of obstruction. But if (with your consent) I just ask to have it fixed on the outside wall of the seventeenth-century part of the old manor house on our new (and lovely) estate at Westwood, where all the Colleges are to be built, it will have a beautiful position, in an old garden, and be seen by all the students and others, including those who live in the Hall. I shall get leave for that site easily. If, when that offer is made, they agitate for the work being put in the University building, we can graciously accede to the request, and there are sites here – I think you might make it smaller – say 20 ft long instead of 30 ft. This will lighten your labour.

Eric set to work and in November 1922 he sent Sadler a photograph. Sadler thought it showed 'splendid promise'.[1] On January 30 Sadler wrote again proposing to bring the matter before the University Council in February, and asking Eric for a drawing to show how the sculpture would look when fixed in position, and for a photograph of the work in its present form. He had now changed his ideas about the site and suggested the wall space near the Library in University Road where it would be more easily seen. On February 21 Sadler was able to announce the Council's acceptance of the gift; if Eric could get the sculpture fixed by May 31 the Prince of Wales might be persuaded to unveil it. In the event, this proved impossible, but Eric had his carving in position well before the end of May – and it was then that the storm broke.

It raged in the columns of the three local newspapers, all of them owned and edited in the Conservative interest; the *Yorkshire Post*, the *Yorkshire Evening Post*, and the *Leeds Mercury*. The first article, in the *Yorkshire Post* (May 18), was bewildered but restrained: it assumed that Eric had been influenced by Mestrovic, and thought that he exaggerated the uncouthness of coat and trousers. The work had been

[1] November 13, 1922.

exposed to the public view for only one day, during which Eric, chiselling in his overalls, was entertained by the comments of the passers-by. These were so mordant that the sculpture was covered up until the day of its unveiling. On May 23 the *Yorkshire Post* devoted a leader to what was by now a subject of bitter and indignant controversy. The writer criticized the work as primitive, formal and lifeless; as too eccentric to have a lasting appeal; and as wholly irrelevant to the war whose dead it was designed to commemorate. The struggle between Justice and Cupidity had been only one element in the fight between Germany and the Allies, and not the most obvious one. Eric would have done better to present a Christ who laid down His life as a ransom for the many than as a scourge for the unjust few.

Letters of advocacy or protest quickly followed. It was pointed out that Leeds University owed its existence to the gifts of rich men, and that it was therefore gratuitous to insult them; an Indian correspondent thought the sculpture illustrated the Hindu maxim that 'the highest can't be spoken'; the local pawnbrokers protested against their effigy; Sir William Rothenstein, opening the new session at the Leeds Art School, described the memorial as 'one of the greatest pieces of sculpture of the last hundred years'; others objected to the Latin inscription – if it were designed to be understood by the University it should be in the Greek of the New Testament, and if it were intended for the general public it should be in English. Two Catholic lecturers in the English Department, one a poet and the other a scholar of rare imaginative gifts – Wilfred Childe and J. R. Tolkien – signed a joint letter of support, with a paragraph of exculpation for the pawnbrokers.

Meanwhile, Sadler was on his way back from Canada. On his return the editor of the *Yorkshire Post* pressed him to abandon the Dedication ceremony, presenting him with something very like an ultimatum. Sadler then summoned the editor of *The Gryphon*, a University paper, and asked for his support. This young man, Philip Murphy, was a Catholic in general sympathy with Eric's ideas, and Sadler was delighted with his long letter to the *Post*. Murphy defended the pawnbroker as an heraldic device for usury, and only questioned the 'L.S.D.' on the clerk's money bags as an aesthetic impropriety. He defended the conception of the memorial on the grounds that just wars were about justice, and he thought it appropriate for a University whose chief concern was truth. The Editor replied that so very personal a conception of justice and truth was inappropriate for a memorial which of its nature should have the widest possible appeal. At the same time Sadler wrote to Eric:

With great care and with elision of much that, in other circumstances, I should have put in, I have given the enclosed to the newspapers who begged me to say something and whose importunity I have put off. I hope that you and I will not take different lines. In deference to your wish, I have deliberately struck out any mention of German economic ambitions which (*me judice*) in their glittering and perilous mixture with honest patriotism and with fear of danger, made Europe inflammable for war.[1]

In his statement to the Press Sadler commended the carving as suggesting 'a Christian view of war':

By Our Lord's act the Christian is assured that force under due authority may be used in a righteous cause. The words which He quoted bid the Christian remember that to execute judgment is a righteous and sacred duty. Our Lord's driving the money-changers and the sellers of doves out of the temple does not condemn honest traffic but teaches us that sacred things must be kept free from thoughts of money gain. . . . Mr Gill's carving has the vitality of Gothic art. . . . I hope that those to whom the design is now displeasing may feel differently about it when time has made it more familiar, and that to those who come after us the carving may have the significance which a Pre-Raphaelite picture has for us today.

Eric may well have wrinkled his nose at this comparison; at all events, he now made his single mistake. He sent his pamphlet, setting out the purpose of the memorial, to the Press, who naturally seized upon its more controversial features. Sadler's soft-pedalling was drowned in the consequent uproar, and Eric received the following telegram from the harassed Vice-Chancellor:

[1] May 25, 1923.

Regret you published without consultation but except on three points am in substantial agreement with your view. Please refrain from saying any more at present owing situation here.

This was amplified in a letter:

I regret that you published the statement without consulting me because we are jointly concerned in the memorial and any interpretation of it ought, I think, to have been in words which either represented our common view or explicitly assigned responsibility for the interpretation which the handbook offers. But, as I said in my telegram, I am, except on three points, substantially in agreement with what you say. The three points upon which I differ are:

I. The phrase 'financial experts' on page 10 seems to me too indiscriminating.
II. The pawnbrokers' calling seems to me not blameworthy.
III. Modern warfare, so far as I know the facts, has not been mainly about money. Some of the most powerful causes of it are deeper and more impersonal than money gain, and the gift of civilization has in it very many noble elements as well as some ignoble. The quotation[1] with which your handbook ends touches only on a fraction of the truth.

The situation is very difficult, not least because the sculpture will be dedicated on Friday morning. Please do not say anything more until after a full consultation with me.[2]

This was a judicious critique of Eric's over-simplifications, and indeed it rather called in question the whole sense of the memorial.

On May 30 the *Yorkshire Post* came out with a reasoned plea that the memorial be unveiled but not dedicated. It took exception to the 'frivolous tone' of Eric's pamphlet and thought it would appear 'in the poorest taste' to those who did not regard the memorial primarily as a work of art. A War Memorial – so the writer argued – might please some more than others, but it should give offence to none. This had given offence to many. Let it stand on its merits as a work of art, but not as 'the lasting public symbol of feelings and memories which were sacred' to those who disliked it. On the same day Sadler wrote to Eric:

[1] From John ii. 15; see above, p. 128.
[2] May 28, 1923.

The row goes on. Two of the newspapers demand that the dedication, fixed for Friday, should be postponed which means, of course, abandoned. The Pro-Chancellor and I have decided that the arrangements will go forward as announced.

And again, twenty-four hours later:

I am under such pressure that I cannot write at adequate length. Though we differ on some points, our agreement on what I believe to be the chief moral issue is complete. The wind blows high here. I cannot deny that the publication of your handbook has made things more difficult. But I have said nothing about it in public and we must keep our ranks. Thank you for silence. The carving will tell its own tale. We may not be out of the trouble yet, but deep down in my mind is a feeling of thankfulness that the issue has been raised and that people have been made to think.[1]

The memorial was dedicated by the Bishop of Ripon, assisted by the President of the Leeds Free Church Council, on June 1. Sadler wrote to Eric that thousands had watched the ceremony and that many wreaths had been laid. 'We are not out of the wood yet, but I hope all will go well.'[2] And again, four days later:

I think the carving is fine, especially the right hand part of it. . . . The controversy still goes on. The embers are hot. But the big issues are getting clear and, though opinion is divided, the discussion will be found, I think, to have done good. It has made people think.[3]

Sadler himself had second thoughts. On the morrow of Eric's death he wrote in his diary:

Eric Gill is dead. A fine draughtsman, a vain poseur, a tiresome writer. . . . He departed egregiously (without telling me until it was too late) from the earlier design I had chosen. And he broke his word by publishing at the worst moment of acute controversy, and sending down to Leeds, a contentious political interpretation of the Memorial's significance. He behaved like a vain, wilful child. The Memorial is a fine piece of work,

[1] May 31, 1923.
[2] June 1, 1923.
[3] June 5, 1923.

but not nearly as good as it might have been. The mood is too obviously underlined.[1] (November 18, 1940)

Sir James Baillie, a subsequent Vice-Chancellor, disliked it so much that he perseveringly tried to grow ivy over it, but an unknown hand just as perseveringly snipped the budding shoots. It has now found a suitable home in the entrance hall of the new Arts building. Courage had been vindicated; but the relevance of the monument to its subject is still not transparently clear, and there is no evidence that it caused the magnates of the West Riding to tremble in their shoes. Eric's original idea had been for a group in bronze. This would have given an extra dimension to the work, of which it is robbed by its position against the wall.

[1] *Michael Ernest Sadler*, 1949.

9

Ditchling continued as a magnet for those who were unable to come to terms either with themselves or with the world – George Maxwell the builder; Philip Hagreen, an artist who had been through the war and come to Ditchling for much the same reasons as David Jones; Reginald Lawson[1] who subsequently entered the Order of St Dominic. It is to him that I owe many sidelights on these last years of the Community while Eric was still a member of it.[2] Maxwell and Hagreen were both married and seemed to take for granted many of those things which for the others were a matter of endless discussion. Lawson lived with David Jones and two others in bachelor quarters known as the 'Sorrowful Mysteries'; this was a cottage converted from a carriage shed, which became vacant when Desmond Chute went to Fribourg.

He arrived with no special qualifications and made a poor start by digging up a plant of thyme that Mary Gill particularly treasured. Charitably and characteristically, she merely observed that she had been thinking of putting it somewhere else, and that now she would have a proper herb garden nearer to the house. Lawson was next put on to brewing beer which often turned out to be flat and cost exactly what you would have paid for it in a public house. Eric would console the company by saying that it must be 'nourishing' when you considered the barley and sugar which had gone into it. Lawson was caretaker of the 'Sorrowful Mysteries', to which a small-holding was attached. This consisted of a meadow, some fruit-trees, three sows and a goat. Since the sows ate up the fruit-trees and someone had to be paid to take away the goat, only the sows and the meadow remained. But thanks to Mary's Guernseys, the community was largely self-supporting. She also had a mare, whose 'points' were

1 Now Brother David Lawson, O.P.
2 The *Aylesford Review*: Spring 1965.

well regarded in the neighbourhood but which imperilled the life and limb of anyone riding on its back by genuflecting at full speed. When Petra produced some mare's milk for tea, the joke was not appreciated.

Casual visitors were bewildered by the reading of the *martyr-ologium* before the midday meal – such reminders of barbarity were thought irrelevant to the twentieth century – and not all of them easily swallowed the Epistle and the Gospel of the day. Spike Hughes describes a Christmas spent at the Crank in 1919:

Its uncompromising atmosphere of Roman Catholicism I found not a little sinister. There was a considerable amount of splashing of Holy Water and the saying of grace before meals, and there was an interminable nightly performance of Compline around a spinet with E.G. taking the part of cantor and singing plainsong in an unmusical voice. . . .[1] Water froze in wash basins, bread and butter were home-made, and eaten off wooden plates; the only lighting was candlelight, and the members of the family were mostly dressed in clothes that had been spun and woven in the colony of Ditchling. But from a purely aesthetic point of view it was no ordinary arty-crafty collection of *objects* that decorated the Gill interior. It was a craftsman's home, but it was the home of a master-craftsman.[2]

Hardly less bewildered was the neighbouring priest, who was chaplain to St George's Retreat and confessor to the Ditchling community. He publicly rebuked the Tertiaries for coming to Mass unshaven and in unpolished boots, and took every occasion to make his disapproval generally known. As a consequence Bishop Amigo of Southwark – a man with very definite ideas – descended on the Common. Reginald Lawson formally received him. He was friendly enough in the remote way of bishops, and could detect no irregularity, either moral or liturgical; but he would not give immediate approval for the reservation of the Blessed Sacrament and clearly had no understanding of what Ditchling was getting at. Later, he refused to consecrate a church at Leatherhead because Eric had carved the Stations for it, and it remained unconsecrated until his death.

[1] Others would have disagreed.
[2] *Opening Bars*, 1946.

Shortly after his conversion Eric had engraved a crucifix for use on altar cards, but being new to engraving he had forgotten to reverse the letters INRI which he had placed within the circle of the halo. Seeing a print of this, the Bishop exclaimed, 'Look there – spelt backwards – devil worship': it confirmed his worst suspicions of Ditchling. The local parish priest also viewed Ditchling with some perplexity. 'I don't go there very often,' he said, 'but whenever I do go Pepler is ordaining Gill or Gill is consecrating Pepler.' Pepler laughed merrily when this was reported to him but Eric – for reasons that will become clear – was slower to see the joke.

Cardinal Bourne who came with his secretary, Monsignor Jackman, was equally remote from Ditchling dogmas; but Bourne was pre-eminently a man of prayer, and whatever else may have been lacking at Ditchling it was not prayer. Like Eric himself, Bourne was a spiritual child of Parkminster; he had commissioned and approved the Westminster Stations; and Jackman became a good friend to Eric as the years went by. At Ditchling itself there was one person who had not hitherto been able to sing to its tune. Clare Pepler had rather complainingly endured her exile from all that liberal world of free thought and free discussion, good plays and new books, which was her natural climate. In March 1922 Eric was writing to Desmond Chute:

I am afraid Clare does not get any happier or any nearer the Church. I gather from David J(ones) that she lives in a permanent melancholy and more or less open petulance. It's really dreadful. Everyone conspires to do what they can to please her and soothe her and all the result is to be greeted with 'I'd better go away, I can see I'm not wanted here'. . . . It's a terrible sore in the family corpus.[1]

On May 1, 1923, however, she was received into the Church, and went radiantly to her first Communion in Hallett's oratory the next day. At Christmas, 1924, it was decided to put on a Nativity play. This was written by Hilary Pepler, and Reginald Lawson was able to tell him something of what he had learnt in a film studio about the value

[1] March 22, 1922.

of slow motion. Philip Mairet, who was himself playing the part of one of the 'Four Shepherds' at the Old Vic, undertook that the Shepherds would appear on the Common, accompanied by the children who could play the other characters required by the Annunciation and the Crib. When they did appear the disparity between amateur and professional status was glaringly apparent. The smocks, which were the habitual dress of the community, and an alb for St Gabriel, completed the wardrobe.

Eric, for all his activity and his comings and goings, was the still, contemplative centre of a life in itself contemplative. You would find him in the evenings whistling the accompaniment to the girls' songs on the flageolet; or see him flicking his cape as he crossed over to the chapel in the starlight; or watch him rolling his cigarettes over a cup of tea. Sometimes your ear would catch a faint buzzing and mistake it for a swarm of bees; but then you realized it was the pure, thin notes of an early piano, and you would find Eric absorbed in the songs of John Dowland and singing in a scarcely audible *sotto voce* the music which he had learnt to love at Chichester. At other times Lawson would join him in a duet. Eric's taste both in music and painting had paradoxical lapses from austerity. 'What do you think of Holman Hunt's *Triumph of the Innocents*?' he once asked Hagreen. Hagreen confessed that he loved it. 'So do I,' came Eric's relieved admission. Or again he would burst into tears while he was singing 'Sweet and Low', and then exclaim, 'I know it's awful rot, but it *is* so sad.'

Contemplatives often give the impression of self-centredness; but in the case of Eric this was no more than self-sufficiency. Deeply as he loved other people and hard as he worked for them, he had resources within himself independent of them. Critics of Ditchling might have described it, not quite unfairly, as a happy family of misfits; however ill at ease they may have been in the world, they fitted easily with each other. There were occasional complaints about the unpunctuality of meals, the men wondering what the women had been doing 'all the morning', and the women replying, 'Whenever we come over to the workshops you're smoking and chatting and having a drink.' But there was very little of the bickering and backbiting which is the occupational disease of community life, and brings so many communities to an end.

Ditchling has survived – although its numbers have diminished and its novelty worn off. Eric's own part in it, however, was now drawing to a close. It had become altogether too novel in the sense that it was altogether too newsworthy. Father Vincent incessantly publicized its virtues. The stream of visitors flowed on to the Common. Some of these were valuable friends – Father Austin Barker, O.P., Father John-Baptist Reeves, O.P., Dr Flood from Glasgow, Christopher Dawson, and Henry John, son to Augustus – 'a bright spark bursting into flame' and soon to test his vocation with the Jesuits. 'You people are like Emile Zola,' he told Eric, 'you take the part for the whole.' Father O'Hea, S.J., director of the Catholic Social Guild, and no reactionary, also had his reservations:

The Ditchlingites are certainly most lovable, holy, unaffected (though they believe the rest of the English Catholics all wrong) and productive but not in the economic sense, for they live on capitalist money ultimately – very largely. . . .

And then, evidently in reply to Eric's objections: 'The CSG does not attempt, and never did attempt, to baptize the system – whatever precisely that means; that there is a *system* at *all* is to my mind a socialist fallacy.' But Eric would sooner have disbelieved in his own existence than have disbelieved in systems – good or bad.

Other visitors came out of curiosity, and Eric was growing tired of them. Pepler, too, had been considering a move, and in 1922 had returned to Ireland where a property 20 miles from Lough Derg, on the border of the six counties, had seemed worth inspection. Nothing came of this, however, but on April 29, 1923, Donald Attwater arrived to spend a few nights at the Crank. Attwater was then living on the island of Caldey off the south coast of Wales where a community of Anglican Benedictine monks had been received into the Catholic Church ten years before. The Community was at that time going through a difficult period. It was the subject of criticism on various grounds, and Eric himself was not prejudiced in its favour.

A slight air of amateur monasticism still clung to it, but Attwater was able to put these misconceptions in a more favourable light. 'We seem to have been wrong about the Caldey monks,' Eric remarked to Pepler. He then told Attwater that he was restless and dissatisfied at Ditchling, but that it was difficult to find a suitable place elsewhere. This prompted Attwater to tell him about Father Ignatius' empty monastery at Capel-y-ffin, 4 miles from the ruins of Llanthony Abbey, where Father Joseph Woodford of Caldey was shortly going to live for reasons of health and where Attwater and his family were also proposing to migrate. Eric was immediately interested, and Attwater returned to Ditchling in September, when there were further discussions with Pepler and Maxwell.

Early in January 1924, Eric met Peter Anson at Quarr Abbey in the Isle of Wight.[1] Now Anson also knew Caldey at first hand, and he has since written a fascinating account of its most picturesque and controversial personality, Abbot Carlyle. He was able to fill in the picture which Attwater had sketched out, and possibly suggested that Eric should go to Caldey rather than to Capel. Indeed it is probable that the purpose of Eric's visit to Quarr was to meet Anson, since on the following day we find him at Caldey where Attwater was waiting for him. He was accompanied by George Maxwell, and discussions took place with the Prior, Dom Wilfred Upson, and Dom Theodore Baily, an accomplished artist in the Byzantine manner who had spent six months in Paris working with Maurice Denis. For the rest, Eric was appalled by the 'artistic slush in which Caldey now wallows'. He thought it 'arty, and ornamental and garden cityish'; but he could see no sign of the more serious troubles about which rumour had reached him, except that the place was heavily in debt and 'at the mercy of financial experts'.[2]

They spent four days on the island and on January 14 proceeded to Llanthony with the Prior, arriving at midnight. 'A marvellous place,'[3] was Eric's first reaction when the sun had risen over the Black

[1] See *A Roving Recluse*, Peter Anson, 1946.
[2] Letters to Desmond Chute, January 12 and 20, 1924.
[3] Diary.

Mountains. On March 7 Hilary Pepler and his son David went to look at the place for themselves. The Attwaters were already installed, and Donald remembers Pepler in a 'rather truculent and overbearing mood',[1] and already prejudiced against the move. He returned to Ditchling on March 10, and two days later set out with his wife, Eric and Mary Gill and Joseph Cribb. They spent the night at Abergavenny and walked up to Capel in the morning, getting a lift for the last few miles in a lorry. They spent the next night in the deserted monastery, sleeping in Father Ignatius' old room, and on March 16 Eric was writing in high glee to Father John O'Connor:

I was in S. Wales (Brecknock) last week looking at a farm. We may buy it! . . . Capel-y-ffin's the name and just describes it. 2,000 feet of mountain wall on both sides and to the north of it – no outlet but to the south. Benedictine monastery 400 yards away – Bd Sacrament and Daily Mass. Good land – fair price – nice little house and 107 acres with some timber and two rushing streams. Sheep run on mountains and stone galore, both for carving and building, *no extra charge*. 10 miles to Ry Station. Postman on horseback once a day. Doctor on horseback, from Hay, once a week. Any complaints? 400 yards approx. to Monmouthshire border! London in 3½ hours from Abergavenny. Exciting prospect. We may *all* Trek. Say good-bye to Burgess Hill. Why not?[2]

When they returned the whole project was discussed at a meeting of the Guild at which the Prior of Caldey was present. Pepler had made an offer for a farm adjoining the monastery, which he was proposing to buy in the name of his son, David, and was now enthusiastic for the move. The Prior, with Father Woodford and Donald Attwater, spent three days at Ditchling early in May, and on June 9 Father Vincent came down to add his voice to the debate. He had a long discussion with the Prior, who had returned to Ditchling on June 10. For the next week Eric was in Bradford working on his Stations of the Cross for Father John O'Connor, and there now appears an ominous entry in his diary: 'Talk with Fr. O'C. re H.P. and finance.' On June 25 he writes to Desmond Chute:

[1] Letter to the author. Anson dates the visit in September 1923, but E.G.'s diary shows this to be a mistake.
[2] *Letters of Eric Gill*, 1947.

I expect you have heard from Hilary, but I don't know if he has warned you of the fact that owing to financial difficulties and, as I think, financial crookedness, on the one hand and attempts of some members to enlarge the scope of the Guild and include responsibility for family affairs as well as workshop affairs there is a serious deadlock and a break up of the whole thing seems inevitable. I hope you will not be worried by it all – I hope you will not see the sepulchre through the whitewash.

Here was the crux of the only serious quarrel that ever embittered Eric's relations with a friend. Pepler had increasingly come to regard Ditchling as a community whose members had mutual obligations; Eric thought of it as an association of independent families, co-operating for purposes of work and prayer but essentially independent. Pepler, with Vincent McNabb, saw it as an essay in Distributism and a move 'back to the land'. Vincent McNabb was the genius, but also in some respects the *mauvais génie,* of Ditchling. His reputation for sanctity gave an alarming impetus to what Philip Hagreen has called 'the icy torrent of his Jeremiads'.[1] It was disconcerting, to say the least, when he sent his casual 'drunks' down to Ditchling in the hope that the experience would cure them! He was an incessant talker and listened reluctantly, and Pepler was inclined to use him as a fire-hose to batter down opposition. Eric himself liked to be self-supporting, but he was less dogmatic a Distributist. Moreover, over matters of money he was meticulous where Pepler was vague. Pepler's large-hearted appeals to *esprit de corps* went over Eric's realistic head. And so the question arose as to what property rights Eric had in Ditchling and how much of them he could equitably take off with him. Pepler, for instance, claimed that Eric's wood-blocks rightly belonged to the Guild to repair the losses of St Dominic's Press; Eric maintained the opposite. The details of the dispute are both difficult and tedious to follow, but they must in honesty be briefly discussed.

On June 18 Eric returned to London, having prepared in the train a statement of his case which he submitted to Father Vincent, now attached to the Dominican Church at Haverstock Hill. Pepler and Maxwell were also present at the meeting. Eric blamed the trouble

[1] Letter to the author.

Teresa and Winifred Maxwell, wood engraving, 1924.

on Pepler's financial methods and on his alleged tendency to 'boss' the family life of what Eric preferred to describe as the 'village' rather than the community. Eric had lent Pepler £25 to be repaid out of a legacy, but when the legacy came there was no mention of repayment. £180 was required for the workshops, and this was to be found by the sale of Debentures. The Debentures were sold, but the money was not handed over. Interest on this was due to Lord Howard de Walden, and Pepler held that the Guild should pay it – which meant that it came out of Eric's pocket. Pepler also held that the Guild should pay the expenses of the trip to Llanthony; Eric disagreed and paid it himself. Pepler declined to pay his rent and subscription to the Guild on the ground that the Guild owed him money for printing; but Pepler never sent in an account. It was agreed that each member of the Guild should pay his subscription and rent in cash so as to meet the rent due to the Spoil Bank Association; Pepler concurred in theory but did nothing in fact. His inability or unwillingness to keep accounts meant that money earmarked for one purpose was used for another, and his borrowings from Eric, Maxwell, the Guild and others amounted to nearly £1,000, not including the £4,000 mortgage on Fragbarrow farm.

These moneys were to come out of a possible legacy to Clare Pepler, but Eric wanted to know whether she was aware of what she would be expected to pay – if and when the legacy came. Did she know how much her legacy would be? Did anyone know whether it would be adequate to pay the mortgage and the debts? How exactly had Pepler bought his farm at Llanthony, and how was it going to be paid for? Presumably it would be bought by David Pepler's grandparents for David Pepler; they would never know that it was really for the use of the 'community'. Neither Eric nor Maxwell questioned Pepler's right to buy a farm for his son, nor did they blame him for not consulting the Guild over the purchase. They merely thought it dishonest that the property should be bought for the Guild under the pretence of being bought for David; and no agreement had been reached as to whether the Guild should own such property at all. Pepler's enthusiasm for the farm had cooled down since his visit – probably under Father Vincent's dissuasion – and he had delayed coming to any final agreement with the owner. The result was general uncertainty.

Again, he had set up a distillery at Ditchling which he operated 'in the interest of the community' but which the community had never authorized. Moreover his operation of it was so indiscreet that there was serious risk of a summons. If this happened, who would pay the fine? Everyone loved Hilary Pepler, but they hated 'his finance, his brutal methods, his dictatorial manner, and his minding other people's business'. He was even beginning to suggest that other people's 'surplus' money – there cannot have been very much of it – should be at the disposal of the 'community'. This would mean, in practice, that Pepler would dispose of it – not of course for personal gain, but it would none the less disappear without being accounted for.

Eric attributed these velleities to Pepler's education and former affluence. He was 'always biting off more than he could chew'. Generous and well-intentioned by nature, he could still be 'brutally insensitive to other people's feelings or responsibilities'. Moreover he had a Manichean attitude to money. Regarding it as intrinsically evil, he was careless about what he did with it – 'rushing into new projects and leaving the consolidation undetermined'. Eric, in common with the others, had regarded these as Pepler's own perilous affairs; but when Pepler maintained that since he had done everything for the community therefore the community must shoulder the burden, Eric put his foot down. Matters had now come to a head because there was no more money to carry on with, and because it was 'absolutely necessary to decide clearly that the Guild is neither founded nor fitted to run a community of families'. Eric reproached himself for not raising these questions earlier; only the general affection in which Pepler was held had prevented him, and others, from doing so. He concluded his statement as follows:

This outspoken statement is wrenched out of me as a result of Hilary Pepler's actions in reply to my decision to take a private house at Llanthony. Hilary Pepler's accusations against me, and his accusations against Mary, make it immediately necessary to clear things up.
　It has not been my intention to clear *out*.
　It is certainly my intention to clear *up*.

Outspoken it was indeed; these were hard words to use of anyone, particularly of a friend, and Eric must have felt very strongly to have used them to his face. It is difficult either to impugn or to endorse Eric's charges; nor do I know what 'actions' Pepler had committed or what 'accusations' he had made to provoke them. Some people blamed Eric for borrowing money for the building of workshops which were wrongly placed and badly constructed; they had started cracking before any of the debt on them had been paid off. Eric was also blamed for spending borrowed money on a chapel which would have been the better for fewer fads and more technical sense in its architecture. The doorway was too low, and the windows and tie

beams too high. Generally speaking, however, a conspiracy of silence
or oblivion has grown up around what is known as the Ditchling
'split'. Neither Eric nor Pepler cared to talk about it, although Eric
wrote about it very freely to Desmond Chute; and one of the very
rare occasions on which he is recorded to have lost his temper was
when he broke off a discussion of Pepler's financial methods to
plunge his knife into a loaf of bread! Always tenacious in argument,
he was never more so than here. Even those who were nearest to the
two antagonists seem to have forgotten the details of their quarrel,
but a clue is given in a letter from Clare Pepler to Eric:

The immediate fault seems to be that it is not until you are corrected[1] for
rushing into Wales do you find courage to tell Hilary your views of his
financial position. But the root must be elsewhere; consider the history
of your relationship with Hilary since there was an oratory at Halletts.
You involved him in a land speculation in order to add a field to your own
estate, he became further involved, but willingly, as the idea of a
Catholic Village developed. It was evident that he was prepared to and did
actually give all that he had to make this a reality. I know of nothing that
he kept back. The result was that we grew poorer, you encouraged us
'hold on as long as the Bank will let you' . . . and we have held on until
our home is sold . . . and are still holding. But you grew richer and as that
happened a change came. 'Hilary has had his fling why should not I?'
Now a Catholic Village is not built on these lines.

It was a grave fault surely to keep back from him the uneasiness you
felt as to Hilary's affairs. It was a grave fault to talk about such things
behind his back (to newcomers like Hagreen especially) considering the
nature of the enterprise you had begun with him.

It was an unhappy mistake to assume that because you were being
prompted by self-interest in beginning the Fragbarrow business that
Hilary should share those motives.

I cannot remember Hilary complaining of your faults, not even when
you appeared in chapel with bare legs.

As to Vincent . . . the matter was as left in June. In our opinion (and
presumably in his until you put reasons to convince him otherwise) your
act in accepting the Prior's invitation was an act against unity (no

---

[1] In a letter written indeed by Hilary, but read by the other two and posted by Joseph
Cribb.

community could exist on those lines) and an act against prudence in becoming involved with Caldey.[1]

This makes it pretty clear that Pepler thought Eric was acting from motives of self-interest, where Eric thought he was acting from motives of self-protection. Moreover he was an artist of national reputation, earning more than the rest of the Guild put together. This led Pepler to expect an altruism in which he was disappointed. My reconstruction of the dispute makes no pretence to be a complete summary; it is no more than an accurate condensation of the statement read by Eric at Haverstock Hill. Meanwhile there is some consolation in the fact that Eric and Pepler exchanged the kiss of peace when the meeting was over; and there was further relief for Eric in a reading of the *Alcestis* in the train from Victoria to Burgess Hill. He was 'quite overcome by it'.[2]

On June 29 there were further discussions at Ditchling out of which it 'emerged clearly that E.G. must sever his connection with Guild because of H.P.'s financial methods and condition, and H.P.'s and Guild's notions of an organized community'.[3] This suggests that some, if not most, members of the Guild were on Pepler's side. Two days later Eric left for Caldey. He stayed four nights, visiting Llanthony on the way back and discussing household rearrangements with the Attwaters. On his return to London he put the Crank up for sale with Knight, Frank & Rutley; went to Sotheby's to arrange for a sale of books; and discussed the removal of furniture. On July 21 there was a meeting of the Guild – 'very difficult and unpleasant – no agreement'[4] – and the next day Eric wrote to Pepler:

I hereby resign my membership of the Guild of St Joseph and St Dominic. My reasons for this are of course obvious and I think you will agree that no other solution is possible as we have lost confidence. You will no doubt let me have at your convenience a statement of what the Guild deems to be my obligation as tenant of my workshop, etc., and I will make out a statement of the Guild's obligations to me. Meanwhile I have

[1] Undated, probably later in 1924.
[2] Diary. [3] ibid. [4] ibid.

handed the £25 gold and the chapel account book, balanced to date, to Joseph.

The Guild made one last effort to keep him; the following letter was signed by Pepler, Cribb and Maxwell:

Our dear Brother,
Some things which are lost are found again, we ask you simply to defer the matter until we have had the opportunity of a conference with Dr Flood in the chair. He will be here for the Feast of St. Dominic, what better day for arriving not only at the truth but at concord?
Your affectionate brothers in St Dominic.

Eric replied, though not in quite the same fraternal vein:

I thank you for your joint note and for its obviously charitable intent. My decision is however unaffected by it. Certainly I hope to have some conversation with Dr Flood and if you like to invite me to your meeting, I will come but I cannot promise to take part in the discussion. . . . There is no need for discord, only for a reasonable settling up.

His personal feelings in the matter were conveyed, without equivocation, in a letter to Father Austin Barker:

Undoubtedly there is a split but I hope it will prove to be a healthy division of forces. I do not understand Hilary's determination to stay on here. I only understand my own determination not to do so. George Maxwell has made things much more difficult – for me anyway. I don't blame him. I think he simply doesn't understand – how could he – after all, he's very much compounded of CSG[1] and CEG[2] elements and his work is very different from mine and he doesn't suffer as I do from the publicity and advertisement of E.G. 'The well-known sculptor who did the stations of the X at W'minster Cathedral!' Fr Vincent is I gather very much against me in the matter and very distrustful of the Caldey people, but, there again, I simply cannot be led in this matter by Fr V. He doesn't understand a little bit – and in practical matters, money, land, etc., well he's simply hopeless and leads Hilary and George more and more into high-falutin and absurd notions. Oh lord – this is most awfully confidential, for

[1] Catholic Social Guild.
[2] Catholic Evidence Guild.

I do love and respect Fr V. very much indeed and that's part of the difficulty for me, for I simply cannot stand by and say, to *him*, that I think his notions all bally nonsense and if I say so to George, it's no good, because, to George, Fr V. is absolute wisdom! Well, anyway, the thing is now settled and we leave here on or about August 12. I have resigned from the Guild, because I do not want to stand in Hilary's or George's way. Personally, I am exceedingly happy. I am more at peace than I have been for years and can actually get on with my work without interminable discussions about lands and family managements. . . . (August 2, 1924)

On July 24 Eric saw his lawyers in Brighton about obtaining the release from his part tenancy of Fragbarrow farm, and on the 26th he attended a party at Fragbarrow. The children 'read the *Pied Piper* very nicely. Gordian was the lame boy: very touching.'[1] On August 4 he was lowering down the head of Christ in profile, which stood with its inscription – *Pastor est tui Dominus* – over the lintel to the Crank; on the 10th he took tea with the Mairets and said good-bye to Edward Johnston; and on the 11th there was a kind of reconciliation with Pepler and Maxwell – this went off 'very happily'.[2] On August 13 David Jones wrote to Desmond Chute:

Eric and the others departed this morning – leaving, what seems at the moment, a very desolate Ditchling. Moreover, you will be pleased to hear that any breach of friendship that may have existed was bridged before the departure – and charity rules the situation.

Dr Flood and Dr McQuillan are both here: Dr Flood I understand helped matters very considerably. By a strange coincidence the quotation from St Thomas on the Calendar for today is as follows: 'Harmony which is the effect of charity does not imply unity of opinion, but a unity of wills.'

Dr Flood said Mass (the Mass for travellers followed by the Benedictus and the prayer for the same) and the company departed. I have just seen the last few odds and ends leaving the Crank by old Evans' Vans of Ditchling.

It was very many years before Eric saw Ditchling again – except the Calvary on the Spoil Bank and the cluster of cottages and huts as they are seen from the railway.

[1] Diary.
[2] ibid.

PART THREE

Capel-y-ffin

1924-1928

I

The family, with the exception of Petra, and accompanied by Philip and Aileen Hagreen, travelled by train to Newport, stopping at the Shaftesbury Hotel. The next morning they took the local train to Llanvihangel, which was the nearest station to Capel-y-ffin. Here Dan Brennan, the farm-hand from Ditchling, met them with a lorry. It was raining steadily as they swayed and jolted up the valley, tightly squeezed and clasping a vigorous and sodden billy-goat. They arrived at Capel in the late afternoon, when the Attwaters had seen to it that tea and fires were ready, and late foxgloves in the flower vases. The monastery, with Father Ignatius' ruined and roofless chapel beside it, stood up on a slope of the mountain built around three sides of a triangle and facing east. Eric and Hagreen stayed the night at the Grange – a house near by, then occupied by Father Woodford, the monk from Caldey. The rest of the party slept on temporary beds in the monastery. Inspection of the land and acquaintance with the neighbours followed, and the furniture arrived from Ditchling two days later. The valley upwards from Llanthony was still a pre-industrial farming community where the seed was broadcast by hand and the flails still threshed the corn.

The ruinous buildings were set in a chaos of big timber. Father Woodford enjoyed felling the trees and hearing them crash, but he was less interested in sawing them up for logs. They sprawled one across the other 'like giant spillikins'.[1] The chimneys had been built for coal and the wood fires needed the constant encouragement of bellows, with the result that the rooms were thick with acrid smoke. In addition to these discomforts the sewers became blocked and sanitation was a recurrent problem. Nevertheless, a familiar routine of life was soon established. On the morning after their arrival they were singing the Mass of the Assumption in Father Ignatius' 'Bible

[1] Philip Hagreen, letter to the author.

Cloister', and on August 24 they were chanting Compline in the ruins of his church. Eric wanted to restart the Guild but Hagreen, and David Jones when he arrived to stay a little later, dissuaded him.

There was no lack of visitors. Dr McQuillan came from Glasgow and the Prior, with Dom Theodore, from Caldey. The Prior and McQuillan did card-tricks after supper. Father John Gray came from Edinburgh as soon as they had left. There were songs in the evening with the Attwaters, varied by a reading of the *Alcestis* to the family; and by September 12 Eric was carving his splendid black marble 'Deposition',[1] which of all his works in sculpture was the one he liked the best. The slab of Hoptonwood stone had been leaning about in his workshop at Ditchling, and he had been fretting at his inability to finish the carving which he had begun. At Capel he was still, at first, incapable of further progress. Hagreen suggested that he was making the job needlessly difficult by his insistence on carving the torso nude. This was contrary to tradition, and it also deprived the sculptor of drapery – which was like depriving a musical ensemble of an essential instrument. Moreover, customers who wanted a nude carving by Eric would hardly want a Deposition, and those who wanted a Deposition would very likely disapprove of the nudity.

At this point Marchant wrote to Eric asking for a small carving to exhibit at the Goupil Gallery. Hagreen urged him to use this opportunity to finish the Deposition and, after the usual objections against the rapacity of art dealers, Eric agreed. He found, however, that he could not work amid the distractions of his temporary studio, which was only separated by a curtain from the Attwaters' living-room; so he took the stone down to a cellar underneath the cloister. Here the light was dim and the damp rusted his tools as quickly as he could sharpen them. Nevertheless after a few days the work was done and was brought upstairs for polishing. A further two days of rubbing by Eric and Hagreen, sitting on either side of the carving, failed to make it shine until, at Hagreen's suggestion, French polish achieved a result which was beyond the power of elbow-grease. The Deposition was sold for £90 and Eric, all objections now forgotten, was so

[1] Now in the possession of the King's School, Canterbury.

cheered by his £60 share of this that he immediately set about carving from an odd lump of soft stone the head of Our Lord asleep,
resting on His Hand, which Marchant sold to Charles Rutherston. It
now forms part of the Rutherston Collection in Manchester and is as
fine a thing as Eric ever did.[1]

Once they had settled in, Mary wrote to Desmond Chute:

It is beautiful here in the Welsh mountains – and the people are most
kind – we love the Monastery – and it is extraordinary how little the
outside world seems to matter. The time passes very quickly – the days
are all too short – for there is much to be done. Betty and Joan are very
good and helpful, and we look forward to Petra coming with her loom.
We want as much as possible to make all our own clothes – and grow
what food we are able – but think it is going to be uphill work, not so
much the work of doing things – as the people around us – it is difficult
and almost impossible to get town bred people the least bit understanding
– let alone enthusiastic! The next generation I hope will have a better
chance. It remains for us to be patient and pray – but it nearly makes me
weep. The people in the Valley are very hard working – and *we* have the
small beginnings of self support – horrid word! Cow, pigs, chickens,
ducks and goats and two ponies, we brought Lasso our little mare, and
last week we bought a biggish Welsh pony – there is still a good deal of
hay to cut – and the weather is very bad.

I am hoping Eric will be able to work here in peace. Unfortunately his
work-shop accommodation is bad at present – he is very busy and very
well and happy. These are absolutely the right surroundings for him, and
I am so thankful he is away from Ditchling – it made me furious to see his
time and energy being wasted – long before we heard of Capel-y-ffin, I
used to feel I must pick Eric up and run off to the mountains – there to let
him work in peace – and live a life of prayer and contemplation.[2]

Hagreen wrote at the same time:

Well – we are settling down here rapidly and all goes well with us all.
Difficulties are many and various, but you can imagine the way in which
Eric tackles them all. What a man! I feel bewildered that Heaven should
have sent me as his companion. If I remain a fool it will not be for want of
an example of wisdom. Eric is writing to you, so I expect he will have

[1] See plate 12.   [2] Feast of the Holy Cross, 1924.

told you all the news, of how well these good monks treat us and how truly neighbourly are the Baptist farmers around.[1]

The saving difference between life at Ditchling and life at Capel was that it never occurred to anyone in that remote valley to describe the Gill household as a 'Community'. For the family, 'community' had become a dirty word, but it was not surprising that the label so firmly stuck. The distinction between a Guild, a group of Tertiaries, and a number of individuals wearing unusual clothes and following a similar way of life was altogether too fine to be drawn by the casual observer. We must never forget that 'Ditchling' started with a single family going to live at Ditchling, and that, as far as Eric was concerned, it ended with that same family going to live somewhere else. But Eric's personality was so charismatic and his ideas so well publicized that other people inevitably gathered round him. Philip Hagreen was the only other member of the Guild who came with him to Capel, but the Attwaters were already there, and as the strange caravan lumbered up the valley road from Llanvihangel a young man, René Hague, was cutting sticks on the side of the hill. He was only 19 years old and had recently escaped, rather precipitately, from the Jesuit novitiate. He was living with Father Woodford at The Grange and, for want of other occupation, was teaching Latin and Greek to a Benedictine novice[2] who was keeping Father Woodford company. The sight of two daughters, one of whom was unattached,[3] floundering out of the lorry with the hens, goats and rabbits was a welcome relief from monasticism. It had consequences fortunate, and not entirely unforeseen.

Hague was a Catholic by birth and anti-clerical by instinct. Ironically, this was fortified by the very new and attractive aspect of Catholicism which he found in Eric. Powerfully drawn by Eric's mind, and at first obediently submissive to it, he would later push Eric's ideas to extremes to which Eric himself was reluctant to go. If Eric's criticism of the existing social order were just, why was the Church

---

[1] September 16, 1924.
[2] Now Dom Raphael Davies, O.S.B., Prior of Prinknash.
[3] Elizabeth was already hoping to marry David Pepler.

everywhere found in support of it? If Catholicism were really a revolutionary religion, why did it contain so few revolutionaries? These divergences were, however, mainly differences of temperament. The Englishman in Eric naturally respected authority; the Irishman in Hague resented it. For the time being he was content to sit with Eric by the hour discussing *Art and Scholasticism*, or listen to him reading Malory's *Morte d'Arthur* to the family. He spent a year at Capel working on the land, and then moved to London. We shall meet him again at a later point in the story.

On September 1 Eric received a surprising letter from Father Bede Jarrett, Provincial of the English Dominicans. Eric hardly knew him, for Bede Jarrett represented a much more central tradition of Catholic thought than Vincent McNabb, and he exercised a different, wider and more balanced influence. He had played no part in the development of Ditchling; indeed he would appear not wholly to have sympathized with it. This is what he wrote:

May I just say that I do hope that if ever I can be of any service to you or yours, you will let me be?

It is always difficult to find one's way in the perplexities, not of principles but of persons and to know in what measure we are to be forgiving and to what measure 'not respect any man'. But if you will allow me to say it, I think you are perfectly right in withdrawing, though I could have wished St Dominic might yet have served you; but you have chosen a pleasant patron whose raven will be a cheering companion, black but beautiful.

Eric had no reason to think that Father Bede knew anything of his withdrawal from Ditchling, or of his proposal to attach himself as an Oblate to the Caldey Benedictines. In fact, Father Bede had learned of this from Father John Gray. Eric replied asking whether there was any ecclesiastical objection to his becoming an Oblate, should he wish to do so, and whether Father Bede would approve. Father Bede answered this letter on September 5:

Of course I thoroughly understand that under the new circumstances it would be more natural to fall under the influence of the Benedictines and since you will be under their shadow it were as well to live under their sunshine.

Canon 705 of the new Order allows the transference from one 3rd order to another *justa de causa* which here certainly prevails. . . .

Really I know nothing save that you have withdrawn from the group at Ditchling. That much gossip reached me. But no more. However, I want no more.

In fact, Eric remained a Tertiary of St Dominic, and generally faithful to Dominican influence. Apart from Father Joseph, a quiet and simple man rather bewildered by his new parishioners, the Benedictine impact was confined to occasional visits by the Prior of Caldey and long talks with Dom Theodore. Eric was in London for a week in October, and had a long and friendly discussion with Father Vincent. But now Father Austin Barker took the place of Father Vincent as a spiritual guide; he was more like a French than an English Dominican, his Thomism a little diluted. Eric himself admitted that he had been 'misled by the logic of medieval Christian theology',[1] and his mind was shifting away from scholastic rationalism and juridicism. Father Austin met this change of direction and Eric was quick to get on easy terms with him. On November 18 he sent him his impressions of Capel-y-ffin before the winter had come to modify them:

Now we are more or less settled for the winter. But the old place is in much need of repairs and alterations so we are not exactly shipshape. The valley is very much what we expected – too good in these days to be true – quite unspoiled – either materially or socially or economically and therefore the spiritual conditions are none the worse – far from it. The people round are all small farmers – kind and friendly and helpful and fraternal. No doubt there is a hidden fund of anti-catholic prejudice but there is nothing to bring it to the surface and we hope it will, if we live right, die a natural death if not a supernatural one. Fr Joseph Woodford, O.S.B., the priest here, is a good kind humble man – and, if *I* may say so, a good religious who knows that contemplation is the secret key to all things.

. . . Of course there is no Guild or Community life here for me as there was at Ditchling. That must be built up anew. Meanwhile we have daily

[1] *Autobiography.*

TO THE DEAR MEMORY
OF OTTOLINE WIFE OF
PHILIP MORRELL AND
SISTER OF THE SIXTH
DUKE OF PORTLAND,K.G.
WHO DIED APRIL 21.1938
IN HER SIXTYFIFTH YEAR

FAITHFUL AND COURAGEOUS
MOST LOVING MOST BELOVED

17. Memorial tablet to Lady Ottoline Morrell, 1938 (photo Edward Sweetland).

18. Eric Gill guiding the hand of W. I. Burch, late Managing Director of the
Monotype Corporation, 1929.

Mass and weekly Confession and many other blessings. Moreover, tho'
the finance of Ditchling is still round my neck like a halter, there are no
financial complications here. Life is certainly cheaper and simpler and of
better quality withal! Communication with Abergavenny (15 miles) is by
pony cart or on the pony's back. We've got 3 ponies, 1 cow, 2 goats and
chickens and turkeys. We've got the use of 25 acres of land – some of
which we've sub-let to neighbours. There isn't a gentleman's residence
(but that of Fr Joseph!) for eleven miles – unless you go over the mountains
(2,000 feet) to Hay which is 7 miles of hard going. . . .

The solid thing that Ditchling stood for in your mind can go on
whether it's at Ditchling or anywhere else. It can't go on at Ditchling
unless Hilary changes his notions about money affairs. It can go on at
Capel if we don't take up with those notions. But here it must be built
up from the bottom again and I'm all alone at present – and don't your
own sins stare you in the face when you're alone!

The sense of loneliness was increased by a doubt whether the
Hagreens would stay at Capel. Philip was suffering from the cold, and
his wife from the double strain of motherhood and a university
education. Joseph Cribb, who was hoping to come, had not yet
arrived. Meanwhile several people had made offers to buy the Crank
– including Pepler – but Eric was reluctant to accept as little as
£1,500. He had spent nearly £3,000 on improving it, and there was
a mortgage of £900 to be met. Furthermore, although Eric had
severed his connection with Ditchling, he could not entirely cut himself off from the Peplers since Elizabeth was eager to be married to
their son. He was bound to remain in touch, and here Clare Pepler
was the intermediary. Eric's letters show a characteristic blend of
humility and intransigence:

Your letter came this morning – I am very glad to have it and thank you
very much for taking my letter in such good part. I am very much
relieved for when I saw your handwriting I felt a bit nervous like. . . . But,
as you knew there would be, there are two sentences which are not so
conclusive. You say '(you) only hoped another member of (your) family
was not going to be made unhappy by one of (mine)'. Of course I know
you mean that Hilary has been made unhappy by me, and I knew you
thought so before, though I don't think it is quite fair to put it just like

that – as though Hilary were the hardly used one and only I the aggressor
or traitor or unkind one – or whatever it might be. But I may be wrong –
the fault, the worse fault anyway, may be all on my side. . . . But human
beings, being material as well as spiritual beings, are largely dependent upon
rational and human aids to the vision of their own faults. Very often God's
grace works indirectly – through other human beings. Here is your
opportunity. Do help. You can be of the greatest help. Tell me, as plainly
and frankly as you can, the faults that Hilary sees in me and which are the
cause of his unhappiness – as you imply. Be the instrument of God's grace
then – as you say for His sake. Of course I am aware of lots of my faults –
but perhaps they aren't the ones he sees or the ones that matter in this
case. I know my constant tendency to incontinence – immodesty – the
physical nature of man and woman seems to me so utterly delightful and
good – to see, to hear, to feel, to know in any way – therefore I find it
difficult to see uncleanness where most people see it and where Holy
Church bids us see it. But this fault is not the cause of Hilary's unhappiness
I guess. Again, I'm not physically courageous on the spur of the moment –
this strikes me as a horrider fault than the other – I don't say it *is* horrider
– I only say it strikes *me* that way – it leads to lying occasionally and often
to a lack of frankness so that I don't speak out when I think it would give
offence. (But there's obviously a good side to this, for often hasty
speaking causes misunderstanding and, besides, it's very difficult to tell
the truth in a hurry, on the spur of the moment.) Again, I'm very 'spoilt'
– anyone can see that. I'm always thinking myself more intelligent than
other people or more in the right in an argument. People are so patient
they don't 'tell one off' and, put one 'in one's place'. But oh! isn't it
difficult not to be conceited when success and applause of one sort and
another is poured on you as it has been on me. 'Whom the Lord loveth
He chastiseth' – When has He ever chastised me? Am I then not one of
His blood? I'm almost too conceited to think that!

Again, I get the 'sulks', i.e. suppressed bad temper. Instead of breaking
something as I would love to do, I fume inwardly and look perfectly
beastly – as indeed I feel. Again – self-indulgent. I always do what I want
to do – or generally always. Again, meanness is a special fault of mine. I
hate parting with things – money or goods – unless the cause seems right –
and that's not generosity. Again, etc., there, I'm telling you my half of
the story – you must tell me yours, and as we aren't likely to meet yet
awhile, or need not do so, you needn't be shy about it but just tell me
straight – never mind how horrid it will be for me – you'll be doing the
Lord's work.

PS. But I see I haven't mentioned the physical faults in me which may be causing annoyance to Hilary. e.g. I hate and detest untidyness in money affairs as well as in houses and workshops. Tidyness is all right but one may be excessively annoying about it. I screwed up my courage to tell Hilary before Fr Vincent where I thought he'd acted wrongly – will he, through you, tell me where I've acted wrongly? Fr Vincent refused to enlighten me though Hilary said he would and could so so!

    E.G.[1]

Clare Pepler's reply brought him little satisfaction:

. . . it's certainly different in kind from what I expected (no harm in that) for when you said you wished H. and I could see our own faults as well as we saw one another's I asked you to tell me the said faults and I expected to hear and wanted to hear what in your view and in H.'s view my faults were. But I misunderstood; you haven't told me my faults but merely my misdeeds as they appear to you. You see a man may get drunk and yet drunkenness may not be a 'fault' of his – it may be a more or less accidental occurrence. Again, a man may tell a lie and yet 'truthfulness' might actually be one of his strong points! However, never mind – I am v. glad to have your letter although it tells me nothing new and is indeed full of misunderstandings and mistakes. It's simply marvellous how human beings misread things – and I'm coming to think that there's no remedy this side the grave – on the other side we hope at last to enjoy 'gaudium de veritate'.[2]

In a subsequent letter Eric summed it up, rather sadly:

. . . I never put it to myself that any harm has been done to me (yet) by any one at D. Common. It's not like that a bit. It's much more like as if 2 persons were playing a game and after a bit they discover they're playing a *different* game. There's no harm done. They separate that's all. There are, incidentally, odds and ends to be cleared up – that takes time and patience. How much time! and how much patience! We all send you our love. . . .[3]

It took a great deal of time and much loss of patience. Not until 1927, when Eric had threatened to bring his grievances to court, was a

[1] November 21, 1924.
[2] December 4, 1924.
[3] Undated.

settlement arrived at. Eric's solicitors informed Pepler that he had at last agreed to 'cry quits', and Pepler's diary has a pathetic entry: 'I am 49 and surrounded by enemies . . . am exercised by my capacity for making enemies.'[1] Each party agreed to pay his own costs. Eric made a conveyance of all his interest in Fragbarrow farm to Pepler, to be prepared at Pepler's expense. He released Pepler from all claims in respect of any building erected by Eric 'for or on account' of Pepler. Pepler acknowledged his sole responsibility for all expenses incurred in the management of Fragbarrow farm and agreed to indemnify Eric from all claims in respect of it. Pepler eventually acquired the Crank, though at considerable loss to Eric. It is fair to say that, where Eric was exasperated, Pepler was deeply hurt by the disagreements. His Quaker upbringing had made him shy of all emotion, but when he received a postcard from Eric on his Feast Day – January 14, 1925 – the terms of this communication were so rough that he turned aside from the breakfast table so that the rest of the family should not see his tears.

Eric declined to sanction Betty's engagement to David Pepler until she was 21, at the same time giving her a lecture on love-making all the way home from Hereford to Capel-y-ffin. This did nothing to dampen her natural inclinations, and she spent a good deal of her time at Ditchling. Eric sometimes appeared to be more attached to Betty than to the other daughters, although Joanna was the one most like him and the one who understood him best. Not wishing to tell Betty himself what he felt about Hilary Pepler, he asked Attwater to do so – but Attwater very properly refused. Betty's good sense and efficiency were stabilizing factors at Capel, and Eric was understandably reluctant to see her go. She was eventually married to David on June 3, 1927, in the Catholic church at Brecon. Laurie Cribb was married there on the same day. Eric and Pepler met in the sacristy – their first meeting since Eric had left Ditchling – but they had no converse 'apart from polite nothings. I sat next to Clare at the breakfast. She was amiable – so was I.'[2] Eric had asked

[1] January 14, 1927.
[2] Letter to Desmond Chute, June 10, 1927.

Donald Attwater to sit down beside him if Pepler looked like coming close – but Pepler kept away. It cannot have been a very exhilarating party, and Eric described it as 'awful'.[1] Desmond Chute had already pronounced his epitaph on Ditchling: Hilary Pepler, he suggested, was something of a 'Peter Pan' and it was 'all unbearably sad', but –

Ditchling was rather crude: we were too self-sufficient and insufficiently self-supporting. . . . Isn't it strange? Who has changed? I'm sure you have not. I know I have modified some beliefs, but modify is the *mot juste*: I don't think continuity has been broken. I await developments of your confraternity, praying with you – but not all that formula, please; I have had to simplify things all round. I mean, useless to try to realize here and now a complete society; one is tempted to limit that society to the available portions.[2]

Reginald Lawson had put similar thoughts in similar words:

The trouble about Ditchling was that there was altogether too much knockabout philosophy.

[1] Letter to Desmond Chute, June 10, 1927.
[2] Letter from Desmond Chute, June 10, 1927.

2

If Eric's intention in moving to Capel was to escape from people as well as from publicity, he must have quickly realized that his effort was foredoomed to failure. Indeed a remarkable feature of the years at Capel is how little time he spent there. The loneliness of which he had written to Austin Barker was relieved by David Jones, who came in December 1924 and stayed for some time. When he attempted to light a fire with a bundle of candles, it was evident that Ditchling had not taught him domesticity. He painted a fresco of great beauty on the walls of what had once been Father Ignatius' 'Bible Cloister' – a Christ on the Cross with blonde hair, blue loin-cloth and twisted feet. The text – *Christus factus est pro nobis obediens usque ad mortem – mortem autem crucis propter quod et Deus exaltavit illum et dedit ille nomen quod est super omnum nomen* – was inscribed in two parts on either side of the figure. He also painted the tabernacle – a Lamb with Cross – above the altar in the chapel, where the Blessed Sacrament was reserved. The altar was simply a stone slab mounted on bricks, and the only other furniture were the choir stalls and a confessional under the whitewashed arch. The windows gave rise to a certain amount of heated discussion, Eric maintaining that the purpose of windows was to let in the light, and refusing the diamond panes which would have kept out the wind and the wet. 'We must pay for beauty,' he declared.

There were other more transient visitors in those early months; Dom Jerome, a tough Caldey monk who enjoyed cutting down trees, and Count Kessler who came to discuss a new edition of Virgil. Eric had not seen his first patron since the war, and they talked German politics by the hour. Kessler's diary gives a vivid picture of his pilgrimage:

After dinner to Abergavenny to visit Gill and discuss with him orders for

Virgil. The address that had been given to me was Capelyffin (pronounce Chapel-y-fin, i.e. Capella ad finem) near Llanvihangel. In Abergavenny nobody knew the place, so I took a car and drove at first to Llanvihangel as I thought that Gill's place would be very near there, and it was from there that he had answered my telegram. My chauffeur too had never heard of Capelyffin. In Llanvihangel we were told that it was still twelve miles further on, high up in the Black Mountains. The chauffeur complained that the road was so bad and narrow that he could not guarantee that we would get there. He himself had never been further than the St Anthony monastery at the foot of the Mountains.

We drove up a beautiful but lonely valley between meadows and hedges along a narrow country road which, indeed, seemed to lead into a wilderness. I had to think of my journey last year in the valley of the Rio Grande. Behind the ruin of the medieval St Anthony monastery the road became still narrower, and my chauffeur became more and more desperate. At last we stopped on a slope, where a local told us that Gill lived high up in another monastery, which had been founded there by Father Ignatius.

I went on on foot between hedges and meadows and, after climbing a steep footpath, finally arrived at the half-ruined building of the monastery. I heard the sound of voices in conversation, and followed the sound through the cloisters which were under repair, and through an antechamber; encouraged, I walked on, and suddenly I found myself in a fairly large room, in which a few women and young girls and two very dignified looking monks were sitting by a huge open wood fire. One of the women, whom I recognized as Mme Gill, came to meet me and asked whether I had not seen her husband on the road, as he had left to meet me a few hours ago. Obviously we had missed each other. Then she introduced me to the two monks, of which one was the prior of the monastery situated on the island in the sea. He was a handsome middle-aged man, very serious, but friendly. He had to leave on the same day for his island as there was some sort of celebration on the following day.

In the meantime I sent my car in order to find Gill who arrived after about an hour. He was of Tolstoyan appearance in his smock and coat, which emanated a half peasant-like, half monk-like atmosphere. He came with his son-in-law, a young sculptor and young draughtsman.[1]

Our meeting after the war, while being undramatic, was not without deep-felt emotion for either of us. Gill remarked that for him and for his friends, as probably for me too, art was now taking the second place, the main purpose being renewal of Life. Before the war people had been

---

[1] Evidently David Jones. Kessler was mistaken in the relationship.

thinking in a much too superficial way, and for that reason they (the Gills) were 'trying hard to be good' which was not always easy. Besides that, one still had to go after one's work even if it were only in order not to starve. Indeed he works a lot. He showed me a number of very fine, small figures made of box-wood and reliefs . . . also numerous wood-carvings and copperplates, images of saints, crucifixions, portraits, etc., everything being of good quality.

He and his wife, and also their children (which is still stranger) like it very much in the solitude of that monastery-like atmosphere. Ditchling had been too narrow-minded: they had only had the choice between the wilderness and London and decided to try the wilderness first; this experiment had been successful so far. They have no servants of any kind and they do everything for themselves, cook their food on the open fire (as we did during the war in Biwak); they lead a squatter-like existence four hours away from London and are happy and contented.

I went with Gill through Maillol's woodcarvings and also the Virgil, discussing with him the initials which he undertook to cut. I took leave in the middle of the night and arrived by eight o'clock in Abergavenny at the 'Angel' which, as a country hotel, is not at all bad.[1]

There was a further meeting with Kessler in London two months later. Here Kessler's impressions (which various entries in Eric's diaries confirm) suggest the tensions of the *quarante ans*; the tight-rope balance between a religious contemplation and a contemplative eroticism.

Eric Gill came to see me and had breakfast with me and with Will Rothenstein. Gill and I discussed his work for my Virgil and initials for the Caslon-scripts, after that we went to the Goupil Gallery, where Gill showed me a very beautiful head of a sleeping Christ which he had just carved in stone. When I asked him whether he would not like to make some woodcarvings for me, he said that he would like very much to make some for a Latin impression of the Hohe Lied on my press. He also suggested an Indian book which he was dying to illustrate; a treatise about Love 'Ananga-Ranga' (French: Le Traité d'amour hindou). In answer to my question as to the contents, he said: 'Well, in reality; thirty-four ways of doing it' (i.e. thirty-four positions of love-making, thirty-four kinds of the act of making love).

[1] *Tagebücher 1918–37*, 1961.

Gill is a completely unspoilt mixture of religion and eroticism. He himself defines his religion (he walks about in a kind of monk's cowl, and his life is like that of a monastic hermit except for the fact that he is married) as being 'fully in love with Christ'.

Gill's appearance is almost that of a mendicant friar: unkempt full beard; rather long, uncombed hair; blood-shot, pure, but energetic, sometimes almost fanatically gleaming eyes; grey-brown woollen cowl reaching almost down to his feet, an old, black felt hat which is nearly grey. He said he found it 'such a comfort' to have all his clothes made at home. One of his daughters was learning to weave,[1] and he hopes, then, that all clothes for his family will be made at home.

He expressed doubts about my intention to have electrotypes made of his initials, because the electrotype process is dependent on modern industry, which means on capitalism which is killing the world. When I objected, he answered that he does not fight capitalism; it is sufficient for him that he himself does not participate in the capitalistic development and simply does 'what is right'. What the others do is not his affair. But he is convinced that the whole of modern civilization will collapse within a few years whether we like it or not, so strong is the indignation against it that is growing everywhere.

All in all, with his great artistic talent, his reckless rejection of modern economics, his peculiar godliness, which is an all-embracing eroticism, his rejection of ethics, his erotic asceticism, union of eroticism and asceticism, which reminds one of the frame of mind of certain Egyptian hermits, he is a very strange and remarkable phenomenon, a parallel perhaps to Van Gogh. Pantheistic lasciviousness.

This confirms the summary of another friend who loved Eric 'this side idolatry' that when he became a Catholic he thought of everything in terms of religion – including sex; and that later he thought of all things in terms of sex – including religion. Eric's next meeting with Kessler was in Paris in 1927:

At two o'clock Eric Gill came to see me in my hotel to collect some money; he had left London yesterday without money, in order to take his little boy to school in France. We discussed everything again, and he promised to come in April to Weimar to work on the Hohe Lied at my place. He meant to begin on Boccaccio in the autumn. I suggested that he come with me to see Maillol in Marly. He declined, as he wanted to make

[1] Petra.

some studies of nudes in the afternoon in some academy; however, he asked me to convey to Maillol his admiration for him as a great artist.

He also remarked that it is high time for one to create works of art that would shake the morals that have poisoned us all to their foundations. I asked him laughingly what his friend, the Abbot of Ash,[1] would say to this point of view. Gill: 'He would disapprove; but all art is a rebellion against everyday morals, and consists of two elements, a moral element and an anti-moral element, the latter being opposed to the former.'

I went to see Maillol in Marly by myself; found him at home with a slight 'flu, but he was gay and happy. I showed him Gill's book. He looked at the etchings and found them 'pas mal, mais trop facile'.

At that time Maillol was etching some quite similar subjects for Ronsard, the act of love, etc., but he was not content with cheap compositions, mere outlines – he could make thousands of that sort; he did not make it so easy for himself – he shaded them to give them form. He showed me a number of drawings, sketches for his illustrations for Ronsard. In fact, the subjects and positions are by necessity very similar to those of Gill, as the positions in which the act of love can be performed are not so various; however, Maillol's have a much greater intimacy and erotic atmosphere than Gill's which are rather cold.

People were interested in Eric's appearance who would never have been interested in his art. It was not that a rather modest man wished to make himself conspicuous, or that an eminently practical man wished to make himself picturesque. Eric's clothes were merely the result of his rationalism. He would describe his tunic as 'the Christian norm' – whatever he may have meant by that – and although there was nothing he liked better than to see women in the nude he would insist that in public they should be dressed in black from head to foot. For Eric almost any woman was so overpowering a provocation that in the interests of security she should conceal her charms. As he wrote against a water-colour drawing:

> If skirts should get much shorter
> Said the flapper with a sob
> There'll be two more cheeks to powder
> And one more place to bob.

[1] I cannot explain to whom Kessler is referring here: probably the Prior of Caldey, whom Kessler had met (see above, p. 165).

In fact, Eric's own clothes were not as practical as he supposed. But if one objected that the pockets were inadequate and inaccessible, he would reply that one had no business to carry a watch; and if one suggested that it was difficult to ride a man's bicycle in what looked like a woman's skirt, he would even go so far as to say that one had no business to be riding a bicycle at all. His leg-wear did indeed bother him a good deal. At Ditchling he produced a pair of peg-top bloomers for inspection at a meeting of the Guild; these were lightly connected and had no buttons. Joseph Cribb, who had a slight impediment in his speech, observed: 'But Eric, are they all right on l - l - ladders?' They were not, apparently, quite all right on ladders, and when he was at work on the sculptures at Broadcasting House, he wore a crimson silk petticoat-bodice and no breeches at all. At other times you would see him in very bright red stockings with bare knees. But the tunic and beret were invariable.

These were the years of Eric's finest achievements as an illustrator of books. He did twenty-two wood-engravings, chiefly decorated initials, for Frances Cornford's book of poems, *Autumn Midnight* (1923), printed at St Dominic's Press. The frontispiece of a girl crouched up in bed with the moonlight falling through an open window most effectively met the elegiac inspiration of the author. But it was in collaboration with Robert Gibbings at the Golden Cockerel Press that Eric did his best work in this kind. Gibbings was an Irishman from County Cork with 6 feet 3 inches of height and a reddish blonde beard. He had acquired the Press in 1924, and was already a founder member of the Society of Wood-Engravers. Many artists were turning to this rediscovered medium, and Gibbings wrote to Eric, among others, inviting his co-operation. Oddly enough, he was the only one to refuse; and the grounds for his refusal – that Gibbings was not a Catholic – were odder still. Shortly afterwards, however, Gibbings was approached by John Wilson of Bumpus with a proposal that he should print a selection of poems by Enid Clay, Eric's eldest sister. Eric had promised to illustrate the poems, and was thus brought into the circle of the Golden Cockerel Press. *Sonnets and Verses* was published in April 1925, and was chosen by the Double Crown Club as the best printed book of the year at its price. Eric's woodcuts of Dartmoor – a country he hardly knew – were particularly striking. His acquaintance with Robert and Moira Gibbings ripened quickly. He paid several visits to their house adjoining the Press, at Waltham St Lawrence, where Gibbings had built a hut-studio, surrounded by trees, at the bottom of the garden. There seems to have been a good deal of larking about on the lawn after sunset; and Eric was soon engraving Gibbings' portrait and drawing both him and his wife in the nude.

His next work for the Golden Cockerel was *The Songs of Songs* (1925). Thirty copies of this were hand-coloured and the eighteen illustrations from wood-engravings said all the things about the poem which Eric had already said about it in his essay for *The Game*. Nevertheless it got him into trouble with the ecclesiastical authorities. Father Austin Barker wrote in kindly protest and Eric replied good-humouredly. In a previous letter he had disarmingly compared himself to a 'naughty boy'.

I must however reassure you on the 'naughty boy' business! It's not what you think a little bit. First of all I hang on to S. Paul's saying: 'all things are lawful to me but all things are not expedient.' As to what is *expedient* that is for authority to say and command and execute. Now then comes the 'naughty boy' sentence and you took it all the wrong way. Let me give you a small but clear example. Imagine us choosing Hymn tunes for Sunday benediction! I say 'let's have such and such – it's a jolly fine tune.' Someone else says 'oh, but Father doesn't like it – you know he only likes sweets. . . .' I say – 'never mind, let's wait till he stops us.' What? Then I feel quite naughty. It's only my silly tender conscience – been brought up so gentlemanly – can't bear hurting anyone's feelings – wouldn't hurt a fly. Then you bring out all your big guns and tell me off for not taking my 'lead from authority', 'guarding its spirit' and so on but, you see, they, the guns, wouldn't work. And when we consider the state of modern Europe, the high level of its culture, the beautiful churches (as at Hawkes-yard), the keen interest taken by Catholics in all that pertains to *reality* (as opposed to appearance), their contemplative spirit as evinced by all their words and works (what more contemplative than wireless and poison gas?) well, well, well – it makes you long 'to be dissolved. . . .' As for 'the Cantab'[1] – I gather that book is not the S. of S. As for the girls sniggering in the bookshop – well, so do small boys over the Bible. But, you wait till we meet and we'll have a good talk about all this.

In a series of postscripts he added:

The spirit of authority is precious little help – its weight is all on the wrong side – that's the trouble. . . . The adolescent sniggering of Birmingham school girls does not suggest to me a standard. Fr Vincent once told me of a young lady who confessed that for her the Crucifix was an occasion of sin! His advice to her was to look hard at Crucifixes till she got over it. . . . and all said and done I did what I did with the *approval* of a responsible priest.[2] I believe he's right. (I'm not thinking of the Biblical criticism question. I know nothing about that.) I also know that very few would agree with him . . . authority apparently preaches one thing and prastices another or rather does not preach but writes it in Latin where it cannot be found or if found understood. . . . You don't seem to realize that 'authority' has only authority today in telling us 'what no fellow should do'. As for what any fellow should *make* – it has no authority whatever – nor respect, nor reverence. I don't give a bad halfpenny for present-day authority in such a matter – it's disreputable – corrupt – disgusting. Authority gives me the 10 commandments and the penny Catechism. I accept and obey. If I am to remember Chapter IX of Maritain's book, let authority give a glance at Chapter V (but it wouldn't understand it).

When can you come to C-y-ff? We desire to sit under you for a spiritual retreat, after which you shall be sat upon for a spiritual attack.[3]

The long winter evenings with *Art and Scholasticism* had inspired Eric to wrote his own essay on the subject – *Id quod visum placet* – also printed, in a limited edition of 150 copies, by the Golden Cockerel Press. This was equally prompted by a complaint from Dr McQuillan that in the matter of aesthetics St Thomas was not really much help. Eric had profited by conversations with Dom Theodore Baily, and on Dom Theodore's copy had written:

[1] A novel by Shane Leslie which had proved offensive to pious ears.
[2] Probably Dr Flood, or Father John O'Connor.
[3] March 15, 1926.

Through ineptitude or stupidity we often fail to make things beautiful;
we need never fail to make things well.

e.g. He said to me 'I do not call that beautiful.'

'No,' I said, 'but at least it's well done.'

There was a frontispiece of David beside a tree with a serpent, and a
slug rising out of the ground, and a copper engraving of the buttresses
springing from the walls of St Pierre de Chartres, with the sun behind and Blériot's aeroplane. All these things had their meaning in
what presented itself as a 'Thomist dialogue'. Eric began by considering a number of objections – that Beauty was of no practical
utility because the tastes of the same person varied, and it was
feeling – not seeing – that mattered; that the subject of a picture
prevented pleasure in the picture itself; that appreciation depended
on expert knowledge, and that uneducated persons were insensitive
to beauty; that what pleased the vulgar was obviously not beautiful,
whereas the ugly often gave pleasure. Therefore *Id quod visum placet*
really meant, not that which pleased, but that which uplifted. The
sight of sin might be pleasant, but sin was not beautiful. A slug was
beautiful, but it did not always give pleasure, although inelegant
objects like a hippopotamus gave pleasure to some people. Sight was
not necessary for a perception of the beautiful, since Beauty could be
approached by taste or smell or hearing. The essence of Beauty was
spiritual, and was therefore imperceptible to the material senses.
Moreover there was no authority capable of deciding what constituted true vision and what should give pleasure when seen.

Eric replied that Beauty was not the same thing as loveliness, and
making not the same thing as doing. A deed was a means to an end;
a thing made was an end in itself – and *this* was the cause of pleasure
when it was seen. One must distinguish between the true and the
good. The beautiful was true because it existed and was known to
God; it was good because it was willed by God. It was true because
it was seen by the mind, and good because it was desired by the
mind. Beauty was the radiance of truth and goodness. Ugliness was
the occasion of privation to the mind – like an orphaned family, a

faceless nose, a decomposed egg, or a wicked angel. Since Beauty was a matter of due proportion, it was therefore also a matter of Justice. *Id quod visum placet* referred to the perception of the object itself, not of what it represented or evoked. It did not imply physical pleasure or emotion or admiration of mere dexterity – like a carving by Grinling Gibbons or the organs of the body or the working of a watch – although pleasure in these things was not forbidden. It did imply the delight of the intelligence spontaneously resulting from the sight of the object itself. Displeasure in the face of Beauty was due to accidental causes; a Plymouth Brother would not admire a heathen idol. It was the same thing with pleasure in face of ugliness; some people liked useless elaboration on carved furniture. Beauty was the cause, not the object, of emotions. Tastes differed – Eric quoted here from Father Joseph Rickaby's *Moral Philosophy*: 'but not right tastes; and moral notions, but not right moral notions.'

Id quod referred to a painting itself, not to some other thing of which the artist might have presented the illusion. The ikon of Our Lady of Perpetual Succour *was* Our Lady of Perpetual Succour in paint – the subject in paint rather than represented in paint. True seeing did not depend on expert knowledge but on right reason; if people did not see the beautiful, it was because they were blind or blinded. Pleasure in ugly things was either sensual or sentimental. The maker was not concerned with the effect of the object on the beholder, and there was no sense in objecting that the sight of sin was ugly or beautiful, because sin was not seen. It resided in the will. There was pleasure in the sight of a naked body, even though its exposure might be an act of immodesty, and pleasure in the antics of a drunken man, even though drunkenness was a vice. Slugs were unpleasant because they destroyed the garden, but they were not on that account unbeautiful. For human beings all knowledge came through the senses, and as for authority, this was merely the human mind rightly used. Tastes inevitably differed because men could not rid themselves of prejudice and predilection, but instinct and tradition must be brought to the test of reason. 'As a good life is a mortified life, so good taste is mortified taste.'

These sleeves-rolled-up arguments were reminiscent of a Domini-can *disputatio*; they were more to the taste of Father Austin Barker than Eric's illustrations to the *Song of Songs*, though he might well have seen how the illustrations illustrated the argument. But Eric had little hope that they would interest anyone else, for in the letter from which I have already quoted he writes:

It is becoming clearer and clearer that arguing about it won't help anyone (except the author) and least of all will it help priests and those who, like priests, are 'invincibly convinced' of the unimportance of the subject – they won't approach the business except in the mood of half amused tolerance or half bored intolerance. Like the rest of the world they are only interested in getting and spending, keeping an eye meanwhile on their heavenly home and a sort of list of things no fellow should do – I mean that while their only real interest is in getting and spending (at what pains they are to prove that Catholics are just as good at 'science' as non-Catholics and that Catholics are just as 'progressive' as anyone else!) they, remembering that they've got to die some day, take care not to infringe against the rules. For the rest, talking about 'art' or 'beauty' is just, for them, so much nonsense – and as for the things themselves (as distinct from *talking*), well, they regard them as just so much museum stuff – nothing to do with life except to titivate the drawing room or the Church (make the altar look pretty). The state of modern Europe – the masses of people totally engrossed in getting and spending – is apparently what they approve. Their only complaint is that so many things that no fellow should do are done! Be an absolute bloody fool, make a vast fortune out of potted meat, live at the Ritz or at Tooting, have a season ticket to Brighton – you're welcome, nay you're worshipful – but don't, oh don't – steal more than a penny, don't use swear words, don't ever get drunk, and above all don't, oh I beg you, don't ever even so much as think of any other girl's legs! Love God? Ah, yes – of course – but remember that life here below is like being in the W.C. (quite pleasant, not necessarily sinful, but only a dirty function). Such is the apparent attitude of our spiritual fathers!

A letter from Father Bede Jarrett reinforced Father Austin Barker's objections; both his English reticence and his very English romanti-cism shrank from Eric's realistic acceptance of the flesh. Eric was patiently and courteously obdurate.

19. Ariel and Children.

20. Ariel between Wisdom and Gaiety, designs for sculptures for Broadcasting House, Portland Place.

21. Eric Gill at Pigotts, 1935 (photo Howard Coster).

In reply to your letter of July 18: I am obviously at a disadvantage. It is not proper that I should argue with you unless you expressly ask me to do so: moreover an artist (i.e. a workman) is not, as artist or workman, an exponent of faith or morals. He is not a propagandist. Rather he is an instrument in the hands of others. But, as a man, he is a responsible being and it is incumbent upon him to criticize the person or authority of which he, as artist or workman, is the instrument. My best defence therefore, as it is the best defence of any artist or workman, is not argument [sic] but the naming of my authority. Yet I do not wish to do that for, though certain priests, and one in particular, have expressed approval of the work to which you refer, I do not wish to drag other people into a business for which I am perfectly willing to take the blame. I simply ask you to believe that I have not been acting without the cognizance and approval of at least one competent and responsible Catholic priest.

Knowing however that you will forgive me, for your letter is almost an invitation to me to do so, I will say one or two things which seem to me to have an important bearing on the matter – asking you to remember that I disclaim any direct interest in propaganda.

1. The following quotation from Maritain's book (*Art et Scholastique*, trans. Fr O'Connor, p. 107) seems to me to contain a truth: 'As to the arts of which men can use the works well or ill, they are lawful, and yet, if there are any of which the works are put to evil use *in the greatest number of cases*, they ought, though lawful in themselves, to be extirpated from the city by the office of the Prince, secundum documenta Platonis...' (*vide* also p. 178). This seems to me to place the burden on the right shoulders – it leaves the artist free from the business of being either a propagandist or a critic – for neither of which roles is he fitted and both are detrimental to him as workman.

2. In your letter you name several categories of forbidden things, adding in every case except 'for grave reasons' or 'very grave reasons' or 'the gravest reasons'. Speaking for the moment in the role of propagandist I should say without hesitation that grave and very grave and the gravest reasons exist justifying the work to which you refer. I may name in particular the 'Marie Stopes propaganda' and the whole movement which tends to deprive the sexual act of its connection with fertility. On the other hand Catholic priests (e.g. the Bp. of Pella lecturing on Marriage at Cambridge, *vide* report in *The Universe*) insist on that connection but deprives it almost completely of any but, so to say, 'clinical' significance. (It is only reluctantly and after considerable effort that priests can, in private conversation, be got to admit that lovers may, without sin, regard

the act as anything but 1°, a means to fertility and 2°, a sanitary function. Indeed it is but rarely that one may meet a priest to whom one can speak in any degree frankly on the matter at all. They seem to regard it as a matter for the confessional solely. They give the impression that one is placing an undue strain upon them as celibates – that it is only by the strictest avoidance of the subject that they can avoid occasions of sin – that as one would refrain from dilating upon the subject of wine in the presence of inhabitants of the U.S.A. so . . . etc. The consequence is that people grow up, in general, with minds quite uncultured in this matter. It is a joke – or it is filthy. It is sacred or it is sanitary. That is all. There-fore, speaking again for the moment as a propagandist – looking at the matter from the outside – forgetting that I have ever carved stone or engraved wood – it seems to be desirable that while on the one hand we are invaded by those who say that the sexual act has no necessary connec-tion with fertility and on the other, those who say it has no connection with anything else, there should be the balanced voice proclaiming that the act is *in se* meritorious and is only made wrong when fertility is prevented or when the children resulting are born out of matrimony – and of the two the latter is probably the lesser evil in the long run.)

3. It seems to me that your strongest line of argument – the one which naturally disturbs me most – is that wherein you say that the catholic tradition has always been such and such – that there is no Catholic precedent for such books, writings, pictures, etc. The argument like all argument from precedent is weighty. I admit its force. I am much moved by it. Nevertheless it is conceivable that a uniquely evil civilization (and in some respects our present civilization is uniquely evil – no ancient nation had such material power for spreading corruption wholesale) requires unprecedented medicines. It is not for me to say. I do what I am moved to do so far as I am allowed. I am prepared to give reverent atten-tion to the words of priests and especially Dominicans; but I must point out that, in my experience, the Catholic priests of Europe and America are, with a handful of exceptions (and that handful quite powerless and unrepresentative) wholehearted supporters of the civilization which I have called above 'uniquely evil'. As they approve what I wholeheartedly condemn I do not find it surprising that they wholeheartedly condemn what I approve. (You will of course believe me when I say that I write this quite impersonally – it is quite accidental to my argument that you are a priest.) And just as I have said I know hardly one priest to whom one can talk frankly about sex, so I can say that I know hardly one priest with

whom one can talk about *work* ('art' is only a name given to work applied to things 'made' as distinct from 'done'). They simply do not understand – nor are they interested . . . I do not say these things in a spirit of bitterness (though sometimes it is cause for bitterness – but in such moods it is easy to find a layman who understands) or in a spirit of complaint. It seems to be an inevitable state of affairs. I write simply to point out that if I am told that 99 per cent of the priests of England condemn the work to which you refer, as, in fact, they condemn all my work, I should simply say: well 99 per cent of the priests of England approve of the material achievements of modern industrialism – so that's that. I mean that tho., as exponents of text books moral theology, one may respect priests very much indeed and tho. in the confessional one may find no cause whatever for complaint – nevertheless one may still be justified in holding the opinion that they do not know a good thing when they see it.

You see what an absurd and difficult position I place myself in – as tho. I were the only intelligent person. I am sorry. All the same I know that very many laymen and women are on my side of the argument. It may be said that laymen and women are not competent to judge. On the other hand it must be allowed that the practice of sexual intercourse is very much a matter in which lay people are concerned. What we laymen think about it, how we act in the matter, matters very much indeed. Mrs Stopes opens the door wide to hedonism – the Bp. of Pella shuts it against anything but utilitarianism – in the turmoil the facts are forgotten – blotted out – stamped upon.

Do I hold any opinion about sex or marriage which is heretical? I do not think so. I hold that as Christ loves the Church, so a man shd. love his wife. It does not appear that Christ loves the church only in order to beget Christians but also because She is herself adorable and delightful and lovely. Can it be imagined that those Divine Lovers could so unite as to enjoy one another and yet to frustrate the begetting of Christian souls? It is unimaginable. In the same way the act uniting man and woman is robbed of all its admirable qualities if it be performed as to frustrate fertility. Nevertheless the union of man and woman is not a merely useful act. It presents a state of *being* as much as a process of *doing*. 'Birth control' will never be 'scotched' until this is recognized and proclaimed – just as industrialism will never be destroyed until it is recognized that money is meant to be spent rather than 'invested' and that a thing made is properly not so much useful as enjoyable.*

Please forgive me for my imprudence in writing thus to you. If

I am wrong in thinking that your letter invited it, I am very sorry.
I am your affectionate Son in St Dominic,

Eric Gill T.S.D.

* nevertheless the usefulness of a thing must not be frustrated. Or, I
might have written, a thing made is properly as enjoyable as it is useful.
But I think the parallel is clear. (July 25, 1926)

Father Bede wished him to suppress the book, but Eric explained
that this was impossible:

I am afraid there is no going back on this, but perhaps the harm will not
be very great as the edition – at 2 guineas – was limited to 200 copies of
which only 175 were for sale (the edition is sold out). In case you have
not seen the book, I make bold to send you a print (which please destroy
if you wish) of the offending plate. I find it difficult to believe that this is
or could be alluring in any evil sense, or an occasion of sin to any. But I
see that if the subject is illegitimate *in se* there is no more to be said.
(August 22, 1926)

Father Bede, with characteristic magnanimity, then invited Eric to
carve a statue of St Dominic for Blackfriars, the new house of
Dominican studies at Oxford.

Eric's third work for the Golden Cockerel Press were his illustrations for the *Passion of Our Lord Jesus Christ*: the 26th and 27th chapters
of St Matthew's Gospel in the Latin text. One of these wood-
engravings – of the Agony in the Garden – has an extraordinary
beauty. In the dark foreground the three Apostles are crouched
asleep; in the middle the figure of Our Lord is stretched across
several layers of rock, and the Angel of the Agony, holding a haloed
chalice, stands above Him; and the upper part of the picture is again
dark with the foliage outlined in white. Eric never did anything
better in wood-engraving. Here, and elsewhere, the figures have the
formal impassivity of an ikon – diagrammatic rather than descriptive
– and the same method was applied to a wood-engraving which appeared in the *Labour Woman*. This was entitled 'Safety First'. It
showed various females being rescued from 'the stormy seas of industrialism' by the good angels of the Trade Union and Labour

Movement with top-hatted capitalists folding their arms in the back-ground. Eric had momentarily forgotten that industrialism was the last thing from which the Trade Union and Labour Movement wanted to rescue anybody.

Further trouble was at hand with the publication of *Procreant Hymn* by E. Powys Mathers. Mathers was a huge fat man, with a pear-shaped head, who had translated the Arabian Nights and cer-tain Eastern love-writings. He was the original Torquemada in *The Observer*. He had the reputation of being a kind and pleasant person; and Eric thought that he was probably 'very good and very naughty. I think the times are hard – the right and proper naughtiness of life, as God made it, is classed by the police with mere filthiness. I think it well to go ahead doing what seems good – however naughty it be.'[1] This description of Mathers tallies with the account of David Jones who accompanied Eric to his flat in Lincoln's Inn Fields where the walls were plastered with pornographic postcards. These were too much even for Eric's indulgent attitude to pornography. 'If I were not a Catholic,' he remarked to Jones, 'I should have been like this.'

Eric was not, of course, in the least like that. His conversation was neither prurient nor Rabelaisian, but he was the prey to an ob-sessive curiosity. Dr Flood once showed some examples of his *erotica* to a psychologist who said that Eric was more than a highly-sexed man; he must have had a particular phallic fixation. This did con-siderable damage to his work – Kessler was right to remark on the 'coldness' of his erotic drawings – but it does not seem to have inter-fered with his contemplation. The Pauline – or Augustinian – dual-ism of flesh and spirit was something he neither experienced nor understood. He was a very simple person and sex did not complicate him; it merely affected his judgment. In this same letter, for ex-ample, he told Chute that he thought Mathers' poem 'very very good. You shall have a copy if only to burn, for you may think it unkeep-able. I think no modern writer and very few old ones have got as close to that subject as P.M. has done without falling into either coarseness or obscurity – mere animalism or mere verbiage.' This

[1] Letter to Desmond Chute.

was an extraordinary opinion. In fact, *Procreant Hymn* was disagree-
ably steamy stuff of no literary merit whatever. Moreover, Eric had
been put in a false position by the publishers' blurb which he
thought 'very low . . . thoroughly disgusting'.[1] Even so trusted and
understanding a friend as Desmond Chute – now ordained – could
issue a word of warning:

Of course I never doubt your love of the creature to be entwined with
love of the Creator. The utmost doubt is lest at times your Julia's leg
seduce you to overstep the barrier which divides aesthetic fruition from
la vie effective. Admit a drop of the latter and you cloud the pure liquid of
art (speaking aesthetically). I mean that the male's enjoyment of woman
actual or imaginary is itself as foreign to art as the sentimentalism of the
Doctor[2] – tho' both may serve as a starting point for good (and bad) art.[3]

Father John O'Connor, on the other hand, thought Eric's illustrations to the poem – if not the poem itself – 'extra good'.[4]

Now if there is one person whose word on Eric Gill should be
taken above all others, that person is John O'Connor. He knew Eric
intimately both as a friend and a confessor. Eric would confess his
sins to John O'Connor when he would confess them to no one else –
and Eric went very frequently to confession. John O'Connor looked
not unlike the Father Brown whose prototype he was, except that
you would never have believed his name was Brown. He seemed to be
the *locus classicus* of the Irish Parish Priest. At other times he seemed
to have strayed into his presbytery from the Irish music hall, and
never more so than when he was lying back in his chair and singing
some popular song of the '98 – 'The Croppy Boy . . . at Passage
was his body laid'. But this cheerful, round-faced and rubicund
simplicity was deceptive. John O'Connor had folk wisdom in his
blood and many other kinds of wisdom in his brain. He knew a very
great deal about mankind; and he saw what Eric was getting at, both
in his life and in his art.

[1] May 5, 1926.
[2] I do not know to whom this refers.
[3] Undated.
[4] Quoted in a letter to Desmond Chute, July 5, 1926.

When he saw a photograph of strenuous action, e.g. Lenglen making an impossible return, he undressed it at once in a drawing. This he made a work of piety, just as others make piety consist in covering up the nude of every sort of thing, animate or inorganic. . . . It was when the aforesaid pious persons were uncertain whether to cover Eric's nudes or to smother Eric under obloquy that I evolved my own apology for leaving him free. I remember telling himself and David Jones in this room that people cultivating the sheltered life ought to consume their own smoke about the nude in art. Whatever tends to make sexual attractions normal, and to keep them so, deserves well of the commonweal. Because we priests and such who have to be ready for anything, any disease of the soul, and keep cool about it, like the hard-mouthed surgeon, were aware that it is ill-treatment of the question that produces abnormality, and this is a much harder nut to crack than any vulgar misbehaviour, even. A Redemptorist Father of long experience told me when I was very young that it was the rude girls in the mills who saw and said everything they had a mind to, who were much more to be trusted out alone than those whose innocence was founded on ignorance. Nothing has ever occurred to make me doubtful of this.

There. I have said enough in reason to account for the faith that is in me towards Eric Gill.[1]

With the faith that was in him towards Eric Gill, John O'Connor was well placed to commend Eric and G. K. Chesterton to one another. Chesterton would have been disturbed by Eric's eroticism if he had known about it, but in that – as in so much else – his innocence was probably angelic. They both had similar ideas about the decent ordering of society, and one suspects that when they were on their knees they prayed in very much the same way. Eric was the right person, therefore, to illustrate Chesterton's poem *Gloria in Profundis*, as the fifth in the series of Ariel Poems published by Faber & Faber (1927). Chesterton looked back as ardently as Eric to a Middle Age more golden in fancy than it had been in fact, and Chaucer was ground on which they would have met completely. The Golden Cockerel edition of *Troilus and Criseyde* with Eric's wood-engravings – most of them borders – was published in 1927. *Troilus and Criseyde* is a pagan love-poem with a Christian postscript. It was better worth Eric's *expertise* than *Procreant Hymn*.

[1] Letter to Stormont Murray, January 21, 1941.

3

In January 1925 William Rothenstein offered Eric an appointment as visiting professor in wood-engraving and stone-carving at the Royal College of Art. Eric declined because 'I am not of one mind with you and the aims you are furthering at the College, and, may I whisper it, I think there are too many women about'.[1] He was also afraid that he would not be able to 'keep God out of it'. At the same time John Rothenstein was proposing to write a study of Eric's work.[2] He read him the introduction, after which they went on to discuss religion and its auxiliary moral problems until 2 a.m. Later the young Rothenstein paid two visits to Capel-y-ffin – an incongruous figure from the Oxford 'twenties on that desolate hillside. In a later address at the opening of an exhibition of Eric's work at Monotype House, Rothenstein justly emphasized that Eric's sculpture suffered from the limitation of being conceived and executed in the flat. This predilection may be linked to his habit of always drawing his portraits in profile; the only things he aways drew in the round were his nudes.

It is a sign of mental health when a man returns to *The Prisoner of Zenda* in his middle forties, and Malory at the other end of the scale indicates the range of Eric's reading. It was assiduous and quite unsystematic: from Ronald Knox's *Viaduct Murder* and *The Psychology of Sex* by Havelock Ellis – which occupied him till 5 a.m. – to *The House of Pomegranates* by Oscar Wilde, *O'Flaherty V.C.* and *The Ancient Mariner* – all of which he read to the children; from *Heartbreak House* to Wells' *Christina Alberta* and *The World of William Clissold*; from *Dubliners*, *The Portrait of an Artist* and *Ulysses* to Conrad's *Shadow Line* and Maurice Baring's *Passing By*; from Plato's *Symposium* to Frank Harris's *My Life and Loves*; from *The Forsyte Saga* and *The Silver Spoon* to *The Constant Nymph* and Rose Macaulay's *Crewe Train*;

[1] Quoted in a letter to Desmond Chute, July 5, 1926.
[2] *Eric Gill*, 1927.

from Belloc's *Campaign of 1812* to Mottram's *Spanish Farm*. Eric's curiosity and surprisingly catholic taste kept him in touch with the older and the newer masters as well as with the ancient and the modern myths.

Meanwhile there were changes at Capel. The Hagreens left early in May 1925, and Laurie Cribb came at about the same time. Joseph Cribb came and went because his wife could not stand the climate. Eric himself was away a good deal – cutting the inscription for Epstein's *Rima* in Hyde Park, where he found the stone 'jolly rotten to work on'[1] and the surrounding 'grass dotted with lovers and every tree supported by the same'.[2] The public row over *Rima* was as raucous as the public row over the Leeds Memorial. Eric thought that *Rima* was 'what one would expect it to be considering how it was done'.[3] A committee chosen for the variety of its misbeliefs would inevitably follow the advice of its most forceful 'high-brow'. We now find Eric staying the night with the Chestertons at Beaconsfield, and talking till midnight in spite of a tooth that had to come out the next day; and drawing from the nude in Oliver Lodge's studio in Glebe Place. Here the model was a Miss Turpin who would always slip into her fur coat when the sitting was over and exclaim 'Oh, I'm off!' as she jumped into her Austin Seven.

Several new friends now come into the picture. Stanley Morison the typographer; Douglas Cleverdon, who ran a bookshop in Bristol, persuaded Eric to design his signboard, and became a close friend of the family; and Denis Tegetmeier. Morison was typographical adviser to the Monotype Corporation and as early as 1925 Eric was discussing with him the possibility of translating his own style of letter-cutting into a type suitable for the printed page. One would like to have seen them *en tête à tête*, clambering into a No. 11 bus from Westminster Cathedral to Fetter Lane – Eric sturdy and four-square in his beret, smock and golfing stockings, Morison lean and almost predatory in his unvarying black broadcloth looking like any man's

[1] G.K.'s Weekly, June 20, 1925.
[2] Diary.
[3] G.K.'s Weekly, June 20, 1925.

picture of Dr Moriarty. And one would have liked to hear Morison telling Eric that Aquinas was all very well but that it was time he made the acquaintance of Marx. When, two years later, Eric came to Monotype House in Fetter Lane to discuss a new sans serif type face, these were the impressions of a mechanical engineer:

What surprises me most when I look back to that first impression of him is just the fact that there didn't seem to be anything 'peculiar' about the man. You'd never have put him down as a famous artist. You'd sooner have said he was a good mechanic – or anyway some good workman who knew his job.[1]

The staff were struck by his lack of standoffishness, by the common-sensical twinkle behind the thick-rimmed glasses, and by the memorable phrases dropping from the light, matter of fact voice.

He had that one quality by which the sane man is most surely distinguished from any sort of crank, namely Humility – in the old and vigorous sense of the word. Once that fact is established, it is easier to get down to the nature of Eric Gill's profound and refreshing 'unlikeness' to anyone who could have been ticketed and pigeon-holed as he came past Temple Bar.[2]

Morison took to Paris the model alphabets which Eric had made in 1925 and commissioned a series of hand-cut punches from Charles Malin, the last of the highly-skilled artisans whose craftsmanship was doomed by the Benton punch-cutting machine. On Morison's advice the Monotype Corporation had resisted the temptation of seizing too precipitately the credit which the cutters of the new type design would naturally acquire:

It had scored indubitable successes meanwhile by type faces which restored to use the masterpieces of the centuries when type punches were whittled and filed by disciplined hands. If the new Perpetua was to be as book-worthy as the roman that Martin cut for John Bell, it might as well have its trial cutting by the same arduous technique.[3]

[1] *The Monotype Recorder*, Vol. 41, No. 3, 1958.
[2] ibid.
[3] ibid.

abcdefghijklmn
opqrstuvwxyz &

1234567890

....

ABCDEFGHI
JKLMNOPQR
STUVW&XYZ

Preliminary designs for the Perpetua and Felicity faces, 1926.

By the end of July (1926) Malin was sending Morison the smoke-proofs of Eric's Roman Capitals and Numerals, and his lower case was already in hand. 'You will have a beautiful letter there,' he wrote.[1] Malin's punches were in due course struck and fitted by the Fonderie Ribadeau Dumas, and they were the origin of Monotype's Perpetua. This developed through trial cuttings and discussions at the Type Drawing Office in Salfords. Eric

– had taken only a mild interest in the Paris smoke-proofs and saw the hand-cut founts for what they were – an astonishing feat of dexterity which had succeeded all too well in reproducing, on the tiny scale of type, the shapes and details of a stone-cutter's model letters. From the Drawing Office at Salfords, however, Gill knew that he had something to learn: not how to cut punches skilfully, but how to put critical intelligence and technical precision to the normalizing of a type face by making sure that it would not distract the armchair reader by any detail that would look fussy and arbitrary on the printed book page.[2]

The full story of Eric's typography belongs to a later chapter, but in July 1928 he was already designing a sans serif lower case and italics. Selfridge had asked for an alphabet for the notices in his shop and Eric worked on the sans serif capitals which Johnston had designed for the London tube. He made certain changes in these, working out his letters on squared paper so that they could be copied easily. He then cut them out with scissors and stuck them on a black card. The first experiment was a pair of notices – MEN – WOMEN – which were put up, one on each side of the chapel, at Capel-y-ffin. Eric thought it indecent that husband and wife should kneel together. Another sign was painted outside the chapel, indicating the way to it.

Among these new friends, Douglas Cleverdon was a bookseller of fastidious taste, who also published in a small way. He presented Eric's essay *Art and Love*, printed at the Golden Cockerel Press, in a limited edition of 260 copies. Eric was here concerned to draw an analogy between the Christian and pagan treatments of love:

[1] July 28, 1926.
[2] *The Monotype Recorder*, Vol. 41, No. 3, 1958.

From the Canticle of Canticles to St Bernard and St John of the Cross, from St Teresa of Avila to Saint Thérèse of Lisieux the theme of love has never been without vivid and unveiled expression. And if the paintings and sculptures of medieval Europe are less unclothed than those of India, the differences of climate and race are sufficient explanation. In all cases, however unconsciously and with whatever accompaniment of philosophical error and uncouth theology, God has been worshipped as the lover, the fount of love, Love itself. The blatantly phallic art of Central African tribes is no more a degradation than is the blatantly photographic art of modern Europe – no more and no less. Both are departures from the norm of human understanding, both are the products of mental decay. The norm is seen in the early art of Greece, in the early art of medieval Europe, in the peasant art of all the world, in the Plain Chant of the Roman Church, and in all such music, and pre-eminently in Rajput painting and the sculptures of India and China. But to all these arts the photographic is abhorrent. All are hieratic arts; all are the arts of peoples for whom religion is the main motive and of whose religion love is the beginning and the end.

Denis Tegetmeier had served in the First World War, and had an ex-service grant to study at the Central School of Arts and Crafts. He had come to know Eric at Ditchling where he was helping him over the New College War Memorial. Eric offered him an apprenticeship, but this he declined and he never joined up with the Ditchling community. During Eric's years at Capel-y-ffin Tegetmeier was in London, doing any odd job that came his way and occasionally 'pointing' Eric's carvings. He had a remarkable gift for delicately mordant caricature, which was afterwards placed at the service of Eric's revolutionary ideas. In 1925 he was living in rooms on the first floor of a large house in St John's Wood; this became a rendezvous for anyone up from Capel and Eric subsequently rented a small room in the basement. The ground floor was occupied by a friend of Tegetmeier's, John Polimeni. He was the son of a Sicilian expatriate, who had married an Alsatian Protestant and started a business in the City of London. Polimeni had musical talent and showed some promise as an operatic tenor. Eric and he would go together to concerts of Bach and make their own concerts in St John's Wood with Edward Rose, the organist of St Patrick's, Soho Square.

On December 20, 1925, Eric with Mary, Elizabeth Bill (his secretary), and Donald Attwater, joined a pilgrimage to Rome. As the train for Newhaven passed Ditchling Common, members of the community waved lanterns in greeting. They arrived at Genoa the next morning at 8 o'clock. Here they were met by Desmond Chute, and spent two hours of ardent conversation. In Rome they stayed at the Ospizio Santa Marta immediately under the shadow of St Peter's; followed the usual pilgrims' round of visits to the basilicas; had a general audience with the Pope (Pius XI) in the Sala Ducale; and watched the closing of the Holy Door. As the long procession of cardinals and bishops went by, Eric observed – perhaps with some surprise – that they formed a remarkably varied and encouraging collection of human faces. On Christmas Eve he walked with Attwater to Midnight Mass, celebrated by Cardinal Bourne, at San Silvestro. There was still time for the catacombs and the Colosseum and Trajan's Forum and the tomb of St Catherine of Siena in the Minerva church, and the children being baptized at St John Lateran. Eric was especially moved by the catacomb of San Callisto and – once again – by the upper church of San Clemente. He admired the outside of St Peter's with its unexpected colour and Michelangelo's dome looking like a soap bubble, but the interior seemed to him all 'swank and aggrandizement'.[1] He was not insensitive, however, to the splendour of its architectural form:

If some future Pope would have the courage and the power to carve off all the carvings in the Vatican Basilica and remove all the mosaics and paintings, we should have a building so stupendously beautiful that even the lilies of the field, who can quite easily hold up their heads before a rather gaudy eastern potentate, would agree that art improves on nature and that that is what it is for.[2]

In the Vatican he was impressed by the mixture of pomp and informality – the officials with manners as elegant as their clothes, and then a ragged woman with three children wandering about the Sala

[1] Diary.
[2] *Clothes*, 1931.

Eve; wood engraving, April 1926.

Regia. Perhaps his fondest memory was of a baby boy rolling about naked on the floor of a *trattoria* where they called in for a drink on Christmas morning. Elizabeth Bill had told Eric of a villa to let at Salies-de-Béarn in the foothills of the western Pyrenees, and in May 1926 he went over with Petra to inspect it. Robert and Moira Gibbings accompanied him to Paris. The Villa Cubaine was a sizeable and comfortable place, painted green and pink on the outside, with eucalyptus trees in the garden, a balcony along the first floor, red tiles in the kitchen, and curly red tiles on the steeply gabled roof, old dressers and cupboards, steel dogs in the fireplaces, and an iron table – as at Ditchling. Eric was taken with it and arranged to bring out the family. He had time to visit Sauveterre and make a very exact drawing of the church before returning to Paris and its infinite varieties. He saw Grock at the Palace and Josephine Baker's *danse de ventre* at the *Folies Bergère*. He called on Maritain at the Institut Catholique and looked in at 'a strange place'[1] – of which Gibbings had the address – where girls were lasciviously posturing in the nude. He drew from some models at the Académie Chaumière; visited Zadkine in his studio; heard Mass at Saint-Séverin and Saint-Julien-le-Pauvre; made arrangements with the Galerie Briant-Robert to handle his affairs; and then lost his portfolio of prints in a taxi.

One evening he attended Julian's Fancy Dress Ball with the Gibbings. He painted Robert 'with a face all over his chest and stomach – nipples for eyes and navel for mouth'.[2] Petra had been sent to bed, but she returned home the richer for a long cigarette holder and a lipstick. Eric had had a mouthful of Paris, sacred and profane, and he was back there within a week with Betty and Elizabeth Bill. Zadkine had managed to recover his portfolio, the contents of which Eric valued at £100, and Eric went out to Marly-le-Roi to see Maillol. There was no longer any question of apprenticeship; the two sculptors were now meeting on equal terms. Eric attended six more life classes at the Académie Chaumière before coming home; no doubt it was for these, and for the recovery of his

[1] Diary.
[2] ibid.

portfolio, and a second glimpse of Grock, that he had paid a second visit to Paris so soon after the first.

He took Mary and the girls to Salies in February 1927. Once again the Ditchling community waved to them as they went through to Newhaven. Joanna was accompanied by a harp – never a convenient article of luggage – and her playing of it disconcerted the other passengers in the train from Paris. They arrived at Salies in time for the Mardi Gras. Eric revelled with the others in purple 'dread-noughts', short skirt and purple scarf. There were games of *pelote* to watch on Sunday, and medlars for sale in the market, and long conversational evenings at Lousteaud's café, and a fire at the Hotel de la Paix which extinguished the electric light. Joanna, not to be out-done by Petra's lipstick, had her ears pierced. They stayed until the end of April through the soft spring weather. It was Eric's first experience of living in a rural and Catholic community which would never have dreamt of calling itself anything of the kind – so much were these things which he valued taken for granted. At Salies Gordian went to school for the first time, and in September Eric saw him off in the train from Paris for the autumn term.

The occasion was a good excuse for further life classes at Chau-mière. Eric and Mary were in Salies for a further short stay in April 1928, when Eric made a large pencil drawing of Saint-Vincent with the steps and railings leading up to the church door. David Jones was with them and they went to Chartres on the way down. All the chairs in the nave had been stacked away, so that the worn and undulating expanse of floor made its full effect. There was a seizing contrast between the pure Gothic and dark jewel-like brilliance of the Cathedral and the late Gothic of Saint-Pierre which seemed like a casket of light, the colour of the stones hardly differing from the white glass of the windows. When David Jones said that he found Saint-Pierre almost more felicitous than its neighbour, Eric laughingly protested. They argued – not necessarily about this – all night long in the train; and when a small boy – the only other occupant of the carriage – was asked by his mother at Bordeaux whether he had been able to sleep, he said that the two Englishmen had talked so long and so loudly that he had not been able to sleep at all. One day Eric went over to Lourdes and met the Hagreens who were staying near by. The place confirmed his worst apprehensions. 'The Bishops ran loose,' Eric recounted afterwards, 'I chased one all round the Grotto to kiss his ring, but I didn't catch him till the afternoon.' One would like to know which prelate was thought worth such arduous pursuit. 'There are a lot of queer smells here,' Eric complained, 'but garlic is the only one that really makes me feel ill.' He must have felt ill for a great deal of the time, and there is no wonder that he took his lunch up the funicular and ate it on the Pic de Jer. In Paris, on the way home, there were more life classes, and sportive tricks at the Bal Colonial with Robert Gibbings and his lady.

Apart from a caryatid made out of a Wellington pine at Capel, Eric had done relatively little carving in wood, but a commission from Rossall School to design and execute their War Memorial gave him a chance of exercising his skill in this medium. Eric's name had been suggested to the Headmaster and Council by Charles Rutherston,[1] but the commission was only offered to him after much debate and in face of opposition from William Temple, who was then Bishop of Manchester. The altar-piece in oak measured seven feet in width and three in height. It consisted of three panels in six sections. In the first John the Baptist is baptizing Our Lord; the second shows the penitent thief looking towards Him and the fifth the other thief turning away; the third and fourth are occupied by Christ on the Cross with the Blessed Virgin, St John, and St Mary Magdalene; the sixth shows the beheading of St John the Baptist. Some of the figures overlapped from one section to another.

The carving drew warm admiration from D. S. MacColl writing in the *Burlington Fine Arts* magazine. Eric's difficulty had been to adapt a subject which is usually represented in height to a space more suited to a landscape. He had resolved this by placing certain figures grouped around the Cross on their knees, thus linking them with those who would stand or kneel before the altar when the carving had been fixed in position. There was a freer movement and a

[1] William Rothenstein's elder brother, and a notable patron of artists.

greater fluidity of form than in Eric's previous work and the relief was well adjusted to the effect that wood-carving was calculated to give. When the preliminary cartoon was exhibited at the Goupil Salon, the heads of the nails on the hands and feet of Our Lord were made a decorative feature and the haloes were gilded. This accentuation was omitted from the finished work. P. G. Konody in *The Observer*[1] found Eric 'unquestionably the hero' of the Goupil exhibition, and the Rossall Memorial 'as impressive in its own severe way' as Stanley Spencer's *Resurrection*.

In March 1928 fifteen examples of Eric's sculpture were shown at the Goupil Gallery. In size and ambition his kneeling figure of *Mankind*[2] in Hoptonwood stone towered above the rest. The woman's body ended below the neck and above the feet, and it followed a more classical design than was usual in Eric's carving, suggesting to one critic that he might be a Phidias if he chose. Other comparisons were made with Mestrovic and Maillol. The sculpture, beautiful and impressive as it is, does not hold its own quite so certainly today; and the doubt expressed by *The Times* whether so large a figure did not demand a more monumental treatment, a sacrifice of grace to grandeur, seems confirmed. Other works, more characteristic, included a superb group in Portland stone of 'Two Clasped Lovers Embracing' and a portrait – 'Susan' – in Beerstone, where the strong personality of the sitter easily survives the austere and formal modelling. 'Head-dress'[3] – a sophisticated and rather mannered reminiscence of Assyrian modes – was less successful, though Eric himself thought it one of his best carvings. The exhibition captured the imagination of the connoisseurs; they discerned in it an advance from craftsmanship to art of which Eric was probably unaware. He would not have admitted the distinction.

[1] October 30, 1927.
[2] Tate Gallery (see plate 15).
[3] Coll: Sir Edward Maufe.

4

Eric's diary always gives the sign-post that his biography requires; on May 8, 1928, we find the following entry: 'To Pimlico with M(ary) E(thel) house-hunting.' Capel-y-ffin was a dream too good to last, and there were times when the women folk found it a nightmare. Eric admits frankly in his *Autobiography* that any family establishment depends on the women, and when the women find a way and place of life impossible, the way and place must be changed. Eric must have realized for some time that he had made a serious mistake. The buildings were beyond repair and the local stone was difficult to carve. He was inaccessible to customers, and to earn his bread and butter he was forced to absent himself for long periods of time. Where Ditchling had held, or constantly recalled, him with its social challenge, its liturgical routine, and its tissue of mutual obligations, the life at Capel – for all its Daily Mass and Compline – was essentially a family life without much *raison d'être* when the head of the family was away. The practical inconveniences were enormous. No housewife can live by scenery and shepherd's pie consisting only of potatoes, however regularly she bakes her own bread; and the stones for carving got broken in the Welsh carts as they lumbered up the valley.

In these years between Ditchling and Pigotts Eric's life takes on a colour which one is tempted to describe as hectic – were it not that 'hectic' seems too strong a word for so naturally calm a man. He certainly enjoyed his visits to Paris and Salies-de-Béarn; to London and Bristol and Waltham St Lawrence. Capel-y-ffin was little more than a base camp from which he set out in all directions; a beautiful base camp, to be sure, with picnics and moonlight walks on the Dôl field, and the company of Donald Attwater and Douglas Cleverdon – a constant visitor – to stimulate the mind. But there was something in Desmond Chute's comment when Eric had left:

Never shall I forget my visit to the Vale of Ewyas nor the green light that trickled deliciously into the Guest Room nor the good cheer and the good talk and Betty singing the *Sally Gardens* for J.K.M.R.[1] Yet I am glad you have left it. A splendid place, yet somehow not you. Wales is not you, nor mountains you. In that once to be written preface I would fain have said that your work was purely English, and to be judged in company with Purcell's music and Hepplewhite chairs.

But where was he to go? Like many people who find the country too much for them, he resigned himself to London. Work was in London, and many friends. John Polimeni found a house for sale in Kilburn – Kilburn was no steeper a descent from Capel than anywhere else, though Pimlico might have been more convenient. There was also the possibility of building a house on a site in St John's Wood. Eric was examining this with his lawyer on June 19, when Denis Tegetmeier heard of a property high up on a spur of the Chilterns near High Wycombe. On the following day he took Mary down to see it. Eric himself followed a week later. It was what he wanted – and, more important, what Mary wanted. A commodious farm-house at the end of a lane, with spacious outbuildings and several acres of land, surrounded by woods. Eric decided at once to buy, and there were further visits through August and September while necessary repairs were being put in hand.

In the meanwhile there were visits to the Monotype Works at Salfords with Stanley Morison; games on the lawn in bathing costume at Waltham St Lawrence; a last visit to Caldey where Eric discarded his bathing costume, and the Prior showed his cinema after supper, and the Trappists were foreclosing on the mortgage; work on a gravestone at Stanmer Park for Lady Chichester; and a meeting with Pepler on July 30 when the hatchet was buried as far as it would go with two men incapable of understanding one another. On September 25 Eric began designing his Perpetua and Felicity types, and on the following day he dispatched to Caldey the font he had carved for them. The first days of October were taken up with packing; the chapel was dismantled and the furniture vans arrived; and on

[1] John Rothenstein.

October 10 the last loads disappeared down the valley. The next day Eric left with the family; but there was a difference between his departure from Capel and his departure from Ditchling. Life in both places had been both difficult and idyllic, but at Capel-y-ffin he left only happy memories behind him, and he was always glad to return to it. His inscription on a headstone standing among the seven old yew trees in the churchyard – 'Remember Charlie Stones Carpenter' – is a reminder of the years he spent in the valley and of the art in which he most excelled.

PART FOUR

Pigotts

1928-1940

I

Eric, with Mary and the children, arrived at Pigotts in the early evening of October 11; Laurie Cribb and his family came the next day in a lorry with three crate-loads of chickens, two dogs, four cats, one broom and a large bundle of blankets. The difficulties and delays of settling in were less daunting than at Capel. This was 'leafy Bucks' and High Wycombe was only 4 miles down the valley. Nor was Pigotts itself impracticable as Eric measured practicability. It had the convenience and cohesion of a quadrangular setting. Facing north you saw a row of four open sheds, suitable for workshops. On the right hand, or eastern, side of the main buildings was accommodation for Eric's studio and the family quarters; on the left, or western, side were the mason's workshop and a cottage for Laurie Cribb. A low wall connected the two parts of the building.

The Gills' living-room was long and spacious, and the entire side of the southern wall was taken up by a huge dresser made by Romney Green and bright with pewter plates to match the pewter tankards that Eric had acquired from a 'pub' which had gone over to glass. Another room was turned into a chapel, with a staircase leading up to the room afterwards occupied by a resident priest. Later, the chapel was enlarged so that the plain stone altar stood, as Eric – anticipating later liturgical developments – had wished it to stand, surrounded on two sides by the congregation. Laurie Cribb had carved the Predella, and statues of St John Bosco, Christ the King, and the Blessed Virgin suckling the Holy Child – all by Eric – were fixed along the walls. His Crucifix with the blonde hair and beard hung in the sacristy. In the chapel there was also a carving of St Dominic in oak by David Jones, and a copy of the Proclamation of 1666 banishing Popish priests and Jesuits and enforcing the laws against recusants. It was some time before a resident chaplain came to Pigotts, and the family had no alternative to attending Mass at High Wycombe. When an anonymous article in *Order* – the first, short-lived manifestation of the Catholic Reformation in Great Britain – suggested that 'cultured people' had 'got to take church-going as a penance ("for your penance go to the 10.30 Sunday Mass at High Wycombe or make the Stations at Quex Road")' there was no longer any doubt of the author.

Order gave Eric – under the scarcely veiled anonymity of an unmistakable style – an excellent forum for his views. One correspondent described the periodical as 'a mingling of St Thomas and B(aron) von Hügel and Fr Martindale and Eric Gill and youthfulness and an Oxford flavour and many other lesser elements and a firm belief in the Catholic Faith'. This was not at all unfair. A cartoon by Denis Tegetmeier contrasted a rich couple who could afford to have children and didn't have them – they preferred a trio of dachshunds – with a brawling family of the poor, and the caption: 'Poor men are not so fond of children.' This alone would have justified Father Vincent McNabb's reaction to the first number, where his disapproval of Eric can be heard in rather more than an undertone:

Once, when I was trustful – and conceited – I nearly championed the obscene. . . . I can judge of the group that are behind *Order* only by hearsay, because their anonymity preference makes an impenetrable veil. Now, from what I hear of their views of Art, Morality, etc., I think I would as soon commit a canary to a cat as commit my name to the men (the young men?) behind *Order*.

This was the nearest Father Vincent ever came to a public condemnation of Eric. What had provoked it? It seems that Eric had made a woodcut of Christ and a figure representing the Church locked in a nuptial embrace. Eric had protested that there was no reason why the Church, commonly described as the Bride of Christ, should not behave like a bride. Father Vincent replied that such a relationship should not be visually shown and made Eric promise not to exhibit the drawing. Eric agreed and put it away in a cupboard, but the incident – coupled with Eric's illustrations to the *Song of Songs* – left a lasting impression on Father Vincent's mind. 'Once,' he told a fellow Dominican, 'when I was quite a big boy at school, a much younger boy came up and did something unspeakable to me. I nearly killed him, but I didn't. That's how I felt about Gill.' These were not Father Vincent's last words or sentiments about Eric; and Eric in his innocence probably had no idea that Father Vincent felt as strongly as he did. He certainly bore him no grudge. Eric was quite capable of rancour in personal relationships, but he had never wavered in his admiration for the holiness of Vincent McNabb, nor in recognition of the debt – intellectual and spiritual – which he owed him.

Order fired four salvoes of protest against current Catholic shibboleths before it ceased publication. It was born thirty years before its time, and the Church would have to ride out the divisive trauma of clerical Fascism before the decks were clear for *aggiorna-mento*. Eric's hand can be traced in articles entitled *Tuppence Coloured* and *The Right-Mindedness of Modern Art*. In the first he argued that –

Farm Street and the Sacred Heart at Quex Road are as like as two peas – not even sweet peas – and are representative not of the best people in Mayfair (heaven forbid!) or of Kilburn, but of the worst people in Manchester or Munich. We do not believe there is a single house in North London which would tolerate one of the Quex Road 'stations' in its drawing-room. Certainly there is not a house in Mayfair which would tolerate the furniture of Farm Street. This is a curious phenomena – for the people who are found in the houses of Mount Street attend church at Farm Street, and what they would hate in their homes they appear to think quite satisfactory in church. Why should there be such a difference in standard?

Eric might have added that the clergy who were content with the horrors of Repository Art because they kept the people in the churches never gave a thought to the people they kept out of them. Meanwhile the only remedy was 'to take the road to whitewash and carving off the carving, and wherever possible' to 'employ such good individual artists as are known to us'. Eric did not despair even of the rank and file of his co-religionists – 'Burns and Oates is very nearly as *démodé* as Gounod' – and architects were already 'showing that grandeur of proportion and mass are obtainable in concrete and iron at half the cost of Gothic stonework'. It is interesting that such an admirer of Chartres could see the Gothic as a 'downfall' from the Romanesque, and the tomb of Edward III as a 'downfall from that of Edward the Saint'. Good taste was mortified taste, and the best periods of artistic achievement were the periods of artistic austerity. It was time that the Church applied to its masonry the same standards of mortification that it applied, unrelentingly, to its morals.

In the second article Eric tried to steer a rational path between the notion that the artist was a purveyor of useful or pleasurable objects and the notion that the artist was a seer. Tolstoy was right in saying that art was the expression of emotion; and Clive Bell was right in saying that the business of the artist was 'to find a form to fit the emotion'; and Roger Fry was right in saying 'the question is not what a work of art represents but what it makes you feel'. But Eric maintained that he himself was 'also right in saying that the artist's job is making things which are delightful to the mind'. He then made a list of works of art which gave delight to a variety of minds – and here it is easy to pick out the ones that gave particular delight to his own.

They included the Pyramids; the Forth Bridge; the new concrete church at Bâle; Matisse's *Turkish Girl*; Frank Dobson's *Cornucopia*; Spencer's *Resurrection*; Cézanne's landscapes; Ming, Tang or Sung pots; the Book of Kells; Joyce's *Ulysses*; the *Morte d'Arthur*; *The Song of Solomon*; the Cave Paintings of Ajanta; Plainchant; Waterloo Bridge; Modigliani's portraits; San Clemente; the Nave of Gloucester; *The Tale of Genji*; *The Ballad of the White Horse*; *Love and Mr Lewisham*; and *Moby Dick*. From these we descend in order of predilection to the *Venus of Milo*, the *Sixtine Madonna*, the *Mona Lisa*, Titian's *Bacchus* and *Ariadne*, and Renoir's *Parapluies* to Sargent's *Wertheimers*, Luke Filde's *Doctor*, Gounod's *Ave Maria* and *Lead Kindly Light*. As a feeble gesture of anonymity Eric Gill's *Mankind* figures in the list – just as in another article the same anonymity had been betrayed by the revelation that when the parish priest came to tea the best works of art in the house were hidden away by the author – or the author's wife. Eric saw modern art as 'primarily a religious movement . . . away from frivolity and hypocrisy and flattery and worship of mammon'. In their attempts to discover and manifest true religion modern artists were to be praised; but 'in the absence of philosophical unity and religious guidance, they' were 'bound to flounder in morasses of eccentricity'. It was Eric's right-mindedness in matters to which even the greatest art is tributary that preserved his own best work from the eccentricity he deplored in others, and from the affectation to which he was himself occasionally prone.

An important study of Eric's achievement and ideas, presented by Joseph Thorp with an introduction by Charles Marriott, was published by Jonathan Cape early in 1929. Thorp was dramatic critic of *Punch*, who wore his flowing bow ties with a Bohemian air and nourished an unconcealed nostalgia for the Society of Jesus to which he had once tried to belong. He was not naturally of Eric's world and his admiration for his work did not go very deep; but the book was lavishly illustrated and Thorp was justified in pointing out that no one looking at the photographs would take them as representatives of 'plain craftsmanship'. For all his pretentions to impersonality Eric was an artist of marked individual style and his reputation was further attested by Stanley Casson's essay on *Some Modern Sculptors* (1929). Here he was considered with Maillol, Rodin, Mestrovic and Gaudier-Brezska.

In the spring of 1929 he was commissioned to carve three of the 'winds' on the walls of St James's Park Underground Station. The connection between 'winds' and subterranean transport was not made clear, but Eric did not now regard himself as responsible for the conception of the works he was called upon to execute. He was associated with six other sculptors, including Epstein who carved the figures of 'Day' and 'Night' on the base of the building, and with whom he had an 'irate and emotional'[1] meeting in the office of the Clerk of Works. Eric was put in charge of the team for the 'winds'; Henry Moore was a member of this, with Allan Wyon, A. H. Gerrard, Eric Aumonier, and F. Rabinovitch. Eric himself did the two figures on the eastern faces of the transverse arms of the building, which are clearly visible from Tothill Street. They have just the

[1] Diary.

right quality of relief, dictated by shadow, and are happily related to the building by the horizontal folds of drapery. His third figure – a man – was fixed on the northern face of the head of the cross. If you had asked Eric what business this irrelevant decoration – however skilfully executed – had on a building whose purpose was to house the offices of a public utility, he would perhaps have quoted Scripture in support of making friends with the Mammon of unrighteousness. He certainly did not deceive himself that he was embellishing an everlasting dwelling. Nevertheless the St James's Park sculptures introduced a decade of compromise with a world that Eric denounced in proportion as he was obliged, economically, to come to terms with it.

In an address to the Liverpool Architectural Society (November 21, 1928) he pleaded, a little disingenuously, that he was 'neither a social reformer nor a preacher of religion. The artist must take things as they are. He is the realist *par excellence*.' Nevertheless he maintained that:

From the Pyramid of Cheops to the bare interior of Westminster Cathedral (before they ruined it with marbles and mosaics) beauty and sublimity in architecture have never been dependent upon carving and ornament. Today, when such things as carving and ornament are not to be obtained (save as the rare product of individual artists whose connection with building is a mere fiction – a survival having no reality) it is more than necessary that architects should be independent of them. . . . There is one drawback to the plain building unadorned. That is, the man in the street doesn't like it. But a wise artist is one who makes things people can like for the wrong reasons. Plain building is cheaper. Let the man in the street comfort himself with that.

Eric's whole argument boiled down to this; that since the architect was himself essentially a sculptor, he had no need of sculptured ornament. It was only because the modern architect had no sensitiveness in his fingers that he was forced to call upon the sculptor who had. Ironically, Eric was answered by an architect – A. Tristan Edwards – who pleaded that it was enough for the architect to have the sensitiveness in his mind, and that Eric's suggestion that modern buildings should be without ornament was a counsel of despair. He was too polite to ask why, if Eric so disapproved of ornament on buildings, he exercised his skill to put it there. The man in the street had reason on his side; the current predilection for lean, stark buildings represented 'a passing, Puritanical phase' which had 'little philosophic backing'. It was at best 'an architecture of protest', and ornament must be born again. If the sculptors would not collaborate, then the architects must set to and create the sculpture for themselves. Eric was caught up here in a contradiction between his preaching and his practice which no rationalism could resolve. He was learning that the artist cannot create in the void; like any other man, he is subject to the laws of supply and demand, and the twentieth century was not disposed to accept his own drastic legislation.

Eric's later work rarely achieved the perfection of his earlier, and this may have been due to the necessity of turning out too much. The first volume of the Golden Cockerel *Chaucer* was published in the autumn of 1929. A good deal of the illustration is pretty mechanical; these etiolated borders do not quite match the richness and the occasional earthiness of the text. There is even a hint of decadence which is the very reverse of Chaucerian. At the same time *Art Nonsense*, a collection of Eric's essays – many of them reprinted and revised – was published by Cassell and Francis Walterson. Joseph Thorp justly pointed out that the book was so well printed in Eric's own Perpetua type that if you were exasperated by the author's 'dogmatic assertion of some quite dubious' thesis, your delight in its presentation stopped you from pitching the book to the other end of the room.[1] All the old nails were hammered on the head, and indeed one could not be told too often that 'what is important is what the workman has in his mind, not what some model has in its body'. Thorp raised the objection that if the only cure for the spiritual miseries caused by capitalism was the wiping out of three centuries of human achievement, then those miseries were beyond cure because such an annulment was inconceivable. To this objection, and

[1] *The Spectator*, October 8, 1929.

to the integral pessimism to which it led, Eric had no reply; neither he, nor his critics, could imagine that the splitting of the atom would before long place the whole of civilization – Chartres Cathedral and Cheop's Pyramid as well as the Crystal Palace and the Albert Memorial – at the mercy of a madman's trigger. But a sentence from his essay on *Clothes* (1931) has a prophetic reverberation:

It may well be that our civilization, before many generations have passed, will be at the mercy of nations more practised in mechanical warfare and less reduced in numbers.

On November 10 (1928) Eric watched the Lord Mayor's Show from Anderton's Hotel in Fleet Street. It was the kind of spectacle he enjoyed – gay and popular – and he described it in his diary as 'most thrilling'. But there was a special reason for his presence among the curious and excited onlookers. The new Lord Mayor, Sir William Waterlow, was a member of the firm of Waterlow & Sons, Bank Note and General Printers. Printing had been called 'the art preservative of all the arts', and printing was the *leit-motif* of the procession. Here were the typefounders with a bearded Caxton receiving a proof from a boy, and on the same car was a modern composing cabinet. Here were the ink-makers, with Byron's words for motto – 'a drop of ink which makes thousands – perhaps millions – think!' Here were the papermakers and the typesetters with Gutenberg, Fust and Schoeffer set against the linotype. Here was Petrarch dictating to his scribes, and a stone with lettering by Eric himself; and here was a woman sitting at her cottage door and receiving her Christmas cards from a postman. It was a pageant of printing that went by, with the cars gliding through the streets like ornamental barges, each with its blue and white fascia and panels hiding its wheels.

With Eric in the window of Anderton's was Stanley Morison, and through Morison he had made the acquaintance of Beatrice Warde. Very shortly the Monotype Perpetua would make its first public appearance in the VIIth issue of the *Fleuron*. Eric's note ran as follows:

These drawings were not made with special reference to typography – they were simply letters drawn with brush and ink. For the typographical quality of the fount, as also for the remarkably fine and precise cutting of the punches, the Monotype Corporation is to be praised. In my opinion 'Perpetua' is commendable in that, in spite of many distinctive characters, it retains that common-placeness and normality which is essential to a good book-type.

Eric's original italic, to have been called Felicity, had been considerably modified. In the meantime the suitability of Perpetua capitals for a titling fount was evident, and cutting began on these in 1928. Printers and publishers saw in them an authoritative, classic 'roman' letter for title pages and letter-heads. And even before Perpetua was ready for the Trade the Monotype commissioned a set of titling capitals in sans-serif style. Eric agreed, with some amusement, to Morison's suggestion that the new series should be described as 'Gill Sans'. It was in connection with this that Beatrice Warde wrote of Eric as:

the man who has not only designed the most generally useful sans-serif type but has also created a classic letter which, as Perpetua roman, may well be the 'original twentieth-century book face' for which we have been waiting. There is nothing paradoxical here: Mr Gill's sans is designed along 'the lines of least resistance', as a face for machine casting, while Perpetua was originally a letter evolved for the most famous stone-cut inscriptions of our generation, and has happened to become a type because a machine was able to cut, cast and compose it, and because there was a need for such a type. Few critics would say that Mr Gill's deliberate experiments in designing type for hand composition are in any way as successful as Perpetua, the by-product of his work with the chisel. (*Commercial Art*, January 1932)

In February 1929 Eric was drawing trial letters freehand on the scale of 18 point, and working out what had been tested on that realistic scale over the enlarged figures of the pencilled alphabet. In March he was correcting drawings and visiting the Monotype Offices in Fetter Lane for further discussions. His attraction to typography was the natural result of his attraction to lettering, and he explained it in his *Autobiography*:

Lettering has this very great advantage over other arts; at its very base, conjoined and inseparable, are the fair and the fit – most obviously useful and depending for its beauty upon nothing but man's musical sense. The shapes of letters do not derive their beauty from any sensual or sentimental reminiscence. No one can say that the O's roundness appeals to us only because it is like that of an apple. . . . We like the circle because such liking is connatural to the human mind. And no one can say lettering is not a useful trade by which you can honestly serve your fellow men and earn an honest living. Of what other art are these things so palpably true? . . . Letters are things, not pictures of things.

And so, as 1928 drew to its close, we find Eric at last within easy reach of both work and recreation; designing an alms-dish for the Goldsmiths' Company; paying two visits within a week to *This Year of Grace* at the London Pavilion; walking home to Pigotts after Midnight Mass at High Wycombe, and playing cards till 6 a.m. on Christmas morning.

2

A visit to Pigotts was always something of a pilgrimage, but the piety was less obtrusive than at Ditchling and the place was infinitely more accessible than Capel, where visitors were warned not to precede their visit by a telegram in case they might be asked to deliver it themselves. Some of the pilgrims were the same, but there were a number of new faces and new friends. Even when the caller had been rather a bore, Eric would always stand at the door of his workshop waving them good-bye: 'I can't help it, you know,' he would say, 'I must stand here until they've turned the corner of the house. Silly of me, isn't it?' Stanley Morison and Beatrice Warde – neither of whom were boring – are escorted down the steep lane to catch the bus. Tom Burns – the anonymous dynamo of *Order* – and his brother Charles, the child psychologist, are constant visitors. Bernard Leach arrives with three Japanese friends. Jim Ede, assistant director of the Tate Gallery and author of an important book on Gaudier-Brzeska, soon becomes an intimate. Herbert Read lives close by at Seer Green; and Eric meets Chesterton at a garden fête in High Wycombe, when they draw each other's portraits. After the telephone has been installed at Pigotts, Chesterton is the first person Eric rings up. Prudence Pelham, daughter of Lady Chichester for whom Eric had engraved a tombstone, comes for lessons in carving and Eric does her portrait. She too will become an intimate of the household.

As usual, Eric was continuously on the move. He was at Oxford lecturing to undergraduate societies in Merton and Lincoln, and he was present at the opening of Blackfriars. The Dominican influence persisted, but now Father Victor White and Father John-Baptist Reeves take the place of Father Austin Barker. At Cambridge he dined at St John's with Dr Coulton; and after dinner the two doughty controversialists walked up and down the gardens till midnight, arguing about the Middle Ages. At Jesus he was at work on a carving

of the arms of the College visitor, Leonard White-Thompson, im-
paled on those of his see of Ely. This stands over the gateway leading
into the Chapel Court. The official history of the College records
that 'the angelic supporters of the shield soon caused the gateway
below them to be called the Angel Gate'; it does not record that
some of the more squeamish Fellows had requested the angelic
buttocks to be reduced. Eric was invited to the 'feast' at Jesus in
December. Here, for the first and last time, he met Dean Inge. Once
as he was listening to John O'Connor's translation of *Art and Scholasticism*, O'Connor had asked him what he was carving with his
pocket-knife, and Eric had answered: 'I'm carving Dean Inge because it's as like Dean Inge as anyone else.' But then Inge was rather
deaf and Eric's voice was 'gentle and low' – O'Connor compared it
to Greta Garbo's – so perhaps they did not have much conversation.

On August 3 he was called to Wittering where his mother lay
dangerously ill. 'Mother went by name through all the family, as it
were rehearsing all the names and allowing the sight of each one to
come to her in imagination for a few seconds. She said, "I have
loved you all very dearly." '[1] She died on the 6th – which was the
anniversary of Eric and Mary's wedding. All through the next day he
watched over the body, and followed it to Brighton for the burial.
Later he drew the inscription for the gravestone. There was much
sorting and burning of papers at West Wittering, and the question of
Mr Gill's retirement was raised with the Archdeacon of Chichester.

On January 7 (1930) Petra was married to Denis Tegetmeier and
René Hague was formally betrothed to Joanna. There was breakfast
for eighty-five people at the Red Lion in High Wycombe, and a
reception at Pigotts afterwards. At the end of June Eric went to
stay with Count Kessler at Weimar, stopping at Cologne on the way
for the Feast of SS. Peter and Paul, and admiring the new concrete
bridge across the Rhine. John Rothenstein and his American wife
Elizabeth were also staying with Kessler; and Maillol, in precipitate
flight from Paris with a model, had been lent a cottage near by. He
was in terror of pursuit by his son. Kessler, with an aristocratic re-

[1] Letter to Cecil Gill, August 5, 1929.

Book plate engraved for John Rothenstein, 1920.

spect for the conventions, had made a lightning descent on London to warn the Rothensteins, *père et fils*, that Elizabeth would have to meet a situation more irregular than any she had been accustomed to meet in Kentucky. The danger was lessened by the fact that the model spoke no English and that Elizabeth spoke no French – and in the event she was called upon to meet something much more startling than an attractive Frenchwoman who happened to be living in sin.

We were gathered together after lunch one day in the drawing-room waiting for coffee to be brought in. I remember we were standing by a large table on which lay some of the Cranach Presse books and Kessler was showing us these. Gill left the room and came back with the sketch book and began turning the pages. They were all drawings of a female model and started fairly conventionally. Even so I noticed considerable distress on Count Kessler's face. *The* drawing I remember because of the startling pose and the exact drawing of a certain feature was turned up with all the candour of a child by Gill. I winced from it involuntarily and Kessler was outraged. I remember I said weakly to try to ease the embarrassment and tension, 'Who was your model?' Gill replied, 'Oh, she was the librarian at High Wycombe.'[1]

The Kessler party went on an expedition to Naumburg where they saw the cathedral, and to Dornburg with its three castles, where they sat over their coffee on the terrace arguing about birth control and war. A few days later Maillol and his model joined them for a second

[1] Letter to the author.

26

Two facing pages from *The Song of Songs,* with a wood engraving and two initial letters, 1931. Printed by Count Harry Kessler at the Cranach Presse, Weimar.

QUOD EST SALOMONIS

Statura tua assimilata est palmae,
et ubera tua botris.
Dixi: Ascendam in palmam,
et apprehendam fructus ejus;
et erunt ubera tua sicut botri vineae,
et odor oris tui sicut malorum.

UTTUR tuum
sicut vinum optimum,
dignum dilecto meo
ad potandum, labiisque
et dentibus illius ad ruminandum.
Ego dilecto meo, et ad me conversio ejus.
Veni, dilecte mi, egrediamur in agrum,
commoremur in villis.
Mane surgamus ad vineas;
videamus si floruit vinea,
si flores fructus parturiunt,
si floruerunt mala punica;
ibi dabo tibi ubera mea.
Mandragorae dederunt odorem.
In portis nostris omnia poma:
nova et vetera, dilecte mi, servavi tibi.

UIS mihi det te fratrem meum,
sugentem ubera matris meae,
ut inveniam te foris,
et deosculer te,

expedition to Inselburg. They had tea on the top of the mountain at the Prussicherhof, and visited the castle of St Elizabeth at Wartburg. Eric drew portraits of Kessler, Maillol, Frau Foerster Nietzsche and the Rothensteins; made some experiments in gilding for the Cranach Press; and worked at his essay on *Clothes*. From Weimar he went on to Frankfurt-am-Main from which he drew an appropriate lesson about town halls; town halls were as subject as temples to architectural abuse:

Anyone who has visited the Komer at Frankfurt and has passed from the modern Council Chamber, with its elaborate and costly grandeur, its fatuous historical paintings, its sumptuous upholsteries and candelabra, to the ancient hall of the Imperial elections, with its noble simplicity, its complete absence of architectural display or physical luxury (anyone, that is to say, who is not himself as stuffy as a suite of Maples furniture) will see that nothing can be of any avail to save us but a great bonfire, a great pillage, a great iconoclasm.[1]

Eric finished *Clothes* at Salies-de-Béarn where René and Joanna joined him. They watched the games of pelote played *aux mains nues*, and were vastly entertained by Pinter's Circus which Eric described as 'one long thrill'.[2] In the train back to Paris he read passages of his essay aloud while Joanna slept on her fiancé's stiffening knees. There was further drawing at Chaumière's, the usual pilgrimage to Chartres, and a glut of liturgy at Notre-Dame, Saint-Séverin, and Saint-Eustache – all on the same Sunday morning. Eric's drawings at Chaumière's[3] are little more than five-finger exercises, done – one supposes – to keep his hand in. His latest London model, provided for him by Oliver Lodge, was a more serious subject – an extremely pretty girl called Enid who wore no underpants and contrived to fasten her stockings to her vest.

Towards the end of September 1930 Eric had an attack of what would once have been described as brain fever. He suffered for two days from intense headache and told Dr Burns that the only thing he could bear to look at – the only thing which distracted him – was a

[1] *Clothes*, 1931.
[2] Diary.
[3] Most of these are in the collection of Mr S. Samuels.

copy of Lutyens' plans for the projected Catholic cathedral at Liverpool. Judging from Eric's subsequent opinion of these plans, one is
tempted to suggest that Sir Edwin Lutyens was responsible for his
illness. However that may be, Dr Burns took him in an ambulance to
St John and St Elizabeth's hospital in St John's Wood, where the
neurologist was puzzled by his condition but thought it probably a
case of benign meningitis. Eric remained in hospital for the first
three weeks of October, and fearing that his life was in some danger
he made his confession to Father John-Baptist Reeves. When he had
received absolution he asked with characteristic simplicity:

'Well, father, do you think I'm all right?'

Father John-Baptist reassured him, but suggested that he should
'make it up' with Father Vincent McNabb.

'But I've nothing against Father Vincent, and I hope he has nothing
against me.'

'Still you've drifted apart, haven't you? Won't you see Father
Vincent if he comes along?'

Eric replied that of course he would be delighted to see Father
Vincent, who subsequently paid two visits to the hospital. The two
men – master and disciple – had not met for a long time, and no
mention was made of the matters which had estranged them. But
when Father Vincent returned from his first visit, he was in a state of
unaccustomed emotional disturbance. 'I loved that man,' he exclaimed, pacing to and fro, 'I still love him.' Hilary Pepler also called,
but Eric was not well enough to see him. John O'Connor and Desmond Chute came, however, and Desmond brought him Holy Communion; and before the end of the month he was back at Pigotts
dictating his essay on *Typography* to René Hague. Early in November
Robert Gibbings motored him to West Wittering, where he re-
cuperated for a few days in a coastguard's cottage. On the 19th
René and Joanna were married by Father John Gray at High Wycombe. The music and choir were under the direction of Fernand
Laloux, the organist from Farm Street, and Edward Rose from St
Patrick's, Soho Square. The breakfast was again held at the Red
Lion and sixty guests came up to Pigotts. On the following day

Petra's eldest daughter, Judith, was christened, and two days later a Mass of thanksgiving was held for Eric's recovery.

His work on the Underground Station at St James's Park had an important consequence, for he was now commissioned to execute the sculptures for Broadcasting House. This took priority over a number of smaller jobs, including the illustrations for *Lady Chatterley's Lover*, and it occupied him over the next two years. No one would have accused Eric of believing in broadcasting; a radio set at Pigotts would have been as unexpected as a statue of St Antony of Padua in St Paul's Cathedral. The dissemination of views and news and entertainment – high or low – by mechanical means was a natural corollary of State capitalism, and there was a time when Eric would have had nothing to do with it. But the result of making a national reputation in his own way was the necessity, forced upon him by family cares, of extending it upon objects in which he was uninterested or of which he disapproved. He was not in the least inspired by the notion of Prospero and Ariel – he had little knowledge of Shakespeare and not much liking for him. The idea was a convenient 'gimmick' and as good as any other. How he approached it can be read between the lines, as well as within the lines, of an article he wrote for *The Listener* when the work was finished:

The Governors of the BBC imagine they are playing a very high game indeed. *Deo Omnipotenti* are the first words they hurl at you in their entrance hall, and so the choice of what should be placed in the niche over the main door was obviously a difficult matter. It was eventually decided that a sculpture representing 'Prospero and Ariel' would be appropriate. Who are Prospero and Ariel and why are they appropriate to the BBC? They are characters in Shakespeare's *Tempest*. Prospero is called 'Duke of Milan', and Ariel is a good servant; his very name has affinity with the apparatus of radio broadcasting. His business in the play is to do the will of the beneficent Duke. Had this pleasing but superficial appropriateness been all, then the sculptor's job would have been simply to devise portraits of two Shakespearian characters clothed in stone versions of Clarkson's best theatrical costumes. It seemed obvious, however, that there was more in it than that. . . . A man might be called Duke of Milan and yet be no duke at all. A certain man was called Prince of Juda who was infinitely more than prince of a little Syrian province. This Duke of Milan, of what powers is he shown to be possessed? Were not the gods subject to him to play their little scene before him? Prospero, commander of the immortal gods! Who, then, is Ariel? The heraldic attitude in which he stands in the carving suggests a possible answer. So this stone carving is to be regarded as heraldic rather than architectural sculpture. It is only a work of art in a low sense of the word. . . . This carving is supposed to be a useful object. As walking sticks are useful to lame men, so this carving is intended to be useful to the passer-by – useful as a sign and a symbol, like a cross on a tombstone or the three balls on the shop of a moneylender.[1]

Eric further explained that Prospero was clothed in an alb because he was spirit, not body – this suggested an odd misreading of Shakespeare – and his attitude was of one sending out a messenger. Ariel was not clothed because he *was* the messenger; he was airy but not invisible; he was a spirit who had 'assumed incarnation'. Here again Eric seems not to have realized that invisibility – to be assumed or discarded at will – was among Ariel's chief prerogatives. He was holding a pipe because the pipe was the simplest of musical instruments – the one that shepherds used and children followed – and his attitude was of one offering himself, of one restless and anxious to be gone. 'Others also,' Eric added, 'have found the cup bitter.' Eric was right in reading a theology into *The Tempest*, but his interpretation of Ariel suggests an analogy with the Second Person of the Trinity rather than with the Third. Nor was Prospero quite so beneficent as Eric imagined; he could send Ariel on his errands, but it was Ariel who taught him forgiveness.

Ariel also figured on the bas-relief panels below the projecting towers of the building. In the first of these he was shown borne up by two angelic figures. This idea was taken from the figure of Mary of Anjou, similarly supported, on her tomb in Naples, and it was designed to illustrate Ariel learning 'the music of the spheres'. In the second he is seen piping to children – a plastic illustration of the Children's Hour. In the third Ariel, his pipes now slung over his shoulder, stood between two figures whose identity is not very easy

[1] March 15, 1933.

to determine. It caused some discussion, and the claims of Wisdom, Justice, Faith, Purity, Temperance, Beauty and Imagination were carefully examined. Eventually Wisdom and Gaiety prevailed – a nice balance between the Home Service and the Light Programme. There was a risk at one moment of the Children's Hour being sacrificed to the General Overseas Service; it might be easier and more economical to show Ariel piping to distant lands which would not be seen than to a group of children who had to be shown. But in the end a dolphin or two rearing their heads above the water suggested the shorter wave-lengths.

These analyses were satisfying to the Governors of the BBC, but it was certainly not of broadcasting that Eric was thinking when he conceived his Ariel, nor even of poetry. It was surely of music, which meant more to him than any other of the arts and in which he had his own quiet proficiency. And so it was important for him to find the right model for his musician. Here he was singularly fortunate in the fact that Leslie French happened at that time – January 1931 – to be playing Ariel in the Old Vic production of *The Tempest* at Sadlers Wells, and playing the part better than it had been played within living memory. He had the right physique, small and supple, and his voice, light and delicately inflected, was a perfect instrument for the verse. He entertained Eric to dinner at his flat after a matinée performance of the play, and gave him several sittings at Pigotts.

It was nearly always very cold, I remember, and as I was posing in the nude Mary used to see that there was always a good fire burning in the studio. I think it was a stove. At first I was rather embarrassed at standing about so long in the altogether. Mary used to come in to the studio during the sittings bearing a tray with hot soup and since she was the perfect mother figure I was never for one moment embarrassed. . . . Eric used to draw on a very large drawing block which stood on an easel; he drew many sketches all of which I thought were perfect, but nearly all of which were immediately destroyed. He never seemed to get what he wanted until he had done a great many 'attempts'. I could not bear to see these drawings being ripped from the great pad and being screwed up and thrown away for ever. While he was drawing and I was posing we used to keep up a running conversation. . . . Eric used to write to me quite often, usually on a postcard. That beautiful handwriting of his usually meant another visit to Pigotts. One postcard simply said: 'I'm coming to Regent's Park again to hear you say: "I do hear the morning lark." '¹. . . It is entirely due to those sittings with Eric that I took up painting myself. During a session I said: 'How I would love to be able to draw and paint.' Eric said: 'You can – everybody can – here, you can have a go,' and he handed me a charcoal and I lashed about on his drawing pad for a few moments. We must have looked an odd couple – he in his monk's habit posing for me – drawing happily as I was. I gave up very quickly – we laughed a lot, but I had been smitten with the idea and when Eric said 'There are only two kinds of picture to have in your house, the very best or those you have painted yourself', I could not afford the best and so I began to paint for myself.²

But more than Prospero and Ariel were required to meet Sir John Reith's challenge of *Deo Omnipotenti* in the entrance hall of Broadcasting House. Nothing less than the parable of the Sower could illustrate the good seeds that were being sown by the BBC, and here again Eric met the challenge with a combination of skill and scepticism. He worked hard at the carvings, first of all at Pigotts where he made the small scale models, and afterwards *in situ*. He worked in all weathers until his smock and biretta became part of the landscape of Langham Place. He could perfectly well have been provided with a proper shelter, but he preferred to be treated like an ordinary mason, and stood on a plank platform, reached by a ladder and protected by a strip of sacking. On one occasion the platform was blown down. He worked, as he always did, conscientiously. But this did not prevent him remarking to a friend who was passing underneath the platform: 'You know, this is all b - - - s!' In matters of making Eric never deceived himself, and he would not have been unduly elated by the general approval that was given to the BBC carvings. The only dissentient voice was Violet, Duchess of Rutland, and even she was relieved that they had not been perpetrated by Mr Epstein or Mr Henry Moore.

¹ Leslie French's Puck was as memorable as his Ariel.
² Letter to the author, January 15, 1965.

3

Eric had a special reason for dictating *Typography* to René Hague while he was still convalescent from his illness. The Hagues and the Tegetmeiers both had living quarters at Pigotts, and Eric now decided to set up his own printing press with Hague as his assistant. *Typography* was among their first productions, 500 copies on hand-made paper, printed from 12 point Joanna, published by Sheed & Ward. After recalling Maritain's summary of the modern world as 'spiritually dominated by the humanism of the Renaissance, the Protestant Reformation and the Cartesian Reform', Eric got down to brass tacks. His reasoning, as usual, was relentless. The trouble with the world was that it was not yet wearing the right clothes. The majority of people still thought Gothic architecture appropriate to churches, although Gothic was simply a method of building appropriate to stone and was no more Christian than Hindu. They still wore collars and ties, whether they were kings, clerks or furnace men, although there was no necessity for collars and ties in any of these trades or vocations. Industrialism had its own mechanical merits but, logically speaking, there was no place in it for ornament. 'Plain lettering, when properly chosen and rationally proportioned, has all the nobility of plain words', and fancy lettering was as distasteful to the artist as it was irrelevant to the engineer. The parish church of Saint Pierre at Chartres was an example of pure engineering – 'as free from sentimentalism and frivolity as any iron girder bridge of to-day', although it was the engineering of men 'raised above themselves by a spiritual enthusiasm'. Eric's words, like his lettering, could not have been plainer.

Letters were 'signs for sounds' just as, he might have added, sounds were signs for thoughts. But Eric's typographical aesthetic was not quite so Puritan as it appeared. The return to normality, bare and unadorned, need not forbid an occasional excursion into fantasy:

Moreover, it seems clear that as a firm and hearty belief in Christian marriage enables one not only to make the best jokes about it but even to break the rules with greater assurance . . . so a good clear training in the making of normal letters will enable a man to indulge more freely in fancy and impudence.

Eric distinguished between the typography of industrialism which must be fancy-free if it were to be honest, and humane typography which might be uncouth but which gave scope for variety and experiment. The beauty produced by machines was the 'beauty of bones'; the beauty that radiated from the work of man was 'the beauty of holiness'.

These were familiar arguments, but Eric had now ceased to expect the conversion, or the collapse, of industrialism. He accepted the two worlds – the world of machines and machine minders, and the world of men – living side by side; all he expected – though even here his expectations did not run very high – was that each would produce the works that were proper to them – 'industrialism becoming more strictly and nobly utilitarian as it recognizes its inherent limitations, and the world of human labour, ceasing any longer to compete with it, becoming more strictly and soberly humane'. He went on to consider the technical problems of punch-cutting and the spacing of words on the page. Was it better that all the lines should end evenly at the cost of varying spaces between the words; or should the line endings be sacrificed to evenness of space? Eric held that books were made primarily to be read, not to be looked at; and he thought the reader was assisted by an even spacing. This was how he printed *Typography*, and the result justified his preference. Here again he pushed the argument to a point where only he would have conducted it:

The discovery, then, of what is meant by 'pleasantly readable' involves more than questions of eye-strain, important tho' that question is; it involves first and last a consideration of what is holy.

Holiness meant 'what is reasonable no less than what is desirable, the true no less than the good'.

Finally there came the question of the book itself. Eric admitted a certain plausibility in the argument that the size and style of a book should be governed by its contents – 'that elegant poetry should have elegant type, and the rough-hacked style of Walt Whitman a rough-hacked style of letter; that reprints of Malory should be printed in ''Black Letter'' and books of technology in ''Sans-Serif'' ' ; but he held that the reading, and not the reading matter, should always be the primary consideration. Who was going to read the book, and in what circumstances? A missal to be read on an altar, a dictionary to be read on a table, and a novel to be read on one's knee, would each demand a different type and size, not because their contents were different, but because they would be read under quite different conditions – standing at an altar, sitting at a table, or sitting in a train. Eric was opposed to startling title pages, as he was opposed to all advertisement: 'a smart title page will not redeem a dully printed book any more than a smart cinema will redeem a slum'.

Typography ran into four editions, and to the last of them Eric added a chapter on phonography. This was indeed a flight into the cloud cuckoo land of crankiness. If a 'good piece of lettering' were as 'beautiful a thing to see as any sculpture or painted picture', why replace these signs by shorthand? Eric replied that pot-hooks or hangers were no less beautiful than squares or circles. 'There are no such things as shapes except the shapes of *things*, and if the things be good things only fools could deem them ugly. . . . A section of drain-pipe is no more ugly than a circle made with compasses, we only think it so because we don't see the circle and only remember the business of drainage.' Eric strangely ignored that there may be good or bad shapes of the same thing. The most plausible argument he put forward for the universal teaching of shorthand was that people would no longer be forced to scribble. They would have time to write slowly, and therefore neatly and legibly; although whether human character would enter into shorthand as powerfully as it enters into longhand was a question he did not consider. In any event it was paradoxical to conclude an essay on the making of letters with a plea that there was no need for letters to be made at all.

It was almost inevitable that, sooner or later, Eric should write a book on *Clothes* – and indeed, now, as the 'thirties got under way, he was in a mood to write about pretty well anything. He wrote this *au courant de la plume* in an obvious *élan* of high spirits. He was only preaching what he long had practised. 'The whole point of the book', he wrote, was 'to show that man is, by nature, a clothed animal and that far from being a naked animal who puts clothes on, he is a clothed animal who takes them off.' Here – as a friendly Dominican was quick to point out in *Blackfriars* – he was straying from the narrow path of Thomism. St Thomas had held that man was 'by nature a Naked Animal; and only in certain circumstances, by purpose and device, masks himself in clothes'; and that clothing was only natural to *fallen* man. Eric claimed to be transcending the doctrine of the Fall: 'we go behind and beyond any question as to whether Adam wore a fig-leaf or breeches or an apron. Such a question is almost uninteresting; it is certainly irrelevant. We simply do not care.' Father Bernard Delaney thought that Eric ought to care, but Eric replied that God Himself was normally depicted 'in clothes which, they say, but for sin man would never have worn'. The subject forced Eric away from an aesthetic of pure utility; he did not in the least want women to go about looking like the Forth Bridge. Indeed he was happier about women's clothes than about men's; he distinguished clearly between the dressmaker and the tailor to the detriment of the latter. Robes were better than suits, and whenever a man wanted to make himself important he put them on – the least important Scotsman was happier in skirts than in trousers. The essence of a well-made suit was the seam and the cut; but it was an injury to a fine material to cut it. Robes, of course, were cut as well, but here both the cut and the seam were less conspicuous. Eric was particularly severe on the tailor's avoidance of creases, and his arguments drew a sharp retort from the West End:

I have read your book with interest, but you have made me feel very cross. Your remarks about 'cut' and 'fit' may be true of many clothes but you should, I think, allow that there are people who make a study of their business and make *clothes to drape*, when they are allowed to! Tight fitting clothes without any creases are like low-class clothes and I don't like to feel that you should think we poor tailors-cutters are such a poor lot! Give us credit for something! Neither the maker of cloth nor the maker of clothes has any respect for the material as a piece of weaving. This seems to me sheer bunk!

PS. I don't collect autographs.

The drabness of male attire accurately reflected the monotony of industrial civilization. 'Men have preserved the vestments of priests and of civic and military glory, but have left to woman all the panoply of ordinary citizenship.' Even when they were compelled to assume the uniform of their office, they got out of it as quickly as possible. The High Court Judge on his way home from the Temple looked no different from the bank clerk sitting beside him in the tube; and even the minister of religion, unless he wore the gaiters and apron of the Anglican episcopate, was distinguished by his collar rather than by his clothes. Where people had once been proud of their trades, they were now only proud of their sports. There were special – and often splendid – clothes for huntsmen, cricketers, footballers and jockeys. Eric particularly admired the billowing coloured shirts of the jockey – but these were the clothes that people wore in their spare time. 'Business' suits were the same all the world over, but Eric foresaw a time when all men would 'see themselves as mechanics' and would 'clothe themselves in india-rubber'. For rubber was the right material for robots.

Eric's philosophy of clothes was based on his respect for a body which he regarded, very literally, as a 'temple of the Holy Ghost'.

As a thing good in itself, superbly adapted to its functions, it surpasses in beauty all machines and all engineering. As a thing to be desired, it surpasses all fruits, all flowers, all animals and all mountains. All these things, machines, fruits, flowers, mountains, are reflected in it – all massiveness, all lightness, all grace and all sweetness.

Hats were a tribute to the dignity of the human head, and he himself never went abroad without a beret. Boots were more than a protection against stones; to be without boots was as ignominious as to be without a hat. And to go without gloves was to lack 'a proper sense of the enormous significance of contact. The glove is a shield, it hides the hand as much as it protects it.' Clothes had a dual function – to hide and to display – and these motives were common to man in more than his sartorial activities. Just as he hid the relics of a saint in a shrine and carried them in procession; hid the Blessed Sacrament in a Tabernacle and exposed it in a monstrance; invited friends to his house, but frowned upon the unbidden guest – so, in less Puritanical times, he had both hidden and adorned his virility with a codpiece. Eric had flirted with nudism in his day but finally concluded that bathing suits were as appropriate at Brighton as they were absurd in a private swimming bath. The simplicity of good clothing, like the simplicity of good sculpture and engineering, was the result of an enthusiasm which put into it everything it knew and loved, and 'not a single other thing'. Seen thus, the art of making was 'the overwhelming exuberance of a fertile universe'.

Eric's ideal of clothing for men in the civilization he despaired of saving – so he told a journalist who had made the pilgrimage to Pigotts – was 'the toga of old Rome with long skirts and flowing draperies – clothes fit for meditation and the life of thought and gentle occupation'.[1] More immediately practical, however, was 'the tunic, with a belt to bind it at the waist . . . on all accounts the best garment both for men and for women, and if boys and girls are well clothed in tunics which reach but a few inches below the belly, men and women, as befits their greater age and self-consciousness and the more obvious development of their organs, will wear tunics reaching to the knees or below them'. Eric recalled the eurhythmic figure of Isadora Duncan wandering unconcernedly about the streets of London, and the tunic – or smock – was what he wore himself. Indeed he designed such a garment for a writer on the *Manchester Evening News*. Faithful to his preference, he had them made by a dressmaker, not a tailor; and in so far as he wore anything at all in bed, he wore a nightshirt. At Royal Academy banquets his scarlet silk underpants were an eye-opener to anyone who chanced to catch

[1] *Evening Standard*, July 8, 1931.

sight of them; and whatever Capel or Pigotts might have lacked in other amenities, Eric always had his dressing-room – even if it were at the other end of the house.

He was, as we have seen, the last person to divorce making from morals, and the healthy hedonism of this essay – in which his thought remained securely anchored to its ancient moorings – was matched by an orthodoxy which left his critics as nonplussed as it reassured them. He was writing at a time when one might have asked many of the Catholic clergy whether they believed in anything quite as firmly as they disbelieved in birth control. Nevertheless, on this point where others would reluctantly have toed the line, Eric wrote with evident conviction. It had nothing very obviously to do with clothes, except in the sense that 'all things are related with each other', but we find contraception condemned as 'simply mastur-bation à deux, and when, by means of contraceptive contrivances, a man and woman seek the same gratifications they make themselves, homosexual and earn the same condemnation' – and homosexuality was 'the ultimate disrespect both to the human body and to human love'. Like Industrialism, Eric saw contraception as essentially the product of Puritanism, for a disrespect for 'the human being as an artist' was at the root of both. Such reasoning appears a trifle sum-mary today, even to certain moral theologians, but it reflected faith-fully the rigorism of thirty years ago. The clergy who regarded Eric as an enfant terrible would have been no less heartened by his con-demnation of divorce as a 'phantasy of disordered imagination'. Father Vincent McNabb was happily very far from his grave, but if he had been there he could have rested in peace.

4

It is something of a paradox that a man who spent a lifetime denouncing the evils of industrialism should have found it so difficult to believe in original sin. His belief in the goodness of God and the beauty of creation was so profound that it seemed to him next to impossible that anything created could be really bad. For example, if you said 'This rice pudding is horrible,' he was down on you like a ton of bricks. You were permitted to dislike rice pudding, if you chose to be fussy, but you were not permitted to impugn the essential goodness of rice. He was once extremely angry with David Jones because he confessed to a certain distaste for apples. Apples were good; *ergo*, how could a rational man dislike them? Eric was certainly aware of his own imperfections, and this made him easy to confide in. He was quite unshockable. If you told him that you had done something unmentionable, he would merely smile and say: 'Well, do you know, I once. . . .' And the misdeed that he admitted to you was probably as unmentionable as your own – but he had committed it out of pure curiosity. His temptation was to try everything once.

But the problem of evil, and its associated problem of pain, did not trouble him. His nature was compact of gratitude. Eric was Victorian in his ideas of family life and family management, and even his jokes tended to be Victorian. He was no less Victorian in his optimism. People were fundamentally sensible and good – even bankers and industrialists, and he had good reason to know that his own banker was a fount of generosity. It was only a question of getting them round to his point of view. And here we come to what every one agrees to have been the most conspicuous failure – it was hardly a fault – in the character of Eric Gill. He would argue cheerfully – and furiously – about the Middle Ages with Dr Coulton, because Coulton stood clean outside his own circle. But if one of his own family or friends suggested that he was simplifying matters a good deal, or even that he was talking plain rubbish, he got annoyed. He would have given his last shilling to a beggar – and he had a great respect for beggars – but he was never known to have surrendered an argument. As the years went by this created a certain tension between him and René Hague. Like many another man who knows his own mind beyond the shadow of a doubt, Eric was not clever at getting inside other people's. He quite lacked the Shakespearian or the Keatsian capacity for resting in uncertainty. This was due to the same want of imagination that prevented him from becoming a great creative sculptor; he believed in too many rules and he thought that all one had to do was to follow them.

In spite of his habitual self-control it would be false to imagine him as a man entirely free from tension. When one saw him scratching his head, one knew that something was worrying him. Very often it was money. He had all, and more than all, the work he could manage to get through, but a great many people depended on him. If the money was there, he would give it away – not lavishly, but within the limits of a prudent charity. The financial depression of 1931 hit him badly and there was a day when he came into the workshop and said: 'I'm afraid it's every man for himself from now on.' The apprentices gathered round him and assured him that if he wished them to leave they would go; but Eric said that he would much rather they stayed. They would battle it out together. For all his contempt for the principles of businessmen, he was something of a businessman himself. He had been invited to make a carving for a block of flats near Baker Street and begun by disappointing the Directors of the building by turning up for his interview in an overcoat which effectively concealed his tunic. They had been all agog to meet a stonemason who dressed like a monk. When he was asked to cut down the cost he merely replied: 'Oh, certainly. You can just cut out a leaf here – that will be £10. A whole branch would cost you 25 guineas.' Appalled by this realism, they sent Eric out of the room and then, turning on the man who had introduced him, exclaimed: 'This isn't an artist at all; this is a businessman – and anyway he doesn't wear monks' clothes.' When he lectured Eric would ask for a stonemason's daily wage – about £2, one supposes – and first-class travelling expenses because he generally had proofs to correct in the train.

Or he might be worried by his work – the long hours of engraving which tired his eyesight, the repetitive formulas of tombstone lettering. He was inclined to be bored by the things he could do better than anyone else, and to hanker after imaginative projects which were rather beyond his reach. He had an immense admiration for the sculpture of Henry Moore, but he was never in the same class as Henry Moore, who belonged to a world of invention which was not really Eric's world at all. Eric was a twentieth-century medievalist, trying to work and live as if the Middle Ages had been miraculously prolonged – as if Descartes and Marx had never happened. This is why even his best work has a quality of arrested beauty, of intellectual denial. Yet, except in the matter of his later engravings, he had the exacting conscience of the perfect craftsman – a conscience which, at least on one occasion, earned its perfect reward. He had been carving a head of Christ and came into the living-room for tea looking, as he often did, extremely tired. After explaining his difficulties, he broke into a smile. 'Never mind,' he said shyly, 'He assured me that it was all right.'

Eric was not as strong as his energy tempted one to suppose. He needed a great deal of sleep, and if he had come back from London late the night before he would still be asleep at ten in the morning. If he were engraving he would talk or dictate letters at the same time, although he always wrote his articles or the notes for his lectures by hand. He did not in the least mind people coming into his workshop, provided they kept quiet; sometimes he would get them to chip away at a piece of stone. He was punctual for meals, and expected punctuality in other people. He was a gentle but inflexible patriarch. The girls had no formal education – they only knew what they had picked up from the successive *habitués* of the house, which was a good deal. They had also benefited from Eric's reading aloud to them. He was an emotional man under the surface of syllogism, and tears would come into his eyes at certain passages of *The Ballad of Reading Gaol*. But the girls were inclined to resent his pleasure in the company of young women like Prudence Pelham, whose minds had been more systematically cultivated. His attitude to women had the chivalry which feminism has gone far to banish from modern society; once, at Capel, he threw down his cloak to save Mrs Attwater from walking over a puddle. As we shall see later in a more serious context, Eric's simplicity could always inspire him to the *beau geste*.

Just as he preserved the traditional distinctions between men and women in the home, so he preserved them between master and apprentice in the workshop. His friends, and even his acquaintances, called him 'Eric', but to his apprentices he was always 'Mr Gill' – even when they were talking about him among themselves. He wrote to René Hague, before Hague's marriage to Joanna, to say that he would like them to stand in a master-apprentice relationship to each other, just as he himself always addressed Edward Johnston as 'master' to the end of his life. In guiding his apprentices he was infinitely patient. If a mistake had been made, it had to remain; there must be no faking or patching-up. Eric would tolerate nothing that was not true. He would say that 'a workman's bench should be like an altar', and that 'we should be like Almighty God, easy to please and hard to satisfy'. David Kindersley and Anthony Foster were his most distinguished pupils, each standing in a slightly different relationship to Pigotts and all it represented. Foster was a Catholic and Kindersley was not, although he very nearly became one. It was not easy to resist that harmony of faith and works. Eric himself never made the slightest effort to proselytize, although others were not always so discreet; but those who were not Catholic – Prudence Pelham and Douglas Cleverdon among them – could not help feeling a little outside the magic circle as Eric's indefatigable letters were dispatched to the *Catholic Herald*, and the dialectical Dominicans came and went.

Father Thomas Gilby celebrated Midnight Mass at Christmas 1932, and Father Bede Jarrett brought Brother Conrad Pepler over from Blackfriars. He was anxious that the rift between the two families should be more than formally healed, and Eric was present at Brother Conrad's ordination. Charles Burns brought Maritain down from London, and as Maritain spoke no English and Eric no French conversation was not easy. Eric made a slight face when Maritain remarked, on being shown the workroom: 'C'est tout comme au moyen age.' The last thing Eric wanted was to be thought of as a medievalist, even by a Thomist philosopher – and for the matter of that it was the last thing that Maritain would have wanted either.

Howard Coster arrived to photograph Eric and all his works; Diana Bourne, who afterwards married Oliver Lodge, came to sit for him and he found her marvellous to draw; Cicely Marchant, his agent, with whom he often stayed in Abbey Road; Desmond and Margaret Flower. Desmond was in proud possession of a stone carving of Eric's – head and torso of a girl with a comb in her hair – given him by his father for his twenty-first birthday. It stands today, 18-inch high, in his garden at Dorking. Eric also designed his armorial bookplate and Desmond, who edited the *Book Collector's Quarterly*, published a review of *Art Nonsense* by D. H. Lawrence. 'I agree with practically all of it,' Eric wrote afterwards, 'I only hope it didn't spoil his last hours.'[1] It was not for nothing that when Eric carved the nude statue of a man he should have christened him 'Mellors'.[2]

Other visitors were Hubert Wellington from the Royal College of Art and his wife who had been a pupil of Edward Johnston; Walter Shewring, just down from Corpus Christi College, Oxford, who had won the Craven and the chancellor's Latin Prose Prize and was now winning scholarships for Ampleforth; Harman Grisewood; and a Russian physicist, Kapitza, from the Royal Society Mond Laboratory in Cambridge, where Eric had been carving a crocodile. 'Have you ever seen a real crocodile?' asked a lady who came upon him at work. 'Have you ever seen a brick crocodile?' he replied. There was a Mr Butlin who came to talk about phonetic spelling; and Eric's niece Evelyn Cox and his youngest sister Angela Skelton – 'Oh Angela, she's a darling,' always came spontaneously to his lips. Serge

[1] January 30, 1934.
[2] One of the two principal characters in *Lady Chatterley's Lover*.

Chermayev, a young architect, tried to interest him in an *Académie Européenne Méditerranée* which he and others were hoping to found at Le Lavandou – Erik Mendelssohn was to teach architecture, Chermayev interior decoration, Zadkin sculpture, and Eric typography and lettering. For a time Donald Attwater acted as secretary for the organization, and René Hague did the printing. But the scheme came to nothing. Eric's heart was not wholly in it, but that he should have interested himself in it at all shows how far Pigotts was becoming a jumping off ground for various departures. Eric was the most home-loving of men, but he could not afford to stay at home.

It was on Sunday mornings after Mass at High Wycombe that he found it easiest to relax. Then he would drop into the back parlour of a 'pub' and talk till lunch time; sometimes Herbert Read would join them, and such cares as he had were shuffled off in a happy symposium. He was too busy to take part in local activities, but he was interested in everything. He did not know the meaning of boredom. And in the evening he would soothe his nerves with music, playing on the clavichord and vocalizing in his small, pure voice – so small that when he was lecturing in a large hall people found him difficult to hear. It may be true, as Walter Shewring has suggested, that Eric's admiraion for Beethoven was 'tempered with the proper reserves', but he was present at all the concerts in the Queen's Hall at which Schnabel played through the sonatas. And in a rather severe criticism of Charles Morgan's *The Fountain* he could admit that the novel was 'like a Wagner opera and jolly good in parts'.[1] Eric was still fond of exercise when he had time for it – swimming and bowls – and he particularly enjoyed playing deck tennis with Robert Gibbings. He would throw the ring with great velocity and then Gibbings, who was twice Eric's size, would lob it craftily over the net. But perhaps the secret of Eric's equilibrium, apart from a contemplative life about which he was too humble to speak, was the fact that this man who was so passionately eager to set the world to rights virtually never read the newspapers, although he picked up a good deal of what other people had read in them. An occasional glance at the *Evening*

[1] Letter to Prudence Maufe, October 23, 1932.

Standard in the train; a flip through *The Observer*; an impatient look at *The Tablet*;[1] and a close scrutiny of the *Catholic Herald* to see what the correspondence columns demanded of him in reply – that was about all. This gave him a certain detachment. You would find him in the evening in front of a log fire in the large inglenook, sitting back in a big armchair of shiny brown leather. He had bought two or three of these, just as he had bought a magnificent bath of black marble long before there was any hot water to put in it. He would be rolling his cigarettes of rather strong fine shag under the small statuette by Henry Moore and David Jones's portrait of Petra. But while the First World War had passed over his head except when it touched him with personal loss, the commencing agony of Europe could not leave him for long undisturbed. He was soon to become desperately *engagé*.

[1] This was still under the bigoted editorship of Ernest Oldmeadow.

5

On January 30, 1933, Eric was invited to lunch by the Directors of the London Midland and Scottish Railway who commissioned him to design some bas-relief panels for the lounge of their hotel at Morecambe. These represented the story of Nausica and Ulysses, and underneath was an inscription: 'There is hope that thou may'st yet see thy friends.' Nausica and Ulysses are seen on the right of the wall – Ulysses bearded, with the branch of a tree, and clasping Nausica by the hand. They stand among trees, while three girls offer them a cloth, bread and fruit. The work is not one of Eric's best, but it is representative of the commissions which now came his way. It was afterwards reproduced on the menu cards of the LMS. Big industry wanted the best ornament, and they demanded it from their bitterest foe. But the foe, as we have seen, was also a man of business and he gave to business rather more than it deserved. The job involved several journeys to the north, when he stayed near by at Garstang with the sister of Father John-Baptist Reeves, O.P. Oliver Hill, the architect of the Morecambe Hotel, was also a friend, and it was no doubt through him that Eric had been given the commission. The granite cement with which the outside of the hotel was plastered later came out in small cracks, and Eric wondered if this would let in the wet. He didn't mind if it did, but it was 'interesting to watch the behaviour of these patent materials'.

His visits to Morecambe were combined with visits to Manchester, where he was carving the patron saints of the cathedral over the porch of the new choir school. Eric had no particular love for a city which had given its name to the gospel of industrial capitalism. He gave his views, over a cup of coffee, to a reporter on the *Evening Chronicle*. The Gothic Town Hall was 'just mad', and what was the point of 250 columns to give unnecessary support to the Central Library? Nor did Liverpool escape his strictures. Lutyens' 'sham classical Italian' design for the Catholic cathedral was no less grotesque than Gilbert Scott's soaring Gothic a few hundred yards away. Manchester was busy pulling down the statue of Oliver Cromwell; Eric was the last person to think this a bad thing, but he thought that Manchester would be better employed in pulling down its streets and planning them afresh. 'Let them build streets like they built the Forth Bridge, a noble structure. Of course there is the question of money, but we must insist on financial and banking reforms which will release money for these schemes.'

It was many years since Orage and Mairet had introduced Eric to the currency reforms of *The New Age*, later to become *The New English Weekly*. Here he was in good company, for no other weekly periodical of the time was either so serious or so sane. Neither so respectable as *The Spectator* nor so sectarian as *The Tablet*, and far more fundamental than the *New Statesman*, it tried at least to find a viable *tertium quid* between the crudities of Communism or Fascism, and the chaos of a qualified *laissez faire*. The theories of Social Credit were too technical to have a wide appeal and too debatable to win substantial assent; but they tackled the problem where Eric now believed it must be tackled, not at the political but at the economic level. He was indifferent to the privileges of Parliaments, and he would have hardly known what you meant by the Rights of Man. He still cherished the notion that the King should not only reign but rule. So it was not by chance that he insisted to a Manchester journalist on the necessity for 'financial and banking reforms' which would have purposes far more important than improving the face of Manchester. And it was to the Link Society in Manchester that he delivered the lecture afterwards published under the title of *Money and Morals*.[1]

This book, by very reason of its impetuous brevity, introduces the Eric Gill of the later years with what can only be described as a bang. He is not only concerned but angry, not only didactic but impatient. He is a man writing in a hurry; a man who feels that he has not much time and that the world has not much time either. A critic

[1] Faber & Faber, 1934.

in the *Sunday Times* had once compared Eric's style to a cross between Euclid's axioms and the Athanasian Creed, but here it was considerably unbuttoned. The title of the book was taken from a letter of the Bishop of Salford to a friend: 'Money and morals! Personally I have not much of the former, but the latter cause me a great amount of trouble.' Eric was not concerned – as no doubt the bishop had been concerned – with the connection between morals and mortal sin. That was the business – sometimes it seemed to be the only business – of bishops. Nevertheless the bishop took the chair for the lecture, wondering – rather understandably – what he was in for, and a vote of thanks was proposed and seconded by two priests, both of whom were called O'Connor.

Morals, in Eric's present definition of the term, were 'what people do', and he maintained that Christian morals presupposed natural morals, just as Christian faith presupposed certain ways of thinking. You could not hold, with the Hindu, that the universe was unreal and still remain a Christian – any more than you could hold with the Manichee that created matter was bad and still remain a Christian. Industrialism and Christianity could not both flourish at the same time and in the same place. The industrialist, as such, was 'like a modern army General – he only wants cannon fodder – factory "hands". He wishes to God he could escape concern with what they do out of factory hours. He destroys family life and finds himself compelled to provide brothels and lectures on Shakespeare.' All of which was a little hard on Lancashire cotton – but Eric was by now in no mood for understatement.

He was able, nevertheless, to quote Canon Barry as declaring in Leamington fifty years previously: 'Our interminable rows of tenement houses contain many men and women who are not really human, and it is folly to think of Christianizing what is not yet in any fair way of being Christianized': and Father Vincent McNabb as declaring in Glasgow the day before yesterday: 'The economic conditions of the people make abstention from the practice of birth control a matter of heroic virtue.' It was not a question, primarily, of bad tenements or bad landlords or even bad bankers. It was a question of 'bad economics', of 'artificial scarcity in a world of plenty'. He could point, readily enough, to the apples rotting in the orchards because no one would take them away, and the coffee thrown into the sea because no one would buy it, and the factories idle, and the ships laid up. He had been told of a bank in London where for three months the clerks worked overtime in order to adapt the books of the bank to a calculating machine which would render their future services unnecessary. They worked twice as hard as usual in order that they should soon be unable to work at all. These were the economics of Bedlam, and in face of them Eric compared the clergy to 'men standing on the brink of a frozen pond and shouting to men drowning under the ice that they should take good deep breaths if they want to be healthy'. The comparison was illustrated by the mordantly satiric line of Denis Tegetmeier; and Eric quoted twice over from Father (now Canon) Drinkwater, a courageous and revolutionary priest from the Birmingham archdiocese: 'the economic problem fills the whole sky; it is a monster swallowing everything else; nothing can be done, nothing, until the economic problem and the problem of money has been dealt with'.

To cut the argument even shorter than Eric cut it himself, the solution lay in the public control of credit. The service rendered by the banks was the creation of currency and no service could be more public than this. Eric claimed the authority of the financial adviser to the Treasury for asserting that if credit were so controlled there would be no need for any other taxation whatever. The profits earned by the banks were pure usury, for they were profits earned from money lent upon security without any risk. Where Shylock had merely lent the money he had in his bag, the banks lent what they had not got, for they created credit out of nothing – except, Eric might have added, the confidence of those who banked with them. He maintained that since the money held by the banks represented the wealth of the nation, there was no reason why pensions should be limited to the old, the disabled or the retired. Everyone had a right to them; everyone was a beggar. And he thought the Christian, and specifically Catholic, practice of giving money to beggars 'far from being economically unsound' was 'the soundest possible economic policy'.

Up to this point the more sophisticated contributors to the *New English Weekly* would have agreed with Eric, and he was only saying with a sharper emphasis what other Catholic sociologists, like Belloc and Chesterton – not to mention Mr Ezra Pound and Dr Hewlett Johnson – had been saying before him. But now he followed the Dean, not into his cloisters but into his controversies. He asked in whose interest Charles I had been beheaded, and George III written off as a simpleton? (Perhaps, after all, the removal of Cromwell's statue was a belated retort to the Whig historians.) And since there did 'not seem to be the remotest possibility of any modern nation deliberately doing away with machinery', and since 'the machine state' would obviously be 'the state of the immediate future, Communism naturally seems the only just politics . . . for the beehive state everybody seems to want' and 'no one is trying to prevent. . . . Keep machinery, and the consequent "big business" which machinery necessarily involves, and you must choose between Communism and Fascism. Fascism is the sort of state ownership favoured by the big industrialists. Communism is the sort of state ownership favoured by the "proletarians". I admit that between Communism and Fascism I'm all for Communism . . . it seems clear that justice is more likely to be achieved when ownership is vested in men as workmen rather than in men as men of business.' On the other hand he also admitted that the Russians were like 'schoolboys with Meccano' or young ladies with 'my new car'.[1]

All question of personal liberty, and also of economic efficiency, apart – for the second of these questions was begged and the first was not even considered – Eric fell into the classic socialist fallacy of failing to distinguish between the people and the political officers of the community. It might, or might not, be true that of all forms of human government 'plutocracy was the absolute worst'; that Christianity, in any vital sense, was as incompatible with capitalism as with Communism; and that 'we are back in the catacombs –

[1] Letter to *Time and Tide*, September 1, 1935.

whether we like it or not'. It was certainly true that 'nobility is above all things the necessary quality and proper mark of governors'. But it was much less clear that such nobility was the mark of those who had established and maintained the Soviet Union. While Eric knew all about principles, he knew much less about people, and nothing whatever about politicians.

Nevertheless his convictions about the public ordering of human affairs had now described their logical circle. He would have liked to draw it differently. The marginal Fabian of 1910 had become the marginal Communist of 1930. Like the orthodox Marxist, his ideal was not organization but anarchy; but it was a different kind of anarchy, inspired by a different kind of optimism. He leaned towards Communism because he was more logically, more integrally, spiritual. His deviation – to appropriate Communist terminology to Catholic use – would bring him into conflict with ecclesiastical authority as the Catholic Church, in one country after another, cemented its disastrous alliance with Fascism. It set him apart from men like Belloc and Chesterton and their numerous followers, who would have endorsed his diagnosis but contested his cure. For the first time, in his polemical writing, a note of shrillness can be heard which reflects the exasperation of his solitude. Eric Gill, now in his early fifties, was no longer a young man, but he was very angry indeed.

A small book might be written on the disagreement provoked by *Money and Morals* among those who were Eric's closest allies. Father John-Baptist Reeves, in the *Catholic Herald*, challenged his thesis that Christian morality was exceedingly difficult, if not impossible, under existing economic conditions; and that the responsibility for the moral failure of Christians rested with the Catholic clergy. The clergy were always found to be saviours of society when they preached the Gospel, however unintelligently they did so; and that the reform of a system which everyone agreed to be wrong was the layman's business, not the priest's. Grace could operate upon any nature, human or angelic; there were no conditions of mental health for its efficacy. Sin was a personal, not a social evil. 'Who are the sinners of our time? Are they not Mr Gill, and myself, and you, dear reader? If the present economic order is sinful, and if we want to reform it, let Mr Gill and you and me go and show ourselves to the priests.' Another Dominican, Father Ferdinand Valentine, argued in *Blackfriars* that Catholics had lost the capacity either to fast or to pray; asceticism was reserved for athletics, and although there was nothing wrong in the conveniences of modern life, men had lost the power of renouncing them. The writer agreed with Maritain that 'if an almighty love really changed our hearts, the external task would already be half accomplished'.

W. G. Peck in the *Criterion* pointed out that Eric the social reformer was unwittingly at odds with Eric the artist. It was true that if we looked after consumption production would look after itself; and the whole of Eric's attack upon the banks implied that they were 'systematically translating into financial poverty the factual wealth secured by machine technology, *which men ought to enjoy*'. But the artist in Eric here stepped in to maintain that men had no right to enjoy it, and he refused to consider how the spirit of man was 'to master the machine process and employ it for the liberation of mankind'. The machine was an honest product of the human reason which had always been pronounced honourable by the theological authority to which Eric appealed. If he could not explain why the machine was of intellectually evil root, he should 'address himself to the hard problem of establishing an alliance between the reality of mechanical device and the reality of artistic hunger in the soul of man'. *The New English Weekly* argued that the machine was as good as it was used; and the Press comment reached a pinnacle of comic relief with a criticism of Denis Tegetmeier's illustrations on the grounds that there was 'no excuse for hurting anyone's feelings'. Two letters from close personal friends put the point of view of common sense, or what Eric would have regarded as close to common insanity. They indicate the isolation in which he was now increasingly to move. The first was from Tom Burns:

. . .What we have to bother about is not so much *that* the present thing is awry, but *how*, in detail, it is wrong and to be righted. I don't believe there's a gang of arch-crooks who know it's wrong and want to keep it so for their gain; man in so far as he is an economist is a bewildered little creature constantly upset by the interruptions of man . . . as a creature of lust, or pride, or avarice, or imagination working outside the practical order, or love or race or climate or colour. . . . I believe that insecurity, wars, injustices of all sorts are his chronic condition – and as the remote cause of all *that* I posit the consequences of the Fall! There will never be plenty so long as there is jealousy, and there will ever be jealousy. I don't agree with the clean-sweepiness of your paper. A certain security, an absence of squalor is the best that can be hoped for; a thing built up slowly from trading, as it always has been, but on world trading as it now must be, hence on international lending – I see no way out of it so long as there are seven million people in a few square miles of England who need shirts and skirts, acres of cotton fields in Japan to provide the stuff, if it can be got in, if the crop can be sown, if the sowers can be fed, if the shirt-weavers can feed them in expectation of their shirts, if the shirt-wearer can lend the cash. And if in the cotton mills there are men who are now turned into factory hands and to that extent dehumanized it is only a (presumably) transitory imperfection of the machinery which requires the semi-mechanical hand-picking and putting the stuff about; soon the machine will do that, and the 'hand' will need to be an engineer, a most responsible person. Georgian machinery – can you imagine how our grandchildren will jibe at it? (December 12, 1933)

Burns went on to argue that since the profits of the banks went in wages, salaries and shares – that is to say to the consumer – why should the consumer complain? That man was responsible for his deliberate intentions, not for the consequence, often unforeseen, of his acts; that it was not only foreign investments that brought in foreign goods – Argentine beef was exchanged for British steel; and that Eric could not be a credit reformer and a Communist at the same time.

The second letter was from Louis Bussell who was rather closer to Eric's standpoint on these questions than Burns. It was not provoked immediately by *Money and Morals*, but by a subsequent paper in which a number of the same arguments had been propounded:

I do not agree with the line you take about the future and the beehive economy, either on *a priori* grounds or from observation. I feel more and more that the difference between the machine and the tool has become a barren controversy. Since machines (in the modern sense) have only been used in the service of usury . . . the purely repetitive aspect has been overemphasized. It is extremely difficult *now* to see what development machinery would have undergone if it had been approached from a human angle (e.g. alloys, airships, submarines, and properties of electricity would sooner or later have been discovered by the natural activity of the human mind). And so with factories. It is not in the nature of machines to be housed in large quantities together. It was usury which regimented people to save time and 'inefficiency'. An electric motor can be the size of a toy or a tool and as easily controlled and manipulated. Power can be manufactured without servile labour (flowing rivers) and decentralized, and industry with it. (This is already happening.) The machine cannot under these circumstances be said to deprive anyone of responsibility. Nor do I see anything in the nature of the machine which makes for the present ungodly division between land, labour, capital, profit. In fact all these divisions were well in force before the Industrial Revolution. The machine was used (or rather prostituted) to perpetuate this division. . . . Past civilizations have often combined with craftsmanship and 'natural' living a large amount of real bestial drudgery and an ever present fear of famine, drought and pestilence. Such conditions were as hostile to the contemplative life as the sub-human conditions of today. I feel very much therefore that a norm has still to be worked out in the light of the Incarnation. I doubt very much whether it could be found in history. (October 21, 1934)

While all of Eric's friends agreed with him about morals and most of them about money, many of them differed from him about machines.

On May 25, 1933, Eric was at Brighton for his father's funeral. They had never been very close; Eric's Catholicism, his challenge to the accepted values of his time, and also his mounting prestige had created a certain barrier. Max was also at the funeral, and Mr Gill had often been heard to complain: 'Why can't Eric be an ordinary boy like Max?' – though Max himself was far from ordinary. Nevertheless Eric was very much the son of his father. He would have hated to hear himself described as a Victorian born out of the time, but where Mr Gill had in some ways illustrated Douglas Jerrold's aphorism that 'the character of the Victorians was immense, but their thought was impotent', Eric had corrected the thought but maintained the character. If Mr Gill had read of his son's attendance at the Dress Reform Revel at the Suffolk Street Galleries on June 22, he might have had mixed feelings. Beside a clergyman in kilt and clerical collar, and a youth in a pink bow tie, Eric seemed perfectly at ease 'as if he were a member of one of the more severely disciplined monastic orders'.[1] All things considered, perhaps a layman in a cowl was better than a clergyman in a kilt.

[1] *Manchester Guardian*, June 23, 1934.

6

Rather strangely, Eric lacked the curiosity of the born traveller. When he did travel he kept his eyes open, and the vision of Chartres was a kind of sacrament which sustained him all through his life. But he was not Baedeker-minded; he had no gift for languages and not much taste for landscape. Nevertheless it was travel which brought him the principal inspiration of his later years. If Chartres had been a sacrament, Palestine was a viaticum.

In the autumn of 1933 he was invited by Austen St Barbe Harrison, the architect of the Palestine Archaeological Museum in Jerusalem, to carve ten small panels for the outside wall. George Horsfield, an archaeologist who had been the second excavator of Jericho and of Meroe in the Sudan, came down to Pigotts for Eric to pick his brains; and as a result of these conversations, and of suggestions from Harrison, Eric had completed his designs early in the new year. On February 2 he was writing to Harrison:

Herewith I am sending you designs for the ten carved panels. I hope you will approve of them. The sketches are very rough, but you will see the idea in each. I have borne in mind the general notion that the idea is to symbolize the nations that have had a cultural influence on Palestine. Therefore I have tried to make designs which shall symbolize not merely each nation but the cultural influence for which each nation is responsible. I hope I haven't made any bad mistakes or made designs which will give offence to any party. The Persians are the only ones I don't get clearly. I understand that though conquerors of the country they were a pretty tolerant lot and did not bring much but their religious practices which no one else brought. So the flying bull and the sun seem appropriate enough.

You will see that I have as far as possible used all the symbols you suggested. But as the panels are very small and it is important to keep all the carvings more or less in the same scale I have introduced some variations from your scheme. For example you suggested galleys for Phoenicia and a head of Alexander for Greece. It seemed to me that the latter (a head occupying the same size of panel as the galley) would be out of scale. So I thought a whole figure would be better than just a head for the Greeks. Moreover, as I was attempting to symbolize the culture more than to make merely a symbol of the nation, I thought that the figure representing the Athlete would be appropriate. Athleticism is not necessarily humanism but, on the other hand, there is a pretty close connection. For athleticism does imply a certain detachment from mere aggressiveness (whether the aggressiveness be religious, political or warlike) and detachment from commercialism or any other kind of frenzy is a note of humanism.

Of course I'm going to give myself a lot more work by choosing this sort of thing instead of mere heraldic symbols, but this only applies to a few of the panels. You yourself suggested Romulus and Remus and the wolf and the Phoenician galleys and Constantine and Helena and my scheme simply carries through the same sort of things. . . . I hope there will not be too much criticism on archaeological lines – the exact shape of a Phoenician galley or a crusader's helmet. I'll go to the British Museum and the V. & A. this week but I'm sending these sketches without delay so that you may see what I propose and, as I hope, pass them in a general way.

There was, in fact, plenty of criticism from the learned, but this was circumvented and the designs were finally approved as follows:

1. For Canaan: Man and Wheatsheaf.
2. For Egypt: Pharoe with rider.
3. For Phoenicia: Men in galley.
4. For Persia: Winged Bull and Sun.
5. For Israel: Moses and the Law.
6. For Greece: Man as Athlete.
7. For Rome: Romulus and Remus and Wolf.
8. For Byzantium: Constantine and Helena and the Cross.
9. For Islam: The Prophet on a Flying Horse with the Koran.
10. For the Crusades: Crusader kneeling before a Cross on an altar.

The Hoptonwood stones were sent off on February 3, and on March 10 Eric left Tilbury with Laurie Cribb on the S.S. *Rajputana*, travelling in the second class. Eric was soon deep in Dorothy Sayers' *Nine Tailors* and a comfortable armchair in the half-timbered smoke-room whence you passed into the Adam lounge. The first class into which he diffidently trespassed was Louis Quinze with real fires and real grates. The weather in the Bay of Biscay was bad, but not bad enough to prevent him writing letters to *Blackfriars* and the *New English Weekly*.

He was up on deck when the ship anchored off Tangier, but missed the view of Gibraltar as he rembered it from the picture books. In Marseilles he visited the reputed tombs of Martha and Lazarus, lunched in the Cannebière, and walked down to the Vieux Port.

Lovely, marvellous grand huge basin filled with shipping – small trading ships of all sorts, tiny sailing ships and steamers, and grand pleasure yachts and barges and small boats – surrounded by high old houses and narrow deep clefts of streets with washing hanging from houses to houses opposite. The city rising up the hills all round, and on the east on its high rock the ghastly but so well situated as to be domineering, and therefore very impressive church of N.D. de la Garde. . . . we climbed the high hill and went and put up large and white, too white, candles at the shrine for you and you, and you and you and you and all of you, and looked at the naïve pictures on the walls – some very good pictures indeed of ships and families having visions of Our Lady while they prayed for their husbands, sons, lovers and brothers at sea; popular pictures painted locally by people who knew not art but merely practised it – like old douanier Rousseau, only no one brought them up. . . . Do they tell us that Marseilles is one of the most lovely cities in the world? Well, why don't they?[1]

On the next lap to Port Said Eric was able to sit out on deck in Father John O'Connor's old panama hat. They passed Stromboli in the early afternoon – 'the smoke curls and drifts out into the sky, eddies and twists and flutters and yet comes steadily out like a slow-motion picture of a factory chimney'; and later as Eric sat in the stern of the ship while the sun went down, reading Coomaraswamy's book on the transformation of nature in art, the transformations of history were vividly present to his mind:

Rome . . . Athens . . . Carthage . . . Palestine . . . who, happening to be alone in such a place and such peace and warmth would not be moved by the sudden consciousness of the abiding reality of the human thing? There,

[1] This and other extracts from Eric's letters home are taken from *Jerusalem Diary*, privately printed by Mary Gill after his death.

down over the horizon, not straight ahead like Euclid but over the round edge and down the hill of the world – how curious that is – there are Greece and all the islands – there Italy – there, looking over the same round sea, the Romans, the Greeks, the Phoenicians, the Normans sailed.

Two British administrators were aboard and Eric was surprised to discover that they had brains. One was an elderly Colonel and the younger a recent convert to Buchmanism; both were agreed in foretelling the passing of the British Raj. After disembarking at Port Said, Eric came up to Jerusalem by train, changing at Kantara and Lydda, and singing 'Jerusalem the Golden' in the railway carriage. It was 8 a.m. on the morning of March 22 as he wrote on his knee to Mary: 'The guard says "The house to the north on the hill is where Samson was born",' and 8.30 as he continued – 'Bright yellowish emerald green corn, young corn growing in the valley with the mountains grey all round. Bright blue sky, purple and mauve flowers in the rocks, two dark brown small cows. Flocks of black goats, carefully built stone walls dividing little plots, and people ploughing. Men building bridge. Almond trees in full bloom.' At 9.10 a.m. the train came to a halt at Battir; 'This is where David killed Goliath, it really is'; and it was 9.25 as he scribbled on: 'Going down now. . . . Twenty-five minutes from Jerusalem. . . . Malha. . . . Jerusalem is in sight.'

On arrival he breakfasted with Harrison in his house on the hill of Evil Counsel overlooking the city and divided from it by the valley of Jehinnom. Beyond were the Church of the Dormition and the Temple Area and the great mosque; and from the garden you could see the village of Siloam. After breakfast Eric went to the Museum; deposited his tools; and then settled in at St Etienne, the Dominican convent between the Damascus gate and the Anglican cathedral. Here the French Government supported a famous school of Biblical archaeology. The place was austere but comfortable, and the Fathers were extremely learned. With one of the most eminent, Père Vincent, Eric struck a warm friendship. The guests were housed and fed separately. Among them was a Jewish convert René Schwob –

the author of *Moi Juif Posthume* – whom Eric thought 'just one of the best people I have ever met'.

It was the Thursday in Passion Week – the very season of all the year to imbibe the genius of Jerusalem. Eric walked up to the Mount of Olives in the evening; went to Mass at the Church of the Holy Sepulchre; shopped in the bazaars of the Moslem quarter; and watched the camels browsing with their foals around the buried ruins of Jericho. On the evening of Maundy Thursday he went up again to Gethsemane, and on Good Friday followed the Via Crucis through the narrow streets from the Praetorian palace. On Holy Saturday he walked to Bethlehem in the morning and on Easter Sunday he was at the Jaffa gate to watch the procession of the men from Hebron. The next day he walked to the Pool of Siloam with Harrison, and on the Tuesday in Easter Week he began carving his first panel. Argument about archaeological detail had held him up, and none of the stones were in position; so work had to start in a make-shift shed near by. The weather was very hot to begin with but cooled after a few days, and when the wind was blowing from the west the evenings were quite cold. Eric wrote that 'my brown tunic was very nice in the hot spell but at present my Carmelite tunic is just right with Petra's silk vests and a pair of sandals I got in the bazaar'. Later he bought some material from Damascus – black with gold stripes – and had it made up into a *galebra*. This was the usual Arab dress. With the caphia – or head-cloth – and black agal to hold it in place, he was indistinguishable from any other Arab in Jerusalem.

Later in the same week he followed the services of the Greek Orthodox Easter with René Schwob. There were expeditions to the Monastery of St Saba in a secluded valley leading down from Jerusalem to the Dead Sea; and to Nablus, Tiberias and Mount Tabor. On the road to Nablus they stopped at the well where Christ had talked with the Woman of Samaria. Here there was a girl who let down a ring of candles so that you could see how deep it was, and when the ring touched the water there was a little splash and all the water was lit up with sparkling ripples. 'It is a very moving place,'

Eric wrote. 'It makes you weep and pray.' At Capharnaum he rowed on the lake and bathed in it; 'the water was lovely and warm – with cold streaks in it'; stayed at the Italian hospice on the Mount of Beatitudes; and visited the Church of the Annunciation at Nazareth. And so to Mount Tabor, where Christ was transfigured before the three apostles, and back to Jerusalem by way of a 'city called Naim'. Harrison had a little house at Ain Karem – the traditional birthplace of John the Baptist, and here Eric was his guest for a night or two. A photograph taken from behind the bars of a window shows him having just emerged from his bath.

In May he moved to the Austrian hospice. This was run by a Bishop, aristocratic in manners and outlook, who was shocked by Eric's apparent indifference to politics. In fact, as we shall see, he soon became obsessed by the political problems of Palestine. There was a further expedition to visit the Trappist monastery of Latroun, believed by some to be the Biblical Emmaus. René Schwob was staying there. They drank the Cistercian wine, and went on to Jerash where Horsfield was stationed as adviser to the Director of Antiquities in Jordan. Eric stayed with him for several days and discussed the inscription which he was later to carve on the tombstone of Horsfield's mother-in-law, Lady Conway of Allington. He also made a drawing of the Greek alphabet from the big inscription on Hadrian's arch. Gratitude for Horsfield's hospitality was marred by the memory of somewhat acrimonious debate:

I'm upset (Eric wrote) or, shall I say, scratched, by one or two of your remarks – little pebbles not too well rounded – thrown at me. Lack of charity, lack of humility, arrogance . . . and so forth. What worries me, gnaws at me, is that it's not argument to drag these things in so soon – argument is stoppered at the start. I'm reminded of similar occasions – years ago for I've quite given up saying a word nowadays when I meet them – with my three high church brothers. . . . Whenever I started what I thought was arguing with them I saw a sort of more-in-sorrow-than-in-anger look come over them and I knew it was useless – I should only be accused of uncharitableness or arrogance. . . . There is no doubt it's true – can anyone claim to be free from such things? – but it seems to me that these moral judgments ought not to be dragged in at all. (It's as if, two people boxing, one kept on saying to his opponent – 'don't lose your temper', or 'that blow was not given in kindness'. Of course boxers do gibe at one another but it's not boxing and it spoils boxing.) So we don't get any further, either morally or intellectually. The questions of right and wrong don't get touched. You sail off on a high horse of moral superiority and leave me grovelling in the mud of my sinfulness. You say I'm not humble. How can I not agree? Meanwhile the point of view I want to share with you is not shared, the things I want to say are not said. I am left miserable. I think we ought, as between more or less reasonable and friendly people, to assume charity and humility and freedom from prejudices (why, e.g., *assume* that I 'imbibed all the prejudices of English Catholics' when I was received into the Church?). However I'm only saying these things because you left me so jolly unsatisfied, in the lurch, and because it seems so unsatisfactory that discussions between your people and ours should always be thus frittered away in recrimination.[1] (May 27, 1934)

On the following day Eric was joined by David Jones, with whom argument never ran the risk of recrimination; Mary and Joanna arrived a few days later, and stayed with Eric at the Hospice. They watched the marriage dances in the streets at Bethany, and visited the same hallowed sites. These could not be visited too often. But if Eric was happier in Jerusalem than anywhere else, it was not because everything was right with Jerusalem. 'I can't begin to describe it,' he wrote to Graham Carey, 'there is a mad balance (preserved by British Government) between ancient and utter loveliness and mad bestial commercial enterprise – in fact they cancel out. There is also a mad confusion of religions, all worshipping and scrapping at the same shrines.'[2] (April 5, 1934.) It was not only the Christian sites that moved him; he thought the Haram museum 'the most beautiful place I have ever seen and the farthest removed from the Bank of England and all its devil worship, the most civilized, the most cultured, the most quiet and serene, the most spacious, the most spiritually pervaded place in the whole world'.[3] On the one hand were the British and the Jews trying to turn the Arabs into good Europeans.

[1] *Letters of Eric Gill*, 1947.
[2] ibid.
[3] *Autobiography*, 1940.

The water supply was clean and plentiful; malaria and ophthalmia were being successfully dealt with; banditry had been suppressed; and the work of the young Zionist colonies was not only admirable in itself but of great benefit to the Arabs. The Hebrew University and the Jewish hospitals and clinics were excellent. But on the other hand the cheap products of mass production were everywhere for sale, and the 'smart modern Jews' were 'building smart modern prostitution . . . and smart modern factories, and smart modern clothes'.

There was no doubt where Eric's sympathies lay, or where they would lie in the turbulent years ahead. 'Don't think I saw no bad in Palestine. There was bad everywhere. But the good was not yet dead. . . . Palestine was the last of the revelations vouchsafed to me. It confirmed and enfolded all the others. And it was a twofold revelation. In the Holy Land I saw a holy land indeed; I also saw, as it were eye to eye, the sweating face of Christ.'[1] As he wrote these words was he thinking of an incident recorded by David Jones?

It occurred near St Stephen's Gate which leads out from Jerusalem towards the Mount of Olives – I think it is part of the Via Dolorosa. As far as I can now recall we arranged to meet somewhere in that part of the Old City. As I went to my appointment with him I chanced to see him at the turn of a winding street where a beggar-woman sat, hoping for alms. She appeared to have either no hand or some affliction whereby her wrist looked to be no more than a swollen and livid stump. As I caught sight of him, Eric Gill was giving this woman the accustomed coin. He then leaned down and kissed the repellent and distended part, and, unconscious of my approach, moved away. He was wearing Arab dress, as was his custom during his stay in Palestine, so that he was a quite inconspicuous figure in the lanes of the Old City.[2]

Eric's stay was enriched by many who put themselves and their scholarship at his disposal. Ernest Richmond who had been an oriental secretary under the Samuel administration, disappeared on account of his sympathy with the Arabs, and later returned as first

[1] *Autobiography.*
[2] Material for a *Profile* of Eric Gill, British Broadcasting Corporation.

director of the Palestine Archaeological Museum; Dr Meyer, a delightful and learned Jew with a bushy black beard and a specialist in Islamic art, who had written a book on Moslem heraldry; Dr Marcus Reiner, an Austrian Jew and one of Harrison's principal assistants; the Arab Christian guide from the Church of the Holy Sepulchre, who took Eric to his house and introduced him to his family – the tiny grandchild who kissed his hand and touched it with her forehead, and the sisters who brought in the coffee in tiny cups on a painted china tray; Roy Spicer who came from Ceylon to reform the Palestine police and insisted on their posts being built without bars because – as he incredibly assured Harrison – 'Police are *never* on the defensive.'

On the night before he left Jerusalem Eric was entertained to dinner by Sir Arthur Wauchope, the British High Commissioner, for whom he designed an Arabic script for Monotype machines. He was prepared to dislike any proconsul, and this one in particular, but he thought him 'really ready to be decent and not unintelligent'.[1] Wauchope's secretary, Thomas Hodgkin, became a close friend of Eric; and the breakfast table at Government House was enlivened for some weeks to come by arguments about whether Beauty could really be left to Look after Herself. Eric was reasonably pleased with the ten panels but 'miserable' about the figure of 'Man' on the main door. 'I was ill when I finished it. It shows.'[2] In fact his return journey was ruined by agonizing toothache caused by an abscess in the jaw. Dental aid was not available, and he arrived home 'quite unnerved' after 'an excruciating scraping operation'. News came to them at sea that Petra had given birth to a baby boy.

[1] Letter to Austen Harrison, August 23, 1934.
[2] Letter to Austen Harrison, August 17, 1934.

7

Eric's homecoming would have been a happy one if this had been the only news in the family; but he learnt at the same time that David Pepler was seriously ill. He was brought to Pigotts from Ditchling and then taken to Oxford by Hilary and Father Conrad. He died four weeks later. The body was brought back to Pigotts where Eric made a drawing of the dead face and carved a crucifix for the coffin. Afterwards he accompanied Mary and Betty to Ditchling for the funeral. A Requiem was sung in the Guild Chapel, and David's body was carried to the churchyard on a wain drawn by two of his own horses. This was the first time that Eric had been to Ditchling since he had left it; and it was a saddening thought that he and Hilary – but for a single formal encounter in a solicitor's office – should only have met at David's marriage and David's funeral. Long memories – now drained of much of their bitterness – were in the minds of them all as they sat down to lunch at the *Bull*, and as Eric caught sight once again, as they came back from the churchyard, of the chalk dust on the hedges.

Three days later he was at a very different gathering. This has been described by a clerical wit as the Laxton Synod. The Dominican Fathers in charge of the school at Laxton, near Kettering, had invited a number of Catholics for two days of discussion on every subject under the sun. Dr (now Archbishop) Mathew and his brother Gervase were there, with Father John-Baptist Reeves and, among the laity, Tom Burns, Mr Evelyn Waugh, and the present writer. We slept in a dormitory, where Mr Waugh was surprised – not to say affronted – by the night-wear affected by Eric and René Hague. Father John-Baptist tried to prove, by no means to the general satisfaction, that the cinema would be inconceivable in a fully Christian society; and Dr Mathew cautioned the editor of *Colosseum* not to be quite so grim. It was a happy symposium, productive of nothing beyond itself.

On September 18 Betty, with her children, animals and furniture, moved to Pigotts, and these all added to Eric's responsibilities. Hilary and his son Mark came for the night on October 31. It was a busy autumn with lectures at Halifax (on 'Phonography'), Carlisle, Newcastle and University College, Bangor. Eric stayed with Christopher Dawson at Hartlington Hall in Yorkshire, where he was carving a crucifix. He was also at Croydon at work on a carving for St Andrew's Boys Club. Opportunities were taken to see *The Playboy of the Western World* at the Croydon Repertory theatre and the Oxford and Cambridge match at Twickenham. Early in the New Year he paid a fleeting visit to Capel-y-ffin, where Betty was shortly to set up a school with Miss Reeves; and then went on to Bradford where John O'Connor had commissioned a statue of St John Bosco, and where Eric was careful not to miss the pantomime. In London he was working on the sculptures for Dorset House, and in his spare time designing a badge for postmen.

On January 24, 1935, Mr C. L. Stocks, a Commissioner of Crown Lands and a friend of Eric, received a letter from the Commissioner's representative, F. J. Root – acting on behalf of the Foreign Office. He was asked to approach Eric on the question of a sculptured panel for the front of the terrace on the lake side of the Assembly Hall of the new League of Nations building at Geneva. A drawing and photograph were enclosed to show the size of the panel and its relation to the main façade of the Assembly Hall. The proposal was only tentative. The carving would be the gift of the British Government and had to be approved by one of the architects of the building, M. Lefévre, who had been responsible for recent improvements at the Louvre. Stocks had already suggested a carving of Christ's rebuke to Peter: 'Put up thy sword', or of the Good Samaritan with the words 'Who is my neighbour?', as possible subjects; but the Commission felt that it might be unsuitable to have specifically Christian symbols for a building where people of every nation would gather. It was best to think of the League and its new building as 'the biggest attempt yet made in history to organize peace and remove the causes of war'. The shape of the panel and its position in relation to the severe lines of the building seemed to indicate a 'processional' treatment like the Byzantine mosaics in Sant Appollinare at Ravenna. Perhaps a procession of the nations leading to a figure representing Peace, like Lorenzetti's 'good government' fresco in the Palazzo Publico in Siena, or a central group representing 'Peace, Justice and Prudence' with figures in procession converging from either side? But Eric was invited to make his own suggestions as to subject and materials and, if his reply were favourable, the Government would immediately consult the authorities concerned. 'You will know better than I,' the letter concluded, 'how difficult the Treasury have found it to agree to this proposal at all.'

Eric was immediately interested and had an interview with Stocks at the Crown Lands office on January 30. As a result of this Stocks wrote to Root:

I have seen Eric Gill today. He is delighted to accept the proposed work. He is a very ardent pacifist and he will throw himself whole-heartedly into the job. . . . He is inclined himself to choose the large exterior panel, but he will make up his mind when he gets out to Geneva. If that alternative is chosen the size of the job will be six times that of the frieze which he did at Leeds, for which he was paid £1,000. He says, however, that he can arrange to do the present commission for £3,000 including expenses. As regards the theme, he would *very much* prefer my New Testament suggestions (though they were made without reference to him originally), but he understands the difficulties explained in your note, and if necessary he will turn to a non-Christian theme. He hopes, however, to have a chance of discussing the question of theme with M. Avenol, in which case he will represent to him that all artists, whether Christian, Buddhist or Mohammedan, can only do their best work in their own natural medium; and that if each culture is to make its artistic contribution to the League Building in a vague, non-committal, World medium, the result can only be mediocre; and therefore the League would be wisest to invite specifically Christian, Buddhist and Mohammedan presentations, respectively, of the cause of Peace, and can do that without offending any of the three religions. I suggest that we leave Gill to discuss this matter with M. Avenol and others at Geneva, and wait and see what emerges. (January 30, 1935)

Eric went out to Geneva on March 22; attended a lunch party at the Secretary-General's; chose a site for the panel; and dined with Ronald Armstrong, the British Consul. On the following day he met the architect of the new building, and lunched with the head of the British delegation. In the evening there was a cocktail party at the Armstrongs and Eric astonished the fashionable women of Geneva by going down on his knees and exclaiming, 'I thank God for this beautiful gin!' He returned to Geneva in April when he met Lord Vansittart and Lord Cranborne; Vansittart was then head of the Foreign Office and Cranborne Minister of State for Foreign Affairs. The conversation turned not only on the projected sculpture for the League of Nations Building, but on the subject of Hell. Vansittart, as an agnostic, would have none of it; and Cranborne produced an Anglican theory, derived from Mr Gladstone, that perhaps Hell only lasted in each individual case for about 10,000 years. This might well seem long enough, but Eric was most indignant and insisted that eternal punishment was the least compliment Almighty God could pay to the creature he had made. Eric was formally commissioned to do the Geneva panels on April 27 (1935) subject to Parliament's approval of his fee. The conception of the design was described in a memorandum as follows:

The central panel of the sculpture represents the *re*-creation of man, which the League of Nations is assisting.

The hand of man touches the hand of God: the text at the top says: 'What is man, that Thou art mindful of Him?' and the answer in the big red letters is: 'He has created him in the image of God'.

Then, below, the English text enforces the idea, and it is suggested that the guide draws the attention of the visitor to the words where it says: 'Over again I feel Thy finger'. The whole idea is to enforce the fact that delegates and councils of the League are not here primarily to bargain with one another for oil concessions and so forth, but to remember that politics are made for man, and not man for politics.

On the left-hand side, the panel represents the response of the human race to the idea figured in the central panel; and the words of the Latin text say: 'We are His people and the sheep of His pasture'.

On the right-hand panel, the whole created world is symbolized –

animals and trees, and electricity and machines, and the text says: 'He has placed him over all his works'.

So that, in summing up, it might be said that the left-hand panel represents man's gifts to God (that is ourselves, as we have nothing else to give); and the right-hand panel shows God's gifts to man, that is the whole created world.

The execution of the work, however, was subject to interminable delays; in December of the same year Eric was writing to Harrison:

Nothing further has transpired yet about the sculpture job at Geneva. I suppose they're too utterly flummoxed by international politics to bother about such things. I wonder if the whole thing will be turned down. I shall be sorry. I made designs and I was given to understand by Eden that they met with more or less general approval of the British authorities, and the only delay was caused by the necessity of getting official approval at Geneva. It will be a fine affair if it comes off. The central notion is a great big figure of a man – MAN (you know the chap – the chap all the fuss is about) – the notion being that it is not property (land, money, possessions, places in the sun, raw materials and what not) that the L. of N. is really, truly and properly concerned with, but man himself – it is man himself who is being destroyed by modern politics, industrialism, and finance. (December 22, 1935)

But on March 13, 1936, he was able to write again:

The Geneva carving is at last decided and only yesterday I was up discussing the terms of the contract with the financial people at the Foreign Office. The work has got to be done by April 1, 1938. I don't think this will be difficult. The only snag is that I have got to undertake the carriage from here to Geneva and fixing there, and I have no idea what Swiss workmen are likely to charge. All I know is that when I was there visiting they told me 'Lyons 7d tea costs 10s 6d in Geneva'. That's how they rob you, these neutral Swiss.

The contract was signed on May 14, and Eric's only doubt – a very reasonable doubt – was whether the League of Nations would still be in existence by the time the work was finished. But, as he suggested in a subsequent letter to Harrison, the sculpture 'might be anywhere – the fact that it is going to Geneva is just the irony of things';[1] and later again – 'I'm not thinking much about its propaganda value – that's the Lord God's little affair . . . pathetically enough, the contract is between me and King Edward VIII.'[2] Eric had bitterly endorsed an editorial in the *Catholic Times* on the Abdication crisis:

. . . the gist being that the powers of money behind the Cabinet puppets had fomented and taken advantage of the Spencer-Simpson affair to drive the King, the annoying King, the King who (almost for the first time since Charles I) dared to show a sign of independence and disillusionment, to drive him from the throne. They knew he could, had he but one or two able friends to help, get the whole common people of England behind him. He really did threaten their whole show – their whole damned hypocritical finance-ridden show. They beat him! He was only one semi-educated man against all their entrenched powers and vested interests.[3]

But Edward VIII had not many friends to help, and the voice of the common people – about whom Eric did not know a great deal – was expressed by the charwoman who exclaimed: 'If 'e marries 'er, the state of matrimony in this country will be no oil painting.'[4] Few, besides the editors of *The Tablet* and the *Catholic Times*, and Mr Compton Mackenzie, had discerned the profile of Whiggery in Mr Baldwin's pipe and the mitre of Dr Cosmo Gordon Lang.

The central panel of the Geneva sculpture, about thirty-feet by eight, was finished and fixed in place by March 1938, and the smaller side panels by August of the same year. The inscription read: *Quid est homo, quod memor es ejus? Ad imaginem Dei creavit illum*: and underneath, because it was an English gift, were incised the following words from Hopkins' *Wreck of the Deutschland*: 'God mastering me, giver of breath and bread, world's strand sway of the sea, Lord of living and dead, over again I feel thy finger and find thee.' This was the last considerable work that Eric carved for a public building, and

[1] June 26, 1936.
[2] December 16, 1936.
[3] Letter to Austen Harrison, December 16, 1936.
[4] To the present writer.

Drawing of St Mary for a window at Talbot Heath School, Bournemouth, 1935.

much the best. Even now, when the League of Nations has taken its place among the failures of the past, it is at once an eloquent explanation of its failure and a reminder of the only secure basis on which any such association can be built. Comparisons were naturally made with Michelangelo's painting in the Sistine Chapel; but then Michelangelo was not called upon to spare the feelings of those who did not profess the Christian religion, or who did not profess any religion at all. Eric had been remarkably successful in conceiving and carrying out a work of art in harmony with modern aesthetics and not too deliberately offensive to modern agnosticism. It was all that could be expected of him in an age of unbelief. 'They think I'm a prophet and seer,' he wrote to his brother Cecil, 'but they don't believe in my prophecies.'[1]

In the meantime other work of lesser importance had been claiming him. A coat of arms for Bentalls' multiple store in Kingston-on-Thames – this was about as far as Eric went in shaking hands with Mammon – brought him into collision with the owner who claimed that he had 'turned a leopard into a dog' and 'insulted' a family that went back to the sixteenth century. The fault was in the inaccurate

[1] April 15, 1935.

drawing of the coat-of-arms, and Eric replied that he would gladly turn the dog into a leopard if Bentalls would pay.

G. K. Chesterton died in December 1936. Eric had sparred with him about modern art, and Chesterton had written to assure him that he 'would much rather, apart from necessities, have a private controversy with you than a public controversy with most people'.[1] He also declared publicly that Eric was 'one of the greatest men alive'. On reading of Chesterton's death Eric wrote to his widow:

Nothing I can say can lessen your grief – or ours. I am unworthy even to praise him. For thirty years he was at the very core of our life. The war was holy because he was. We have lost, in a physical manner, the best man of our time. But I can't stop thinking of the joy in heaven – oh, that we were there. Every time I think of our grief and of yours – it suddenly seems absurd, is blotted out by the knowledge of that joy. I could laugh and dance to think of it. Of the thousands to whom he was an inspiration and whom he helped I had the inestimable and undeserved honour of his praise. No other reward could be so coveted among men. So I condone to share your joy as well as your sorrow. (June 16, 1936)

Eric was present at the Requiem Mass in Westminster Cathedral, and on the following day he and Mary supped with Frances Chesterton and John O'Connor at Top Meadow. His monument over Chesterton's grave – as fine a thing as he ever did in this kind – stands beside the Catholic church at Beaconsfield.

Not all of Eric's sculpture stands where it did. He was invited by Dr Nevile Gorton, headmaster of Blundells School, Tiverton, to help in the redesigning of the Chapel. The opportunity was important because it enabled him to experiment with certain ideas which he would realize, more radically, when he came to design the church at Gorleston-on-Sea. The chapel at Blundells was originally a small building to which an aisle had been added. The nave had also been considerably lengthened. This had the result of alienating the altar from the main body of the worshippers; and the result was deplorable whether you regarded the altar as a place for sacrifice or as a

[1] June 2, 1925.

table for communion. Remote and insignificant, the altar had become incidental even when it was not quite invisible. Instead of calling in an architect and hired labour, Dr Gorton called in Eric Gill, and the boys in the school worked under his direction. They first brought the altar nearer to the congregation and raised it so that it could be seen. Then they removed its excrescences and created a sense of space surrounding it. They took away the pews which crowded the chancel and raised the level of the chancel itself by creating a circular platform on which the altar was to stand. They also removed the panels from the apse, and the irrelevant pillars supporting the chancel roof, and blocked out three of the five windows in the apse. Eric designed a new altar of stone, with four panels in bas-relief to be designed, carved and coloured by the boys. A cross, also coloured, was suspended above it.

All this was in tune with a Liturgical Movement, which was essentially independent of doctrinal differences. Its aim was to bring the people into a closer participation with Christian worship, however that worship might be conceived. When Gorton was appointed Bishop of Coventry a number of people objected to the altar and in the face of much controversy it was removed. On a subsequent visit to the school Dr Gorton found it lying in a backyard and took it to Coventry. When the present writer inquired as to its present whereabouts he was told, not without embarrassment, that it was in a 'home for unmarried mothers'. A similar fate nearly befell the Madonna which Eric had carved for the Catholic church at Glastonbury. A newly arrived parish priest removed it and it was found lying in the back garden of a convent school next door, where the little girls amused themselves by chopping off the fingers of the hands. Fortunately it was discovered by a retired professor from Cambridge who placed it over his wife's grave in the local cemetery. On the other hand an Ivory Madonna, still proudly exhibited at St John's Abbey, Collegeville, Minnesota, is not by Eric at all. It was carved by Philip Hagreen.

In September 1936 Eric was ill with bronchitis, and for some weeks was in and out of bed. Even when he was in bed he was writing lectures on Sculpture on Modern Building and Art and Revolution, and he began the essay later published under the title of *It all goes together*. He struggled out to speak at a Peace meeting at the Kingsway Hall on Armistice Day, where he made the acquaintance of George Lansbury. But his cough got no better and he was mentally and physically exhausted. On December 5, therefore, he set out with Mary to stay with Desmond Chute at the Villa Raffaele in Rapallo. Christopher and Valerie Dawson were stopping at a pension near by, and Walter Shewring joined the party for Christmas. There were afternoon visits to Montallegro and to Chiavari where Eric ordered beer instead of wine, not realizing that beer was the more expensive drink; and walks up to the point at Portofino Vecchio whence you looked out to Genoa in one direction and to La Spezia in the other. One morning Desmond took Eric along the *lungomare* to the hotel where Ezra Pound was staying. Pound knew that Eric shared his own belief in monetary reform and inferred from this that he must be in favour of the Italian Fascist régime. Eric tried to interrupt the lecture to explain that he was nothing of the sort, but Pound was not an easy man to interrupt and he found Eric an unsatisfactory listener. At other times Olga Rudge would descend from Sant Ambrogio, the mountain above Rapallo. She was a sensitive violinist and, with Desmond Chute at the piano, played the Mozart and Pergolesi sonatas that Eric loved. This was the music of Paradise – its harmony grossly contradicted by the discord of a world that Eric was still struggling to put to rights. Early in the New Year he returned, now thoroughly rested, to resume the battle – pausing to visit Chartres and Le Mans, and the Sphinx dance hall in Paris where 'two nice girls'[1] engaged him in willing conversation.

[1] Diary.

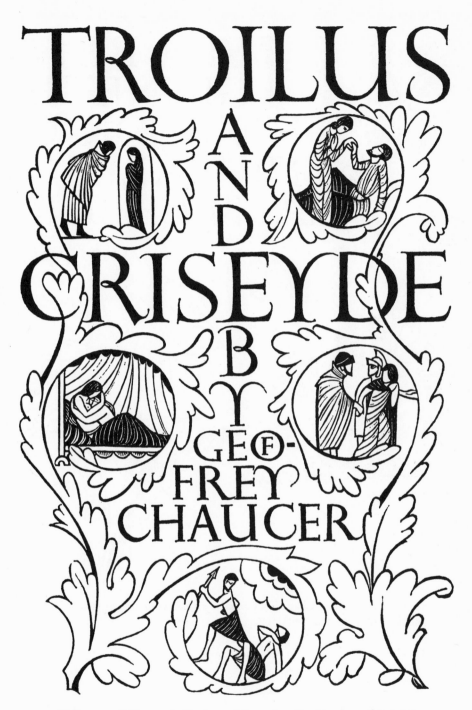

TROILUS AND CRISEYDE BY GEOFFREY CHAUCER

1. Title page of Chaucer's *Troilus and Criseyde*, edited by Arundell del Re, and printed and published in a limited edition by Robert Gibbings at the Golden Cockerel Press, 1927.

2. Opening page of Chaucer's *Canterbury Tales,* volume one, printed and published at the Golden Cockerel Press, 1929.

3. (*facing*) Page 31 from *The Canterbury Tales,* volume one.

As he that wys was and obedient
To kepe his forward by his free assent,
He seyde: 'Sin I shal biginne the game,
What, welcome be the cut, a Goddes name!
Now lat us ryde, and herkneth what I seye.'
And with that word we riden forth our weye;
And he bigan with right a mery chere
His tale anon, and seyde in this manere:

WHYLOM, as olde stories tellen us,
Ther was a duk that highte Theseus;
Of Athenes he was lord and governour,
And in his tyme swich a conquerour,
That gretter was ther noon under the sonne.
Ful many a riche contree hadde he wonne;
What with his wisdom and his chivalrye,
He conquered al the regne of Femenye,

What will ye that I shall do unto you? They say unto him,
Lord, that our eyes may be opened. So Jesus had compassion
on them, and touched their eyes: and immediately their
eyes received sight, and they followed him.

AND WHEN THEY DREW
NIGH UNTO JERUSALEM,
AND WERE COME
TO BETHPHAGE,
UNTO THE MOUNT
OF OLIVES, THEN SENT JESUS TWO DISCIPLES,
saying unto them, Go into the village over against you, and
straightway ye shall find an ass tied, and a colt with her:
loose them, and bring them unto me. And if any man say
ought unto you, ye shall say, The Lord hath need of them;

4. Opening words of Matthew xxi. from *The Four Gospels*, printed and
published at the Golden Cockerel Press, 1931, in a limited edition. The
type is Golden Cockerel Face in 18 point, designed by Eric Gill. The text
of the book was set up in type, leaving spaces to be filled by Gill with
decorated letters.

O HATEFUL harm! condicion of poverte!
With thurst, with cold, with hunger so confounded!
To asken help thee shameth in thyn herte;
If thou noon aske, with nede artow so wounded,
That verray nede unwrappeth al thy wounde hid!
Maugree thyn heed, thou most for indigence
Or stele, or begge, or borwe thy despence!

5. Page from *The Canterbury Tales*, volume two.

THE SOLDIERS OF THE GOVERNOR

6. Opening words of Matthew xxvii. 27 from *The Four Gospels*.

7 Title page of St John from *The Four Gospels*.

of Jesus, which said unto him, Before the cock crow, thou shalt deny me thrice. And he went out, and wept bitterly.

WHEN THE MORNING WAS COME, ALL THE CHIEF PRIESTS and elders of the people took counsel against Jesus to put him to death: And when they had bound him, they led him away, and delivered him to Pontius Pilate the governor.

8a. Opening words of Matthew xxvii. from *The Four Gospels*.

and prayed him that he would thrust out a little from the land. And he sat down and taught the people out of the ship. NOW when he had left speaking, he said unto Simon, Launch out into the deep, and let down your nets for a draught. And Simon answering said unto him, Master, we have toiled all the night, and have taken nothing: nevertheless at thy word I will let down the net. And when they had this done, they inclosed a great multitude of fishes: and their net brake. And they beckoned unto their partners, which were in the other ship, that they should come and help them. And they came, and filled both

8b. Engraving from Luke v. 3–7 from *The Four Gospels*.

8

His weapon was now the pen. In the five years between 1933 and
1938, which included the time that he was working on the Jerusalem
and Geneva carvings and did not exclude tireless lecturing and
public speaking, not to mention smaller works of stone-carving, Eric
wrote seven books of varying length. Of these *Money and Morals* has
already been discussed. Of the others *Beauty Looks after Herself*
(Sheed & Ward, 1933) and *The Necessity of Belief* (Faber, 1936) were
the most important. All of them said many of the same things.
Unemployment (Faber, 1933) and *Sculpture on Machine-Made Buildings*
(Birmingham School of Printing, 1937) were pamphlets; *Trousers*
(Faber, 1937) was a *jeu d'esprit*; *The Lord's Song* (1933) was a sermon.
Art and a Changing Civilization (The Bodley Head, 1934) was a contri-
bution to the *Twentieth-Century Library*, edited by Krishna Menon.
Work and Leisure (Faber, 1935) contained the three lectures given at
University College, Bangor; *Work and Property* was published by
Dent; *Unemployment* and *Work and Property* were both printed
by Hague and Gill, from types designed by Eric; the former from
Perpetua and Joanna, and the latter from Joanna. In 1934 Hague and
Gill had also printed *Engravings, 1928–33, by Eric Gill* (Faber). This,
the second of two iconographies, records 344 engravings, 110 of
which are reproduced. It was a remarkable output.

By now the world knew where Eric stood. *The Necessity of Belief*
was an attempt to explain why he stood where he did. The book
suffered from a lack of concentration – Eric could never resist chasing
his favourite hares – but it was written with an astonishing verve and,
at times, with a moving eloquence. More than any other of his
writings, except for the *Autobiography*, it proved his sheer literary
skill; a cogent style proceeding from a certain mind. Its method was
much more careful than the method of *Money and Morals*, and its conclusions less summary. The dialectical materialism of Moscow was

seen as a logical corollary to the practical materialism of Manchester, and perhaps preferable in the long run; but it was not seen as offering any satisfaction to the deeper desires of human nature. It was not true to say of human society that it was 'a hive in which the members develop individuality. They are individuals to start with, and they take on communal functions; they are not functional units which may or may not end up by developing individual idiosyncrasies. . . .' The Communists had –

thrown away the god whom the capitalists profess to worship and do not, and have accepted the servitude which capitalism has developed and perfected but whose existence capitalists deny. Thus they have not emptied out the baby with the bath water. They have retained the bath water while emptying out the baby. They have emptied out the Baby of Bethlehem only to swallow the foul and befouling bath water of London and Manchester.

In his explanation of the act of faith – to be distinguished from the act of certainty – Eric leaned heavily on Father Martin d'Arcy's classic *The Nature of Belief* where Newman's 'illative sense' had been further defined as the certitude arrived at as a result of converging testimony. For Eric the act of faith was 'to be regarded as the leap of beings capable of *seeing* the truth. A blind man can find his way home by means of a stick; men who are not blind can see their home from afar.'

Eric faced many of the difficulties which were obstacles to religious belief. To those who maintained the insignificance of man beside the immensity of the cosmos Eric insisted on the dignity of man beside the insignificance of the molecule. The telescope was a nobler instrument than the microscope, and it was not for nothing that astronomers were held in special respect. 'Take away your telescope and you know *less* about the moon as a moon. Take away your microscope and you know more about your knife as a knife' – for a knife was a thing to cut things with – neither more nor less. It was not a mathematical formula, however much it might be dissected. Christians might have been taught to grovel before their Creator, but at least they believed that their Creator died for their redemption. The materialist did not grovel before his Creator; he simply grovelled because grovelling was all that he could do. Here Eric underrated the complacency of modern materialism. The materialist seemed only too glad not to have to go down upon his knees. Man alone was important because there was no such thing as importance except in relation to persons – 'to beings who know and will and love'. In a word, to personality; and it was because the extinction of personality was inconceivable that belief in immortality imposed itself upon the mind; and because the complete man was body and spirit – 'both real and both good', as Eric never tired of repeating – that immortal man must be body and spirit also. The bodily resurrection of Jesus Christ might have seemed an irrelevant dogma when Eric sat with Father Anselm in the guest-room at Mont César; now the resurrection of the flesh seemed as certain as the immortality of the soul.

Eric appealed neither to science nor to philosophy – though he had picked up a number of useful hints from Father d'Arcy and the Angelic Doctor. He had submitted his MS. to Father Thomas Gilby, O.P., for correction – and one would like to know which of his Dominican friends he had once seen 'looking like a walking deck-chair in broad red and white striped pyjamas'. His appeal was to common sense. 'I am an ordinary person who refuses to be bamboozled.' Personality was not touched by science, and it was confirmed by consciousness. 'It is only by doing violence to our own minds that we can deny the facts of consciousness.' He next tackled the problem of evil, which he distinguished from the problem of pain. Physical pain was certainly unpleasant, but it illustrated the laws of Nature and was therefore a matter for rejoicing. 'Thank God, the milk will spill. How could I drink it otherwise?' Even death was not a moral evil, although it was the result of man's ill doing – 'the vast aboriginal calamity' which was Newman's definition of original sin. There was no longer any doubt that Eric believed in this; but he did not face the ultimate problem – why, if God were perfectly good, had He created man whose misuse of free will He must have foreseen? Eric would probably have answered that such misuse was inherently possible in any personality that was essentially free, and that was not God. The sufferings of the innocent were justified by the communal guilt of mankind. Man was an individual, to be sure, but he was not an isolated individual. He came into the world burdened with the legacy of his kind and left it enriched – or impoverished – by what he had done or left undone.

Such, in brief and summary outline, was Eric's apologia to a world 'entangled in a web of account keeping' – a world where there was 'double entry but hardly any exit'. Just as he had replied to those who had suspected him of not believing in sin outside the counting-house, so he replied to those who accused him of reducing Beauty to utility. On the contrary he saw the appetite for Beauty as nothing less than the appetite for God, and 'what we clumsily call "the aesthetic approach" as the approach for which man is by nature best fitted and by which he naturally enters into rest' – because 'the beauty of God "was" the cause of all being'. Eric's adversary throughout this essay was Nietzsche who had proclaimed the death of God, and held that there was no 'being' at all, only 'the doing'. All he did was to warn his readers not to mistake their priorities. The artists of Chartres and Ajanta had achieved their masterpieces because they had believed in God; they would not have achieved them if they had assumed Him as a convenient myth. Or, as Maritain had put it, it was 'a deadly error to look to art for the supra-substantial nourishment of man'.

Eric himself looked back to the prophets who had preceded him – to Cobbett who had failed to save the peasantry; to Disraeli who had exposed the corrupt origins of modern banking and the mercantile oligarchy that had turned England into 'two nations' and reduced kingship to ceremony. But Disraeli had 'succumbed to Parliament as Cobbett had succumbed to the police'; and as Ruskin, who had spoken the truth more eloquently than either, had succumbed to madness. And lastly he looked back to William Morris – 'that great man, that most manly of great men, as sensitive and passionate as he was fearless and hot-tempered' who had endured the battle when the battle was nearly over, and failed because he did not perceive 'the point at which humanity was corrupted' and had seen 'no city of God behind his earthly paradise'. Morris had appealed to sentiment where Eric was appealing to dogma.

Nevertheless it was in the poets of his time – or of a time not so far removed – that Eric discovered reason for hope. In Baudelaire who had declared that the dignity of man lay in his capacity for damnation; in the T. S. Eliot of *The Waste Land*; in Stephen Spender who had written that 'literature is a means of understanding the profoundest and most moral changes in the human mind';[1] in W. H. Auden whom Eric both liked and admired. And it was another contemporary poet, and *habitué* of Pigotts, Rayner Heppenstall, who saluted the literary qualities of *The Necessity of Belief* as warmly as he criticized its conclusions. Heppenstall had come very near to an acceptance of Eric's religious beliefs, and his eventual deviation from them perhaps embittered his recollections of a friend. His review appeared in the *Criterion*, and it stressed Eric's 'alarmingly vivid literary eye . . . his descriptions of complicated situations, the virtuoso effects of his understatement, and his flair for manipulating crowded instances'. Heppenstall justly referred to the satirical soliloquy which Eric had put into the mouth of a man of business; and there was another paragraph worth quotation, not for its literary merits alone, but because it tells us exactly how Eric spent the day after he left High Wycombe in the morning and was observed by the astonished passengers to be reading the Little Office of Our Lady in the train:

. . . But what goal is before humanity? Why all this hurry? What's it all blooming well for? To live and not die? Did Christ die in Jerusalem that we might live as we live? Did Christ ever live? Did Christ ever die? There seems no compatibility between such ideas and arriving at Marylebone Station and taking the 'tube' to Oxford Circus, and then going down to the underground urinal and then coming up again and, in danger of an apparently futile life, crossing the road, going to a stationers in Great Portland Street and buying a dermotagraphic pencil (you can draw on glass with that kind – if you want to draw on glass) and a ball of string

[1] *The Destructive Element*, 1936.

(good lord!) and then in a bus to Fetter Lane and up in a lift – 1st floor, 2nd floor, 3rd floor, 4th floor – to talk to a man about designing a new kind of letter for printing. 'Come out to lunch.' Eat soup and stewed steak and potatoes – drink half a pint or a pint. Up the street, take a bus, get out at Piccadilly, go to the bank (marble halls, 'nice day', 'Thank you, yes, still chipping away') walk under the Ritz arcade, nearly killed at the top of St James's Street, by the by. Curious images in shop window of young females in brass and bronze to go on mantelshelves in bachelors' flats, and photographs of 'the nude', very refined. Down in the place by Green Park Station, up again and across to Berkeley Street. Look at the motor cars in the windows (£2,700 for a Rolls-Royce), call on Cicely and talk about wood-engravings. 'Must go.' Dash through Bond Street to Hanover Square. Appointment with architect to discuss sculptures on shop in Bond Street where they sell natty baths for Narcissus. 'Have a cup of tea?' Sit on a high stool, rustle of drawings, calculations of prices. 'Must go.' Squeeze through crowds to Oxford Circus. Take No. 23, catch the 5.51 at Marylebone, just time for 'a quick one', and buy the *Humorist*.

It is interesting, nevertheless, that Rayner Heppenstall should have contributed an appendix to Eric's book on *Art* for the Twentieth-Century Library. Here he was in substantial agreement. The book said little that Eric had not said before. Indeed it would be amusing to go through Eric's writings to discover just how often he had quoted Father d'Arcy to the effect that man 'had been reduced to a condition of sub-human intellectual irresponsibility', or Coomaraswamy to the effect that 'the artist is not a special kind of man, but every man is a special kind of artist'. Obviously, of course, every man is not; certainly twentieth-century man was not, struggling like Laocoon 'with the twin snakes of Usury and War'. And it was a rather ludicrous overstatement – all prejudice guarded – that the modern interior architects were 'the only real architects we have had since the Middle Ages'. There was truth in Eric's assertion that the artist had become 'the presbyter of sensibility', but he did not see that 'sensibility' was itself a conquest – although, like all conquests, it was not won without casualties. An art which would be valid for the twentieth century had to take it into account. The poetry of Eliot, the painting of David Jones, the music of Stravinsky, and the sculpture of Henry Moore represented an accommodation between modern sensibility and the perennial necessity of myth; between the fact – not to be denied – of highly developed individuality and the conventions of that 'unanimous society' to which Eric vainly looked backward. Nor was it true that modern materials necessarily reduced building to functionalism. Corbusier may have been right in describing a house as 'a machine to live in' – though nothing less mechanized than Pigotts could well be conceived – but Notre-Dame de Ronchamps is among the great imaginative flights of architecture. It is not only functional, but gratuitous.

On this question Eric found himself at odds with men like René Hague, David Jones, and Herbert Read, who agreed with him about so much else. It had been one thing to sit up in a shivering attic at Capel-y-ffin and analyse Maritain by the hour; but Maritain had never denied the gratuitous nature of the creative gift, nor failed to point out an analogy between its operation and the operation of grace. The artist *was* a special kind of man, though one need not grant him a special code of morals or suggest that he should content himself with a special kind of God – or perhaps with no God at all. This latest book of Eric's about Art was deliberately unconcerned with aesthetics, but Art is a matter of aesthetics whether one likes it or not. It is a 'making', to be sure, but it is a particular kind of making and it concerns him who receives as well as him who gives. Eric rightly pointed out that while it was no use casting pearls before swine, 'the swine should remember that the blame is not all on the thrower'. Aesthetics are the education of the swine – and it was a branch of education that Eric persistently neglected. Moreover, as he rightly pointed out again, 'the senses are a kind of reason'; and it was difficult to withstand their argument if they said that Tintoretto was as great an artist as Cimabue or that Manet was not inferior to Cézanne.

Eric returned to the same subjects in his collection of essays under the title of *Work and Property*. Here he discussed the relation of Art to revolution, and confessed to a preference for the Brave New World prophesied by Aldous Huxley to the world of cultural Sunday after-

noons organized by social reformers for men and woman at a loss
how to occupy a perfect leisure. 'Fine Art' was bourgeois art and
evidently in its last stages of decline. But it was a contradiction to
assert that the senses had their kind of reason, and then to condemn
aesthetic pleasure because it was 'grounded in the physical rather
than the spiritual'. . . . Eric described the history of music during
the last 400 years as 'the progressive divorce of music from occasion'
and compared the 'high talk' of musicians to 'married love under the
inspiration of Mrs Stopes'. Did he seriously mean to denigrate the
madrigals of Monteverdi and the sonatas of Scarlatti as 'pleasure un-
alloyed'? If the music of Stravinsky meant 'nothing at all', the same
might be said of a Bach fugue. Eric added insult to insensitivity
by adding in a footnote that 'it is significant that many of the most
successful and unscrupulous Jewish money-lenders are notorious for
their sensitiveness to music'. After listening to one of these playing
the piano, Eric had asked him how he made his money – 'Something
to do with the wool trade, isn't it?' 'That's not how I make my
money,' came the reply, 'I make my money by charging a higher rate
of interest on my overdue account than I pay on my overdraft.' The
man in question was a great collector of Chinese bronzes and modern
paintings, but confessed that he could never bring himself to buy a
crucifix. It is ironical, therefore, that the richest private collection
of Eric's drawings, sculptures and engravings should now be in the
hands of a Jewish merchant. A great deal of this essay on 'The End
of the Fine Arts' is repetitious and unreasonable rant; it indicates the
strain from which Eric was now suffering as he contemplated the
British Laocoon struggling between 'Usury and War'.

His pamphlet on *Unemployment* proposed no immediate remedy,
and it was quite false in its prediction that as machinery was perfected unemployment would increase. Just the opposite has happened. The reason, he suggested, why the just master in the parable
had paid the labourer as much for working one hour as the others
who had worked all day long was because wages were not really payment for work but payment for living. Their logical consequence
was the dole. Unemployment was not really a curse – no factory-

hand, Eric thought, would prefer to be in his factory; the only curse was 'the smallness of the dole', and the only remedy for unemployment was the abolition of machinery. Fresh markets were a possible escape from this dilemma; and here again Eric has been proved wrong in his assertion that there were no fresh markets to be had. The most original section of the pamphlet was an appendix in which he argued that birth control was turning Britain into a matriarchy. Women were impregnable since they need not become pregnant, and could therefore be as provocative as they chose. The supreme male responsibility of generation had been shifted on to the shoulders of his female partner.

In *Trousers* Eric resumed some of the arguments in *Clothes*, but a rather conspicuous reference on the cover to 'Man's most precious ornament' provoked Father Vincent McNabb to a fresh *démarche*. He begged his Provincial, Father Bernard Delaney, to remonstrate once more with Eric. Rather reluctantly, Father Bernard went down to Pigotts but seeing on the walls of the smallest room in the house drawings which would have brought a blush to the cheeks of Faber and Faber, and trying to relate these to the pervasive atmosphere of work and prayer, his nerve failed him. He simply told Eric how awfully pleased he was to see him, and there the matter rested.

Eric had found his own way to an acceptance of Christian belief, but it was Coomaraswamy's introduction to the philosophy and practice of Hindu sculpture and painting which had opened his mind to a religious view of life. Here he found a text for his eroticism, and Coomaraswamy sent him reproductions of pictures that in European bookshops would hardly have been seen above the counter. Something of this debt to Coomaraswamy can be read in his own introduction to Mulk Raj Anand's *Hindu View of Art* (1937). Hindu and medieval images were alike in kind, made according to a hieratic canon, devoid of idiosyncrasy, negligent of anatomical verisimilitude, and of public rather than private significance. Here was Eric's cherished synthesis of Ajanta and Chartres. Descending to the secular level, he noted that in the medieval centuries life-like portraiture was rare. The Great Seal of Henry V was the same as the Great Seal of

Henry IV, except for the numerals. Similarly all images of Buddha were alike. 'The best works and the best periods are those in which the nature of the thing to be made is best known and most poignantly expressed – the time and the place and the loved one all together. . . . An early Christian crucifix is a better work of art because it is a better crucifix.' In this matter Eric would have agreed with a writer in *Harpers*:

Yet the vivid throngs of erotic statues on certain Indian temples create in the viewer no uneasiness but are simply delightful to look at. The viewer is kept at a considerable remove by the impossible poses and expressions of the statues. We cannot identify with the persons performing the acts. For the statues do not represent lustful, passionate, guilty, self-conscious, confused people like you and me, but pure beings to whom all things are pure, paradisal folk who are expressing their joy in generation and the body by erotic acts: these are stylized artifices of blessedness.'[1]

The Lord's Song was a sermon, beautifully printed in Eric's *Perpetua* roman and *Felicity* italic type by the Golden Cockerel Press, on a number of his favourite themes. *The Lord's Song* was a love song, and the one song that we no longer sang. The sermon was principally a plea and a lament for freedom:

Our fault has been that we sought freedom – we found an iron law of causality. We sought free thought – we found psychological determinism. We sought free love – we found that we had lost Love itself. . . . The only freedom we did not seek we have deliberately thrown away. We did not seek for freedom of the will. . . . There is no remedy but that which man alone has power to apply. . . . He must reclaim the one freedom he has thrown away; and he must throw away all the other freedoms he has falsely claimed. He must reaffirm the freedom of his will and his consequent responsibility for all his deeds and works.

[1] George P. Elliott, *Harpers*, March 1965.

9

The Spanish Civil War divided the Catholics in England less than it divided them in France, but it divided them all the same. It was indicative of Eric's political sympathies at this time that he should be spending the weekend with the Dean of Canterbury and reading a life of Christ by Conrad Noel; and on the Spanish question he stood well to the left of the neutralist *Blackfriars*. A letter to Michael Sewell[1] reveals his undiscriminating mood:

You believe in your Franco and his Moors – I prefer the blind anger of his enemies. I don't believe, in spite of all they say, the communists and anarchists are anti-Christ or even anti-church. The destruction of churches is another matter and an excellent move. Do you know of any church in this country that would not be better in ruins? I have no evidence re the Spanish elections. All elections are 'rigged' – the whole electioneering business is rigging. Did you ever hear of an election that wasn't?

The holy father is I believe about 80 years old. This is pure religion and undefiled: to succour the widows and the fatherless in their misery . . . and to keep unspotted from the worldliness of property and power and riches and frills and furbelows and titles and estates. . . . I don't wonder they call religion 'the opium of the people!' See how us catholics are doped! . . . Meanwhile I know in whom I believe, and it's not old man Franco.[2]

Eric had given an interview to the *Daily Worker* in which he had said, 'If the (Spanish) Government is out to remove corruptions then we must support it, and if the rebels are out to re-establish those same corruptions we must oppose them.' The *Daily Worker* had suppressed the 'ifs', thus making Eric's views even more categorical than they were already. He admitted in a subsequent letter to Sewell:

[1] Now Father Brocard Sewell, O. Carm.
[2] August 27, 1936.

What a muddle it is! . . . Friends of Christ and enemies are on both sides. But in a general way the clean-up which is necessary is more likely to occur as a result of Left activities than Right. . . . I'm not supporting the Communist programme, I'm only saying that if we persist in industrialism we'll *have* to have C(ommunism) or F(ascism). There can be no Christian industrialism.[1]

Yet even on a matter which moved him so strongly as the Spanish Civil War Eric was forced to a slight measure of compromise. David Kindersley wrote to ask him whether, as a supporter of the Spanish Government, he was morally justified in carving a tablet to commemorate those who had fallen in defence of the Alcazar. Eric replied with characteristic realism: 'Plenty bis – no; no bis – yes.' He did not hesitate, however, to join the signatories – all of them Catholics – of a letter addressed to Archbishop Hinsley and other members of the Hierarchy urging them to protest against the bombing of open towns by the Nationalist forces. They received a very dusty answer. The Archbishop was a forceful and endearing personality, who won the affection of the nation when, a few years later, he so ardently supported a popular cause, but he supported an unpopular cause just as warmly. Even at the height of the Second World War a photograph of the Caudillo stood on his writing table. He told the signatories that he had long ago condemned indiscriminate bombing from the air, because he had seen its effects on defenceless populations in Africa. But he denied, on the evidence at his disposal, that the Nationalists had bombed other than military targets, and he quoted Republican sources to prove that such attacks had come from the other side. The conclusion of the letter showed clearly where his sympathies lay:

You have no right or justification for stating that the Catholic Church in Great Britain has identified itself with the 'Nationalists'. But it is impossible to ignore the facts and the comparison of the conditions prevailing in Government and Nationalist Spain is more than sufficient excuse for the present attitude of many Catholics in this country. . . . In fairness to the Bishops and myself you are under the obligation of sending or

[1] August 29, 1936.

showing this letter to your fellow-signatories, some of whom may then begin to use the right eye as well as the left. This answer to your effusion will be published if you allow your document to become a specimen of the current propaganda for the side you favour.[1]

It is hardly a contradiction in terms to say that Pigotts was up in arms. Mary Gill, Anthony Foster, Michael Richey (a newly-arrived assistant) and Laurie Cribb were all among the signatories; indeed they criticized the original letter for seeming to suggest that the clergy could be justified in supporting Franco if he ceased the bombing of civilian targets.

Among Eric's closer friends Stanley Morison was on his side over all these questions, because Morison believed what the Church had once taught about usury. He reassured Eric that 'one satisfactory feature of the worst scandal of the day – that the Church militant should be in favour of the creditor class – is that the Church militant in this respect does not know what it is talking about'. But Morison disagreed with Eric about industrialism:

. . . I am not prepared to suggest that the present world should go back to the ninth century . . . back to feudalism and serfdom, primitive simplicity, with every physically weak man at the mercy of every physically stronger. In other words, if you ask me to make the choice between what I may shortly call factory ideas and peasant ideas I choose – and without the slightest hesitation – factory ideas. This is in part helped by the fact that I am a born Londoner, and will never live anywhere else, so that my native heath is a concrete flagstone, and I prefer the No 11 bus to the sight of a horse or cow. . . . Allowing all other people a similar degree of bias in the contrary direction, I still cannot believe that the greatest material good of the greatest number of all sorts of men – Christian and non-Christian and anti-Christian – can be assisted, let alone achieved, by the destruction of the machine. No programme, yours or mine, could be put into operation by a single stroke. At this moment, people of your sort (the Anarchists) and people of my sort (the Socialists) are arguing out these matters in the face of an aerial and artillery bombardment by the military and their mercenaries. 'Spain' as a whole is

[1] August 29, 1936.

underfed materially, hence it is comparatively indifferent to me that your people have bombed the churches. It is important that they spare the factories. From what I can see of it, humanity stands in need of more and better churches, and more and better factories, not fewer. I say that we need a more thorough and efficient exploitation of the industrial machine. I wish it to change hands. And the same with the Catholic Church. This super-exploitation of industry can take place if interest is turned into wages.[1]

Eric's reluctant preference for Communism and his blunt statement of the dilemma – that Christian morals demanded collective owner-ship in an industrial society – brought him into conflict with Father d'Arcy. Father d'Arcy denied the argument that an industrial society was essentially an evil one and that a society where there was no individual ownership was better than a society where such owner-ship was handicapped. Reduced to concrete terms Eric's argument had seemed to imply that people were better off in Russia than in England or Switzerland. Communism was an historical phenomenon; it could not be judged in the abstract. It represented the despair of human nature and the denial of free will. Because some people abused their liberty, no one should have any liberty at all – except the officers of the state to whom all liberty had been handed over. Father d'Arcy concluded his letter as follows:

I owe much to the friendship of Eric Gill and I am disturbed by what seems to be his loss of power of judging his ideas. Instead of standing over them and being free, he seems obsessed. His supposedly clear and distinct ideas have no edges and no relations and no background, and I have learnt to distrust such a state of mind as one of mental strain.[2]

Eric wrote privately to Father d'Arcy, claiming that his point of view had been misstated, and Father d'Arcy replied that he had only entered into the controversy with the greatest reluctance and with the fear of 'appearing to denounce so strongly the views of one for whom I have such a great liking'.[3]

[1] September 7, 1936.
[2] *Catholic Herald*, July 30, 1937.
[3] August 1, 1937.

Another well-wisher, Monsignor Jackman, wrote in much the same way:

Carissime,
    You cannot but know that many take amiss such expressions as appeared in the summer in the *Daily Worker* or again the inclusion of your name among the Friends of Russia. I am sure you know what you are about and maybe take a mischievous pleasure in confusing fools and puzzling people like Yours Sincerely.

The trouble had started in 1934 when Eric exhibited with the Artists International; Philip Hagreen had written to him from Ditchling:

Certain communists are crowing triumphantly because they have got you to exhibit at the 'Artists International' show. The purpose of the exhibition is being camouflaged and what has been published about it suggests an attack in which we might join. It happens, however, that I have heard a lot about what is behind the organization and what is connected with it – all of which is 'anti-God'. A great friend of mine has been mixed up with the business and has plenty of documents to prove that point.[1]

Eric replied that he had taken the organizers of the exhibition at their word, but Hagreen tried to persuade him that in this case their word was 'mere humbug'.

They say among themselves that they are using you and Henry Moore for publicity purposes – I have this first hand. Really and truly the organization is Anti-God without any mistake about words. . . . Now do have your things withdrawn from that show. The use of your name there may do a great deal of harm.[2]

Hagreen fortified his argument by reminding Eric that certain Communists had propounded the view that stone and wood were 'counter-revolutionary materials'. But not even that dissuaded Eric from his fellow-travelling. 'What I say is: if you can be against God you ought to be – and I think you'll find that very little publicity will accrue

[1] September 25, 1934.
[2] October 4, 1934.

from my small exhibits. I fear I don't take the matter so seriously as you do.'[1] A severe critique of the exhibition by Herbert Read put the finger on more than one of the fallacies into which Eric was now falling. Read also counted himself 'on the side of the working class against the capitalist class' and called himself a socialist. Nor did he accept the doctrine of 'art for art's sake' – at least in the accepted meaning of the phrase – because art was the expression of the artist's *weltanschauung* which might well include his attitude towards the social problems of his time: 'One might even accept . . . the Marxist position "that the character of all art is the outcome of the character of the mode of material production of its period" ' – thus stone and wood were definitely 'out' – 'provided that by character is meant external features rather than inner form'. But this did not excuse one from aesthetic valuation.

There are good artists and bad artists in every period, and the better an artist is, the more he transcends the limitations of his period. Nothing could be further removed from our own existing 'mode of material production' than the mode prevailing in the Old Stone Age; but the drawings of the unknown artist of the Altamira caves have a definite similarity to the drawings of Picasso – the same concentrated vitality expressed by the same mode of linear abstraction. . . . The true revolutionary artist today is not any artist with a Marxist ideology; it is the good artist with a revolutionary technique.

As far as this exhibition was concerned, Herbert Read concluded that, 'apart from two paintings by Robert Medley and a woodcut by Eric Gill, there was nothing of any interest to be seen'.[2]

Further trouble was at hand when Eric's name appeared on the cover of the *Left Review* with Tom Wintringham and J. D. Bernal. Father Bernard McElligott, the resident chaplain at Pigotts, received the following letter from Monsignor Elwes, the Archbishop's private secretary:

His Grace would be grateful to you if you would convey to Mr Eric Gill (very unofficially, via me and via you, and therefore demanding no

[1] October 5, 1935.
[2] *The London Mercury*, November 1934.

answer) the fact that he is very much shocked and distressed to find the name of such a well-known and highly esteemed Catholic as he on the title-page of such a publication as can in a former number produce the frontispiece that I enclose. His Grace has no quarrel whatever with the sentiments of Mr Gill's letter published therein but only with the associations.[1]

The frontispiece in question – bearing the title *The Rival Firms* – depicted a sandwich-man with two boards, on which were inscribed the words: *God is Love*. He was parading outside a shop window in which various lubricious magazines and contraceptive gadgets were displayed. Eric thought the company of the *Left Review* no worse than other company that Catholics were only too happy to keep; and he continued to support the Artists International, and to exhibit with them. Here he was in the unexceptionable company of Vanessa Bell, Stephen Bone, Jacob Epstein, Duncan Grant, Barbara Hepworth, Henry Moore, Paul Nash and Ben Nicholson. Nevertheless on April 14, 1937, Father McElligott received the following letter from the Archbishop in his own handwriting:

I am still being informed by responsible persons of the scandal given by Eric Gill in giving his support to Communistic activities. The latest one to date is the First British Artists Congress 1937, of which you will see he is a supporter from the enclosed leaflet. In face of the recent Encyclical 'Divini Redemptoris' in which our Holy Father warns Catholics against the deceitful methods of the Communists to enlist even Catholics among their activities, the appearance of a Catholic name on this leaflet is sufficient to cast suspicion upon the sincerity of the person in question. Will you kindly get Eric Gill to read this Encyclical and use all your influence to have him withdraw his patronage from this and similar veiled Communistic propaganda.

Father McElligott passed on the letter and Eric read the Encyclical. He wrote to the Archbishop asking him in what way the British Artists Congress could be regarded as veiled Communism. Some, or many, of the organizers might be Communists, but he had no information to show that this was the case. The stated object was

[1] November 4, 1935.

simply to consider economic conditions as they affected professional artists and to present a united front in defence of 'peace and democracy, i.e. as opposed to war and fascism'. The Archbishop sent Eric the evidence he had asked for, adding, 'not only for you am I solicitous but also for those of my flock whom your example may lead to join a questionable organization. I have no quarrel with your own, or with anyone's political opinions provided that they are not opposed to the teaching of the Church which enforces the natural law.'[1] Eric replied:

I have read most of the papers you sent. I find it difficult to discover any definite Communistic leanings, but of course I know that the most active members of A.I. are that way inclined. I note that someone has marked with blue pencil my name wherever it appears and also references to Fascism, implying that objection is taken to the anti-Fascist opinions expressed. But I see very little reference to Communism itself.

He then expounded his familiar views on the necessity of communal ownership without which 'religion will necessarily wither. For these reasons I support anybody or any party which works towards workers' ownership.'[2] At the same time he enclosed a letter from the secretary of Artists International stating that 'there is no need for all of its members to be Communists, and in fact I imagine that very few of them are; there is no need for them to be socialists either; all we ask is that they should believe in our aims of peace, democracy and cultural development.'

These were honeyed words and Hinsley was too tough a Yorkshireman to take them *au pied de la lettre*. But he sent Eric a kindly and considered reply. Experience had shown that in practice nearly all so-called United Fronts for this and that invariably supported Communist activities; putting the matter at its lowest level, was it expedient that a prominent Catholic should openly associate with such a movement? The Archbishop then tackled Eric's economic arguments. The end did not justify the means. Granted that Eric's reasons

[1] April 20, 1937.
[2] April 24, 1937.

were correct, he could not in good conscience support a party which had been explicitly condemned by the Holy See on grounds of Faith and Morals, even if that party favoured workers' ownership. Moreover, he did not find Eric's reasons altogether convincing.

It is true that the Encyclicals state that as many workers as possible should become private owners. But, on the other hand, the right of private property is upheld in the Encyclicals as a fundamental *human* right. It is not, therefore, *only* workers' ownership that is considered. And, on the other hand, the very doctrine of the *living wage* implies acceptance by the Church of the wage-system, i.e. property-less Labour working for propertied Capital in exchange for a wage. (Of course a wage sufficient for the human dignity of the worker and his family, i.e. a living wage.) The social ideal of the Church is not, therefore, *exclusively* a system of collective ownership.

It was precisely in an industrial world that the Encyclicals had been issued, and they condemned collective ownership. In fact workers' ownership could be achieved co-operatively or corporatively. The Archbishop ended his letter as follows:

My duty to the Church and my loyalty to the Holy See require that I should not hesitate to declare the truth proclaimed so authoritatively. Furthermore, regard for yourself makes it a duty, delicate indeed but necessary, to tell you in all friendship that your attitude is causing not a little *admiratio* among those who are your admirers and co-religionists. I hope that I have not said one word to cause you pain or to make me appear other than charitable and desirous of promoting your best interests.[1]

Eric assured the Archbishop that he would dissociate himself from the extreme left wing parties, and the Archbishop accepted the explanation of how his name had come to be connected with them. It would be quite unjust to regard Archbishop Hinsley as a social reactionary. He was ardently in favour of the Beveridge report and very critical of those Catholics who opposed it. He was heard saying that he would vote Labour at the 1945 election. But Eric would have had a four-letter word for elections; and although he did not live to read

[1] April 29, 1937.

the Beveridge report, he would have seen in it no more than the consecration of industrial servitude. Finally, it is worth noting that when the fastidious eye of Pius XII fell upon one of Eric's books, he observed: 'This man has understood our Encyclicals.'

The threat of war was now so insistent that men on every side were turning to absolute solutions. The advocates of rearmament and disarmament faced each other with increasing bitterness. Already, in 1936, Eric regretted that Gordian wished to join the Air Force Reserve, and his own mind was made plain in a letter to Austen Harrison:

It seems to me clearer and clearer that war, modern mechanized war, is impossible – and there's no other line to take but complete refusal to take part in it.

He was active, with many other Catholics, in the preaching and publications of the *Peace Pledge Union* and the *Pax Society*.[1] The second of these stopped short of dogmatic pacifism, but it maintained that in existing circumstances a just war was impossible. Lord Baldwin had said that 'the only defence is offence, which means that you have to kill women and children more quickly than the enemy'.[2] *The Times* said that 'the object of the bomber is not to defeat the rival air force, but to terrify into submission populations whose women, children and houses are attacked and destroyed by fire, explosions and gas'.[3] The Archbishop of Cincinnati had called for an organization of conscientious non-combatants in his diocese and declared that 'war today never attains its ends'. Nevertheless the activities of *Pax* brought the society into conflict with Westminster. On June 16, 1939, as war seemed inevitable, Cardinal Hinsley, whose hatred of Nazi Germany was quite as strong as his distrust of Communism, requested the Society to cease distributing its pamphlets outside the cathedral or other churches of the archdiocese. It was further requested that any of the Society's publications written by Catholics

[1] A full statement of Eric's pacifist views will be found in an Appendix, p. 303.
[2] November 9, 1936.
[3] January 12, 1938.

should be submitted to censorship. This was agreed to, although Donald Attwater, who was active in the same cause, held that since the Society had never asked for episcopal guidance or authority – that was the strength of its position – it could not therefore be accused of disobedience to the Bishops. Arthur Hinsley and Eric Gill were both fighters, and both disliked opposition. Fortunately, there was one matter – less urgent than the matter of peace and war – on which they had no quarrel.

10

In the early autumn of 1935 anxiety was expressed by many people about the mosaics which were being put up in the apse of Westminster Cathedral. A number of important signatories, headed by Edward Hutton, appealed to the Archbishop to stop the work and appoint a Commission to decide how work more in accordance with Bentley's designs might best be carried out. The Archbishop was sympathetic and by the end of November the work in progress was halted and the Commission appointed. Eric had been among the signatories to the appeal, and at about the same time Monsignor Elwes asked him for a photograph of a statue of the Sacred Heart which he was then carving for Ratcliffe College. He wished to show it to the Archbishop as a proof that 'your "pagan" work is so only for lack of opportunity of expressing youself in more Christian subjects and atmospheres. Clerical circles are, I'm afraid, grossly inartistic very often, as witness these quite frightful mosaics which are ruining the cathedral, and which needless to say I am doing my level best to have stopped.'[1]

Eric had not yet met the Archbishop, and Monsignor Elwes thought the introduction had better be arranged 'casually', not 'formally'. Eric replied cautiously that he had been left wing by nature ever since he had played 'outside left' at school. Shortly afterwards he received a letter from Edward Hutton, urging him to make known to the Archbishop his personal views in the matter of the Westminster mosaics. Eric wrote a characteristic essay to Hinsley, urging the disadvantages of Bentley's proposed method of *opus sectile* and suggesting Lethaby's solution – 'namely to use whitewash for the walls and domes, thus preserving the very great beauty of the building, as such, and giving light'. The Archbishop – by now rather out of his depth – replied that his action in stopping work on the mosaics was

[1] November 27, 1936.

'administrative and financial rather than artistic . . . we need every penny for our schools at the present time'.[1] He ended by asking Eric to call and see him on January 2. Eric, in accepting the invitation, expressed his relief that the work had been stopped for financial rather than artistic reasons.

It seems to me certain that the artistic question would solve itself in the course of time if by Schools and other educative and propagandist means a unanimous state were once again seen in England. It is obviously impossible for people to agree about things like decoration when they do not agree about things like Heaven and Hell.[2]

With this unequivocal rejection of the pluralist society, Eric went to his meeting with the Archbishop. It passed off very cordially. Hinsley had been embarrassed by the publication of the correspondence between himself and the signatories to the appeal; he had it before him on the table when Eric came in.

I did my best to point out that my connection with the affair was simply due to the fact that I was asked to sign the appeal and could not refuse to do so as I agreed with the contention that the mosaic work was spoiling the cathedral. But I wished him to understand that I was not really connected with these artist people, and that I entirely agreed with him that as things are today it would be ever so much better to spend money not on decoration but solely on things required for the service of the Church. . . . I was there for about half an hour and no mention whatever was made of the Communism business, and I did not think it up to me to introduce it if he did not. He was extremely kind and friendly.[3]

The Archbishop quoted the adage – *de gustibus non disputandum* – and when he got home Eric sent him Father Rickaby's reply: 'Tastes differ, but not right tastes; and moral notions but not right moral notions.' But the use of the word 'right', as Eric told Monsignor Elwes, implied the use of the reason: 'and that is why I say look after the good and the true'.[4]

[1] December 9, 1935.
[2] December 11, 1935.
[3] Letter to Peter Anson, January 3, 1936.
[4] January 3, 1936.

In June 1937 Eric was invited by the Archbishop's Commission to make a design for the mosaic in the apse. He declined on the grounds that, not being a mosaic worker himself, the design would have to be 'extremely simple and dogmatical and of a kind which the cathedral people would probably hate'. He also repeated his objections to any mosaic decoration in the cathedral – 'we lack the tradition and the right kind of workman' – and pleaded once again for the lightening effect of whitewash. He was 'overwhelmed with gratification' that the Committee had made him the offer, but wondered whether the Archbishop knew of it. 'I am not at all sure that they would accept the suggestion with pleasure in that quarter.'[1] Nevertheless he did, according to his diary, make a number of preliminary drawings.

But Eric had not finished with Westminster Cathedral and the Westminster authorities had not finished with him. He was commissioned to carve an altarpiece for the chapel of the English Martyrs. This represented St John Fisher and St Thomas More looking up at Our Lord on the Cross, and clinging to the robe of More was his pet monkey. The presence of this charming animal was explained as follows:

St Thomas had a little Zoo of his own at his house in Chelsea and among the inhabitants was a little monkey of whom he was very fond. The sculptor has introduced the little animal as indicating by its very incongruity the deeply human character of the Saint – so completely unlike the conventional stained-glass figure. Moreover the animal does by its caricature of humanity remind us of our lowly state.

The work was not quite finished when Eric died, and it remained in his studio until the end of the war. Shortly after its erection in the chapel, those who had seen it in the studio observed that the monkey had been removed. There was no word of apology to the sculptor's widow or of consultation with the cathedral architect. A great number of letters – many of them unpublishable – were sent to the *Catholic Herald*, but only the lamest explanation was forthcoming. It

[1] April 27, 1937.

was left to be understood that a high ecclesiastical authority had seen the monkey, disliked it, and ordered its removal. High ecclesiastical authorities are not given to owning up; but had Cardinal Hinsley been alive he would have been the last to condone or, still less, to promote such an outrage. A poem, dedicated to 'St Thomas More, Eric Gill, Fr Martindale, Robert Speaight,[1] and all others who see as they do', opened with the following lines:

> And I, if I be lifted up,
> Will draw *all things* to me.[2]

Eric was wiser in his generation than the Canons of light; he had a way of hitting theological nails on the head. In a letter to the present writer Mary Gill summed up the feelings of Eric's friends:

. . . It never occurred to me that such a thing *could* happen. Otherwise I would never have parted with the reredos without some understanding from the cathedral. The original design *with* the monkey was passed by the Committee who gave Eric the commission. Alas! alas! and nothing can now be done about it.

It seems inconceivable that people in high places can be so ruthless. As we had charge of the reredos for over six years, even out of common courtesy we should have been consulted.

I have written to the Cardinal[3] telling him that had he consulted us, we could have come to some arrangement – he was not obliged to accept the reredos, especially too as it had not been finished paying for – it did not *really* belong to them. My only reply was from the Cardinal's secretary thanking me for my letter.[4]

Through his friendship with Sir Edward Maufe, Eric was commissioned to carve on stone a Calvary on the outside of St Thomas's Church at Hanwell, and two statues of St John the Baptist – one to stand over the gateway of St John's College, Oxford; and one for the new Anglican Cathedral at Guildford, of which Sir Edward was the architect. The conception of each statue was very similar:

[1] Fr Martindale and the present writer were among those who had protested most vigorously.
[2] *The Ark*, August 1947.
[3] Cardinal Griffin.
[4] March 10, 1947.

You ask me to describe the statue of St John Baptist: St J-B was a preacher who went walking up and down Palestine. He called himself the 'forerunner' saying there was one coming after him to whom he bore witness. He was an uncouth man, no gentleman saint. He dressed in camel skin and ate rough food. I therefore tried to make an image of this rough man walking and, by the attitude of pointing over his shoulder, to suggest that 'he went before'. As the college chapel is on his left, he is pointing in that direction because the chapel is a Christian church and it was to Christ that St J-B bore witness. The staff or stick he is holding merely indicates his hiking life. It is improbable that he trimmed his hair or beard so I have carved them long. He looks down into the quad because his witness is still needed and he may be thought of as preaching to the people of St John's College as he did to them of Palestine.[1]

. . . you requested that the figure should be of a young man and I quite agreed with this, so, as shown in the sketch, though bearded he is youthful and slim. I wanted him to be wiry and strong as well. He is clothed in a sort of camel hair tunic hanging over one shoulder. With his left hand he holds a stock, which I like to use to indicate that he is a peregrinating prophet. His right hand points over his shoulder to show that he is the forerunner of something other than himself. He is not saying so much 'Come unto me' as 'Go unto Him'. The position of the hand rather close to the head is necessitated by the fact that the figure is made of stone and therefore there cannot be complete detachment of arms and hands.

The head will, in the actual stone, be leaning as far forward as the stone will allow (in fact, I think it would be good if you would see that this top stone projects outwards three or four inches more than the lower stones) so that he looks down over the people entering the porch. His legs are supposed to suggest – but not too evidently – a moving person or one just about to move.

I hope this will be sufficient description. . . . The fact is that the figure of St John the Baptist as portrayed in the Gospels is what I want to make.[2]

Eric would often stay with Sir Edward and Lady Maufe at their house at Shepherds Hill in Sussex. Sometimes he would be left alone there, carving the family coat-of-arms over the front door. On one of these visits the butler discovered him saying his prayers in the middle of the morning, when he ought to have been catching his train. On

[1] Letter to Sir Edward Maufe, July 7, 1936.
[2] Letter to Sir Edward Maufe, December 1938.

Engraved Christmas card, 1937.

another occasion he looked up at the carving and exclaimed: 'God! what an amateur I am!' Other work included a memorial tablet to Lady Ottoline Morrell, and carvings for the choir stalls at Mount St Bernard Abbey.

But Eric's most important work in these later years was the new Catholic church at Gorleston-on-Sea, near Yarmouth. This was an event in English ecclesiastical architecture. There was no trace of foreign influence – although such influences were already making themselves felt. The exterior, designed in the form of a Greek cross, was of red brick and the roof of red tiling. The interior was entirely white, with pointed arches rising straight from the ground. The altar stood, three steps high, on a red floor, and was placed in the middle of the church, with the intersecting arches forming a small square tower above. High up on the wall and facing the front aisle Eric had painted the triumphant procession of Palm Sunday to contrast with the Way of the Cross. The crucifix was of wood and hung by chains from the cross-beams; Our Lord is depicted with red hair and beard, gold halo, and wearing a blue loin-cloth. The figure of St Peter with a fishing net was lightly cut in brick over the north porch. Nothing could have been plainer nor, in its total effect, more appropriate. If the church at Gorleston looks anything but revolutionary today, that is only because Eric's ideas as to how churches should be built, and of what materials, have now won fairly general acceptance. It was opened by the Bishop of Northampton, Dr Youens, a very good friend of Eric, in August 1939, just before the outbreak of war. His first work as an architect, it was also among his last gifts to the world that he had tried to save for peace.

In these hectic and nearly hopeless years Eric often talked of emigrating to America and perhaps of setting up his 'cell of living' in New England. He was in correspondence on the subject with Graham Carey, who undertook to organize a tour of lectures. This would enable Eric to examine the possibilities more closely. But the threat, and then the outbreak, of war soon put the project out of mind. Meanwhile he had more work than he could easily get through. There were his bas-reliefs for the People's Palace at Mile End, symbolizing fellowship, drama, music, boxing and dancing. There were his engravings and type for Dent's *Aldine Bible*, and his designs for the new postage stamps. He was elected an Honorary Associate of the Institute of British Architects in 1935, an Associate of the Royal Academy in 1937; and was given an Honorary Doctorate of Laws at Edinburgh University in 1938. In the same year he was elected an Honorary Associate of the Royal Society of British Sculptors, and he was among the first eleven appointments to the distinction of Designer for Industry conferred by the Royal Society of Arts. He may have smiled at such recognitions, but he accepted them if they came his way. And for sheer relaxation there was a ride in the engine driver's cabin of the 'Flying Scotsman' from King's Cross to Grantham, when the tunnels – as you faced them – looked far too narrow to get through. This was a reward for painting the name of the engine on the name-plate. Eric's first love had been a locomotive, and after fifty years he was still faithful to it. In the summer of 1937 he returned to Palestine – his last and greatest love – carved an inscription for the Scots church, and stayed with Harrison. They went down to Cairo where Eric bought a caftan of wine-red silk from the Suk, which he often wore at Pigotts. Harrison wanted to take him on a caïque round the Greek islands, but time was short and we shall never know what Eric would have thought of the glory that was Greece. He had serious reservations about the grandeur that was Rome.

There was relaxation, too, in his drawings from the nude. The earliest of these studies were the last to be published in book form,[1] and they carried the following dedication: 'Paris 1926, May. (Sketch Book No. 1) for Gordian Gill because it was begun on his birthday and it's the first time I did any life drawings.' 'Drawings from life', Eric wrote afterwards, 'properly comes late in life rather than early. For the training of imagination is the first thing to be seen to, and that is best achieved by life and experience; and in order to make this particular thing, this construction of lines derived from the sight of human limbs and bodies, the artist is more dependent upon his life and experience than he is on any other business.' It came 'when the experience of living has filled the mind and given a deeper, a more sensual as well as a more spiritual meaning to material things'.[2] In a perceptive introduction to the book Sir John Rothenstein drew attention to the lack of volume characteristic of Eric's drawings as it was of his sculpture, and to their sometimes obsessive sensuality – a sensuality which was also 'candid and gay'. Nor could the force of the idea and the delight in the object quite make up for the want of early training,

Twenty-five Nudes (1938) were even more purely linear; animated

[1] *First Nudes*, 1954.
[2] From the preface to *Twenty-five Nudes*, 1938.

diagrams on a dark background; contours looking, now and then, as if they would burst into flame. In a short preface Eric recalled the rightness of the child who said, 'First I think and then I draw my think.' His own drawings suggest that he had said: 'First I feel and then I draw my feel.' It was the passionate mingling of soul and sense, not without humour, in these engravings that made them – in the words of *The Times Literary Supplement* – 'little hymns of joy in creation'.[1] *Drawings from Life* (1940), like the *Twenty-five Nudes*, were all taken from the same model. Eric had confessed to Charles Burns, on one of Burns' later visits to Pigotts, that he had fallen in love. He made the confession shyly, and a little sadly, as if he were a young man who had never been in love before; and the quality of these drawings undoubtedly owed a great deal to the young model who had engaged his affections as well as his artistry. They are lighter in emphasis and more rhythmical in line than his previous studies; but even so they are less interesting in themselves than the introductory essay which explains and justifies them. Eric found his text in a letter from Desmond Chute. 'If naked bodies can arouse a hell-hunger of lust, they can and do kindle a hunger for Heaven.' Eric put the whole of himself into this brief essay. He did not scruple to describe the image of the naked man or woman as an 'ikon', and he admitted that –

the great enthusiasm of the last four hundred years for pictures of 'nature' – landscapes, 'still life' and portraits and figure subjects – has had the effect of greatly deepening our respect and admiration and love for the natural world, the world which God created – its infinite beauty and subtlety, its grandeur and its solemnity, its sweetness and its terrors, even its comicality and, so to say, its Rabelaisian buffoonery and pig-style coarseness. All these things are good and holy, and I don't see how it can be denied that we are today much more aware of these holinesses than would have been the case had we not been through the turmoils and corruptions of the post-Renaissance centuries.

The artist was not only an interpreter of nature – one who discovered the eternal types in the divine mind; he also created new and living

[1] December 24, 1938.

images of God. And so, with a formal bow to prudence, he would omit no detail of the divine anatomy, even laying, as it seemed, an exultant stress upon those features usually prohibited by pictorial convention. He compared these to the 'roses and lilies' and thought they deserved a similar respect. Eric had not only enjoyed the human body, as few men have so fearlessly enjoyed it; he had loved it for its own sweet sake with an almost disinterested adoration. Whatever the standards of the boudoir or the precautions of the nursery might have to say, he would take his stand upon the inalienable prerogatives of love. His nudes are chiefly important to us because they were important to him; but the best of them – like the best of his portrait drawings – have what Frances Cornford had once described as 'the pure, certain vitality' of his line.

II

In August 1939 Eric was at work on a carving for St John's College, Cambridge, and a coat-of-arms for Fisher House. One day the Clerk of Works at St John's remarked to him: 'The Master seems very nervous.'

'Does he think they're going to bomb Cambridge specially?' Eric inquired.

'Coo, the b - - - s would do anything.'

'Well, I suppose we shall do the same – what?'

'You bet, an hour after the war starts the b - - - s will get the surprise of their lives.'

'It's a civilized and Christian state – I don't think.'

At this the man pointed his finger and declared: 'Religion started 2,000 years ago – it's finished.'

The conversation confirmed Eric's pacifism and it set him thinking about what England really stood for. He was interested, as ever, in the subject because he was the most English of men. Well, there were certain things that Herr Hitler could hardly destroy; the English climate, the English reticence, the Englishman's love of fair play, the Lake District, and the South Downs. The defence of these was not included in British war aims. What England stood for in Eric's simplified summary[1] was the Workshop of the World – 'a country devoted to facture for export, having little agriculture and therefore dependent on cheap foreign food'; the Factories, the Banks and the Leisure State; Religious Toleration – 'a country in which, as there is no unanimity about man's nature and destiny, religion is a private affair and doesn't matter'; Democracy – 'neither king nor religious teaching having any authority, a state ruled by financiers and financial cliques'. There could be no doubt, after this, what Eric stood for; he was standing for things which had long disappeared beyond the possibility of defence.

[1] *All that England Stands For*, a pamphlet, 1940.

Life at Pigotts went on very much as usual, except for the four refugee children who arrived on September 5. David Jones came with them. Eric soon put his pen to paper on *Tribunal*,[1] but the workshops were not so busy and grew steadily less so. The cows grazed in the fields and the cob drew the pony cart and the plough; although the fencing was in bad repair and the cattle were continually breaking out. Butter and bread were both made on the farm and the grand-children would exclaim in chorus: 'Shop bread!' when it was bought outside. Dr Flood had succeeded Father McElligott as Chaplain in 1938; the chapel had been recently enlarged; and Dr Youens had given permission for the Blessed Sacrament to be reserved there. Betty's school at Capel had not been a success, but she had remarried, and Miss Reeves – 'Auntie May' as she was called – ran a school at Pigotts for the Hague and Tegetmeier children, and for others who lived near by. She wore a long red dress, with full skirt and tight bodice, and liked to sit at Eric's feet – which rather annoyed Mary. She also taught the children to sing the Apostles Creed – which rather annoyed Eric. No doubt they sang it out of tune. But Eric would always kiss the hands of his grandchildren when they came into the room, and was quite unperturbed if they ran naked about the chapel. In the evenings René Hague and Denis Tegetmeier, Michael Richey and Anthony Foster would go down to the *Sportsman's Arms* at North Dean, where there was loud talk about St Thomas Aquinas and birth control. But Eric no longer joined them. He did, however, occasionally visit the neighbours; among these was a member of the Rowntree family whom he astonished by suggesting that the better he treated his workpeople the more culpable was his conduct. Eric was now in a mood when he would say almost anything.

In November he was writing to his brother Cecil: 'Adolf makes good speeches, doesn't he? – but Churchill is an honourable man'; and in the same month he was at Capel-y-ffin helping to fell a beech tree. At Christmas they were snowed up at Pigotts and Eric observed: 'It's almost like a breakdown of the industrial system – but no such luck.' Gradually the workshops emptied. René Hague – now in

[1] See Appendix, p. 303.

rather sharp disagreement with Eric on many subjects – joined the Royal Air Force; Michael Richey went into the Navy. Pigotts was not very far from the headquarters of Bomber Command, and in May 1940 German bombs fell near by. 'If only they would drop a bomb on Selfridges', was Eric's pious wish. When they did bomb Oxford Street, Eric saw the huge chunks of Portland stone lying about among the ruins; he reflected that perhaps most architecture had to be battered about before you could really see it. Even the Parthenon – which he had never seen – came rather sadly to mind. In the meanwhile he argued the position of a conscientious objector with Stanley Morison, but Morison who had objected to the First World War had no such objection to the second. Eric's own objections found themselves in strange company when he listened to Lord Tavistock's disingenuous pleas for peace.

At the end of February (1940) he was writing to his brother Evan from Capel-y-ffin: 'At present moment I'm in bed . . . with sore throat and cough, nothing to worry about.' And again from Pigotts on April 16: 'Am in bed at the moment with a bit of a temp and a cough.' He had always insisted on carving without a protection for his nose, and it was thought likely that the consequent inhalation of dust had affected his lungs – more particularly after his bronchial trouble a few years before. Now, in the fatal spring of 1940, he could no longer work at the carvings for Westminister and Guildford which were not quite complete. So he accepted Jonathan Cape's proposal to write his autobiography. He wrote it straight from memory, without reference to diaries or correspondence – and a great deal of it sitting up in bed or, when he was feeling better, on the mountain side at Capel. While he was still recovering from a fairly innocuous bout of German measles, the doctor diagnosed a patch of congested lung; but there seemed no cause for alarm, and Eric was able to visit his brother Cecil, who was a doctor in Cardiff. Their sister Gladys was also there. Eric had reached the period of his story where Cicely had died, and they talked of Cicely and of other things all through the night. The weather was warm and the skies unclouded for the Luftwaffe. 'How nice it would be,' said Eric, 'if we could all go bathing naked!'

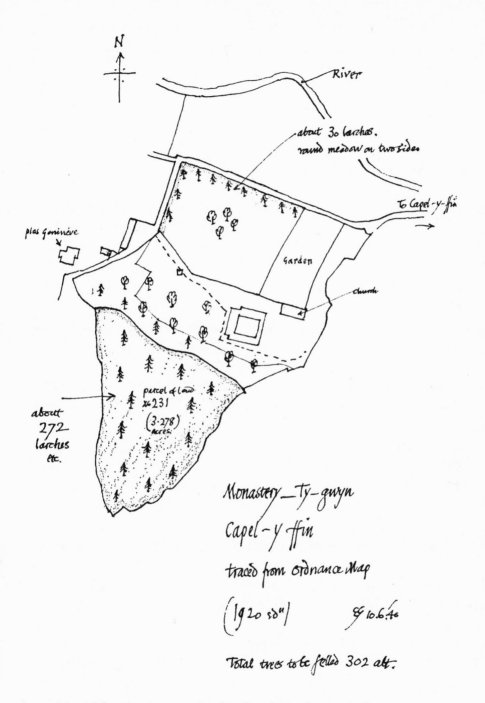

N

River

about 30 larches.
round meadow on two sides

To Capel-y-ffin

plas Geniveve

Garden

church

about
272
larches
etc.

parcel of land
№ 231
(3·278)
acres.

Monastery — Ty-gwyn

Capel-y-ffin

traced from Ordnance Map

(1920 s6")   EG 10.6.40

Total trees to be felled 302 alt.

Map of the Monastery at Capel-y-ffyn, drawn by Eric Gill, June 1940.

In June he was picking the cherries and currants at Pigotts, and lending a hand with the haymaking. Harman Grisewood brought his beautiful wife down for a brief honeymoon, and other visitors were Max Plowman and John Polimeni. The girl he had taken to Chartres in the far off Fabian days came to call, but he would not see her. At the end of the month he went to Birmingham to inspect the College of Art, but on July 3 he was back in bed, with a temperature and an attack of lumbago. He had a bed fixed up in the garden, and it was here that he struggled to finish what was a portrait of himself rather than a story of his life – 'an autopsychography', as he called it. His whole self went into it, nothing extenuated and nothing set down in malice. He showed the manuscript, day by day, to Dr Flood and invariably took the advice of his old friend when he thought that Eric's candour had overstepped the limits of discretion. Eric detested the usual book of memoirs, and when he looked at what he had written he found it 'shy-making': 'I begin to think I ought to clear out before it's finished,' he told Cecil; for here indeed was the man himself, greater than even his most accomplished works, nakedly exposed. Eric's autobiography was the last of his drawings from life. Here was the 'pure, certain vitality' of his line, but the line flowed more freely than in anything else that he had written. It was not that he had changed his views, but he was looking beyond his views; and as his dream of the 'unanimous city' faded in that bright and embittered summer of heroism and hatred, it seemed as if his eyes were fixed on a 'city without foundations whose builder and maker is God'.

'I wish I was well and strong', he wrote to Austen Harrison, 'as I used to be. I'm a crock at present. But I live in hopes – either of living or dying. It's the present neither one thing or the other that wears down the spirit.'[1] His mind went back to Beersheba where he and Mary had sat outside a café and watched the Arabs walking up and down with their splendid swords; and he was greatly heartened to hear that the statue to Allenby in Jerusalem had been destroyed. The war still seemed to him a 'monstrous madness', though his patriotism had flickered during the Battle of Britain and he thought the French

[1] August 20, 1940.

ought to have been ashamed of themselves for putting up such a poor show. He even designed a badge for the Ministry of Information. His mind also went back to Ranjitsinhji batting on the cricket ground at Hove through the long summer afternoons, and the bright red locomotives that pulled the 'Brighton Belle', and the interminable Sunday sermons. He was reliving his life at the same time that he was losing it.

He went to London for the Royal Academy Exhibition in August, and this was followed by three further visits when he had treatment for his lumbago and his lungs. On September 9 he was in Oxford, having tea with Christopher Dawson and staying at Blackfriars; and he was sufficiently himself to engage his secretary in a long conversation about the pleasures of love. He had further books in prospect, if he were unable to go back to his workshop; but on October 10 he went into hospital at High Wycombe for closer examination. In the intervals of X-ray and bronscopy he was writing an article on *Art in Relation to the Incarnation* for *Blackfriars*;[1] it was the last article he ever wrote. Curious as always, he copied out the notes on his medical chart and asked Cecil to translate them. Cecil came down to Pigotts when Eric had come out of hospital, and as Eric sat rolling a cigarette in his workshop told him that he had cancer of the lung. An operation to remove a portion of the lung had been suggested, but Eric was opposed to any extensive mutilation. 'It's sort of impious,' he said. He then asked Cecil to describe the probable sequence of events if the operation were not performed. Cecil told him the truth unflinchingly, and when he had finished Eric merely remarked: 'Well, that's not bad; in fact it sounds far too easy.' He consented, however, to a modified operation and became suddenly quite light-hearted and gay as if he were looking forward to a holiday.

On October 22 he went down into High Wycombe to lunch with Michael de la Bedoyère, who offered him a pinch of snuff. Eric examined the box and hearing that Bedoyère had bought it cheaply replied: 'It may not be valuable, but what I like about it is that you can see where the engraver's hand slipped: nothing prefabricated

[1] December 1940.

about it.' He offered to take it away and engrave its owner's initials on it; Eric's time was running out, and the snuff box remained as the last item on an unfinished agenda.

After writing a letter to the Press on *Machines*, *Big and Small*, and adding a codicil to his will, he spent the last days at Pigotts tidying up a few outstanding affairs and reading R. H. Wilenski's book on Ruskin. Every morning he attended Mass and received Holy Communion, and on All Saints' Day, November 1, he made his confession. On November 4 he was taken to Harefield House hospital in Middlesex, where the Brompton Chest hospital had been evacuated. When the surgeon came to see him, Eric said: 'I don't want to grow old like Rodin, carving ladies' bottoms with great technique and no inspiration.' Further X-rays were taken, and as the days passed he began a translation of the Psalms and started to illustrate some Chinese tales he had been reading. He was also correcting the proofs of his autobiography. Mary and Joanna came to see him, and the Catholic priests from Ruislip and High Wycombe. He had left behind the large notebook in which he kept his diary, but each day he recorded what he had been doing on an odd sheet of paper. The last entry was for November 9.

The operation was successfully carried out on November 11. As he came round after the anaesthetic Eric sat up in bed and exclaimed: 'Well, that's over – isn't it?' – and had to be restrained. He appeared to be progressing well during the days that followed, but on Saturday, November 16, his condition suddenly grew worse. The story can best be told by Monsignor Sutton, who was chaplain to the hospital:

One night there was a very big air raid on, when about midnight I had a phone call to come to the hospital urgently. So I gathered my pyx, with the Blessed Sacrament, and the holy oils, and set out in my car in the dark for Harefield. Guns were banging and bombs bursting all round, but eventually I arrived safely, and made my way to Eric Gill's room. Outside the door was a young doctor who said: 'You have come to visit Eric Gill, I believe.' I replied: 'That's right.' Then he said, 'Well, his life is hanging by a thread, and if you go in and worry him with your last sacraments I won't answer for the consequences, so I must forbid you to enter.' So I said: 'Well, doctor, I have the greatest respect for medical opinion, but I am chaplain to this hospital, and have been sent for, and it is my duty to go in, and I intend to do so.' Thereupon he said: 'I wash my hands of the case. I won't answer for the consequences,' and departed. Then I knocked on the door and a feeble voice said, 'Come in'. Eric Gill was lying in bed, with a cradle over his knees to keep the clothes off, and he raised himself gently on one arm. When he saw me, he said, 'Thank God, Father, you've come.' I then heard his confession, gave him Holy Viaticum, and anointed him, and he answered all the prayers himself in Latin. We said a few more prayers together in English, and I left, and he died shortly after. There was a beautiful serene expression on his face as I left. I can truthfully say I have never, in my 45 years as a priest, seen a more beautiful death. I really felt I was in the presence of a Saint.[1]

Mary spent most of that night at the hospital, and was called to Eric's bedside a few minutes before 5 a.m. on Sunday, November 17. He died ten minutes later.

The body was brought back to Pigotts and lay in the chapel, the craftsman's hands – delicate and strong – entwined around a crucifix. Eric had once expressed a horror of being buried alive and Cecil, remembering this, gently severed an artery in the left forearm.

The day of the funeral, November 21, broke dully, but the sun came out as the morning wore on. The coffin remained unclosed until after the Requiem, which was celebrated by Father Lockyer, the parish priest of High Wycombe in whose favour Dr Flood had generously stood down. The Mass was served by Cecil and Gordian Gill. The congregation overflowed into the hall and on to the half-landing between the chapel and Eric's workshop. A choir, composed of Betty, Petra, Joanna and Denis Tegetmeier, sang the *In Paradisum*, which they had practised the night before. Father Lockyer preached a panegyric, and the poignancy of this farewell to Eric was tempered with a kind of joy – perhaps because many of those present believed that he had wanted to die.

When the service was over, Mary came forward, alone, and with the tip of her finger conveyed a kiss to the face that she would see no

[1] Letter to the author, December 29, 1962.

more. Then the coffin was closed in the presence of the mourners.

Outside, in the roadway, a farm cart with a bed of straw was waiting to receive it. Wreaths from the Royal Academy and the BBC and the Monotype Corporation trailing their gorgeous ribbons, and many bunches of humbler flowers, were piled around it. Immediately following the cart walked Hilary Pepler carrying the cross; he was surrounded by Eric's grandchildren, some of whom were also his own. Mary and other members of the family followed close behind. Dr Flood and three Dominican Fathers augmented the choir which sang the *In Paradisum* at intervals on the way to the burial. A local builder – and friend of Eric – led the horse as it pulled the farm cart slowly down the steep hill.

The little cemetery at Speen adjoins a Baptist chapel. It was appropriate as well as paradoxical that this naïve and intrepid non-conformist should have been buried with the rites of the Catholic Church within the precincts of Nonconformity. Eric had spent many years trying to discover something to which he could conform; and when he had conformed to Catholicism he found that Catholics would not conform to him. The service at the graveside was taken by Dr Flood. Only one hymn was sung – *Jerusalem the Golden* – the hymn which Eric had sung in the train that brought him up to Jerusalem. His grave is on rising ground on the outer edge of the cemetery, and the tombstone, which he had himself designed, bears the simple inscription:

PRAY FOR ME

ERIC GILL

STONE CARVER 1882–1940

Appendix: A Tribunal

This tract is written in the form of question and answer not because any Tribunal is likely to allow a C.O. so much rope but because it is not a mere essay on war and law but is an attempt to answer some of the questions underlying conscientious objection.

E. G.

Q. Are you a Conscientious Objector?

A. Yes.

Q. Do you think all use of violence in support of law is wrong?

A. No.

Q. Do you think all war is wrong?

A. In the abstract, no.

Q. Do you think war is wrong today?

A. Yes.

Q. Why?

A. Because the conditions which might justify war are of two kinds – a just cause and just means. Today it is *doubtful* whether the cause is just and *certain* that the means are not.

Q. I see – ends and means. With regard to ends: what right have you to set up as judge against lawfully constituted authority? If the Government judges it right to go to war, by what authority do you judge it to be wrong?

A. There are two sorts of law-giving, positive and negative – things you must do and things you must not. The former are rightly confined to general principles, as: 'Thou shalt love the Lord thy God', or 'Honour your father and your mother'. The latter are rightly confined to particular acts, as 'Thou shalt not steal'. Positive commands as to particular acts are bad law and are only submitted to for convenience, as when the Government says that every child shall be registered at birth. What the law really means is that the Government chooses to keep a register and demands the assistance of parents and guardians. But it could, if it chose, keep the register without that assistance; the assistance is convenient but not essential. In general it is true to say that people can justly be forcibly

prevented from doing certain things but cannot justly be forcibly compelled to *do* anything. This principle is derived from the facts of nature.
You can take a horse to the water but you cannot make him drink. So, in
this matter of war we may say: you can take a man to the slaughter but
you cannot make him kill. Therefore I say that the Government has the
right to demand that we love and honour our country but no right to say:
thou shalt kill her enemies. I am not saying that there are no circumstances in which enemies should be killed – there may be or there may
not – I am only saying that no government can justly compel a man to
take the job of executioner.

Q. Your contention, that the Government cannot compel particular acts,
will not 'hold water' – what about paying taxes? Cannot the Government
justly compel you to pay?

A. Yes, but that's only saying that it can justly take your money and that,
if you refuse to pay, is precisely what they will do. And may I say this:
that considering the methods of electioneering and the whole corrupt
business of politics today, and, quite apart from the fact that no government even claims to represent all the people, there is no reason why anyone should look up to the government as though it were in any way holy
or to be reverenced. It represents the big economic and financial interests
of our empire even more than it represents persons. It has no unity of
mind upon moral principles – except that its members are almost unanimous in denying that morality has anything to do with economics – and
it has therefore no mandate to teach morality or any power to do so.
As the legitimately constituted authority it is to be obeyed, but only
when its commands are not immoral. As to whether this or that war be
just, such a government cannot judge. Justice is a conception depending
upon the acceptance of certain moral and philosophical principles and no
government today is founded upon such acceptance or subject to it. To
ask the Government for a ruling in a matter of justice is like asking the
keeper of a cat's home for a ruling on ping-pong. In brief, I hold that the
Government has the right, as it has the power, to prevent my doing what
it judges to be contrary to the common advantage, but that it has not the
right, and it has not the power, to compel me to do what I believe to be
wrong or even to do any particular thing, whether wrong or right.

Q. Let us leave all that and let me ask you the old simple question: If a
man threatened your wife with a gun, would you not defend her?

A. Why yes, naturally.

Q. Would you use force?

A. Yes, if I could command it. Failing that, the good thing to do would be to get between her and the gun, and then to throw myself upon him and, before he had time to use it, to wrest the awful weapon from his horrid grasp.

Q. Isn't that, in effect, what the country asks you to do – to defend your wife and children and your home?

A. That's how they express it. But, if you will forgive the slang, they 'kid' themselves. For where is the parallel? Times have changed. What they ask of me in *fact* and not 'in effect', is not simply to join an army of defence but, in accord with the old saying, 'offence is the best defence', to join up in an organization for the destruction of the enemy. But of course no one is deceived (or are you, Sir?) by the talk about only destroying 'military objectives'. We know very well that immediately air-men start bombing they cannot possibly confine their attention to such. They will bomb whatever they can and particularly any centre of population. 'In effect', to borrow your phrase, it is as though, in answer to your question about the man with the gun, I were to answer: yes, I would defend my wife, but I would not give a poker to the baby and rush out of the back door and down the street to my enemy's house and throw vitriol in his wife's face to 'break her morale'. There are in fact 'some things which no fellow should do'. I do not believe that 'all's fair in love and war'. Nobody does really. I don't believe in killing prisoners. I don't believe in killing the wounded. I don't believe in killing children or their mothers or old people or imbeciles. In short, I don't believe in killing the innocent, i.e. the harmless and I don't believe in killing people, whether soldiers or not, who are running away – as we did to the Turks in the last war – that is massacre. And it's no use any longer trying to make out that such things are only done by accident. It is not true and everyone knows it. Do *you* believe in gouging out the eyes of prisoners or mutilating them to break their morale?

Q. You're here to answer questions, not to ask them.

A. Please ask.

Q. Assuming for the moment that you are right in saying that it is the in-tention of our commanders to bomb open towns – though I don't admit it and it is grossly insulting to our Government and to our soldiers – even so, are you not compelled to use the same means as our enemy uses?

A. No, of course not. There's no compulsion about it.

Q. But if we do not, will they not have us at a hopeless disadvantage?

A. Perhaps – but that's no argument, unless you think it's right 'to do evil that good may come'. History seems to show the contrary even if God's word were insufficient.

Q. Would you allow the enemy to ride rough-shod over your country?

A. Not at all. I should, as I said before, attempt to defend it. But I refuse to use evil means to that end. A man may refuse to defend himself but he cannot honourably refuse to defend his wife and children. Nevertheless he can and should refuse to defend them by immoral means. If good means are not sufficient, if, for example, his anti-aircraft guns are not good enough, or his barrages defective, then he must surrender. It cannot be helped. Murdering your enemy's children would be no remedy and you would only stir up hate and lust for revenge.

Q. Don't you think a man is entitled to defeat the enemy by any means in his power?

A. No, I do not.

Q. Are you prepared to take the consequences of your opinions?

A. Of course I am.

Q. Will you join the anti-aircraft corps?

A. Yes, if I am given a written guarantee, which I am allowed to carry about with me always, that I shall not be drafted into the bombing section of the Air Force or into any overseas army of offence.

Q. That is impossible; for it is not only the home-country that must be defended but also our colonies and dependencies and they cannot be defended, as perhaps England can, by anti-aircraft guns or barrages, but only by attack on the enemy in his own country.

A. Very well then. I refuse to join even the anti-aircraft defences. But, I repeat, I will join those defences on the condition I have stated. And I should like to add that in taking part in anti-aircraft defence there is no suggestion of any desire to kill enemy airmen, but only to destroy their machines. In the same way one should endeavour to disarm an intending murderer rather than to kill him.

Q. What alternative service will you accept?

A. Broadly speaking, I will do anything which it would be good to do in any case. For example: The land needs tilling and cultivating. It has been shamefully neglected in the interest of our overseas trade — trade conducted by methods and policies which are themselves very largely the cause of this war and others. Then again, if we are to attain to a just peace, a lot of propaganda will be required to stem the natural tide of hatred and anger which war sets flowing. People who can write should be employed to do this work before it is too late. Again: building work. It would be much better to employ C.O.s on slum clearance and rebuilding work than to shoot them or imprison them. They are anxious to serve their country. Let them do so. Unless you shoot them all, they will have to be fed. Let them earn their keep. But do not talk to us about justice and honour. The present war is not due to Hitler's injustice or deceit, heinous though they may seem, but to economic developments and compulsions reaching back over many centuries. And the beam in our own eye is not inconspicuous. *We* cannot set up as arbiters. Our hands are no cleaner than anyone else's. Therefore I ask for total exemption – that I may serve my country without disservice to God.

21.9.'39.

Short Bibliography

Letters of Eric Gill, edited by Walter Shewring. Cape, 1947.

Autobiography, Eric Gill. Cape, 1940.

Bibliography of Eric Gill, Evan R. Gill. Cassell, 1953.

The Inscriptional Work of Eric Gill: An Inventory, Evan R. Gill. Cassell, 1964.

Engravings by Eric Gill: A Selection, Douglas Cleverdon, 1929.

Engravings, 1928–33, by Eric Gill, Faber and Faber, 1934.

Modern Christian Revolutionaries: 'Eric Gill: Workman', Donald Attwater. Devin-Adair, New York, 1947.

Eric Gill, Joseph Thorp. Cape, 1929.

Eric Gill, J. K. M. Rothenstein. Benn, 1927.

Four Absentees, Rayner Heppenstall. Barrie and Rockliff, 1960.

Index of Life and Works

1. LIFE

Influence and importance, xvi, xvii; boyhood in Brighton, early tastes, 3–10; move to Chichester, study at Technical Art School, 11–14; apprentice to architect of the Ecclesiastical Commissioners, 15–18; first inscriptions, 18; joins Edward Johnston's lettering class at the Central School of Arts and Crafts, 18–20; lodges with Johnston, 21–2; meets Ethel Mary Moore, 23; marriage to, 26; birth of Elizabeth Gill and move from Battersea to Hammersmith, 28–9; teaches masonry and lettering LCC Paddington Institute, 29; contacts with the Fabian Society, 29; meeting with William Rothenstein, 31; visit to Rome, 31; meeting with A. R. Orage, 32; influence of Nietzsche, 32; first visit to Chartres, 33; visit to Bruges, 37; move to Ditchling, 35, 37.

Meeting with Ananda Coomaraswamy, 42; visits Maillol at Marly-le-Roi, and declines Count Kessler's proposals that he should work with him, 44–6; views on funeral monuments, 47–8; carving directly from the stone, 46, 48; friendship with Epstein and Roger Fry, 48–54; Rothenstein on erotic bias of E. G.'s carving, 55; conversion to Catholicism, 59–67; Edward Johnston comes to Ditchling, 68; E. G. moves to Hopkins Crank, 69–70; commission for Westminster Cathedral *Stations*, 72; Hilary Pepler comes to Ditchling, 75; adoption of Gordian Gill, 91; meeting with Desmond Chute, 92; E. G. called up for military service, 94–5; basis of his spiritual life, 98–102; views on war memorials, 103–5; visit to Ireland, 106–9; David Jones comes to Ditchling, 111–12; E. G. writing for *The Game*, 114–19; Fr. Martin d'Arcy S.J. on E. G., 120; Desmond Chute leaves Ditchling, 122; E. G.'s visit to Fribourg, 123; influence of Jacques Maritain, 124–6; Leeds War Memorial controversy, 126–34; Philip Hagreen, George Maxwell and Reginald Lawson at Ditchling, 135; Spike Hughes on a Christmas at Hopkins Crank, 136; E. G. and Pepler propose to move from Ditchling, visit to Capel-y-ffin, 139–41; E. G.'s dispute with Pepler, 142–6; letter from Clare Pepler, 146; last days at Ditchling, 147–9.

First days at Capel-y-ffin, 153–6; E. G. and René Hague, 156–7; correspondence with Clare Pepler, 159–61; settlement of dispute with Pepler, 161–3; Elizabeth Gill's marriage to David Pepler, 162–3; Count Kessler on a visit to Capel-y-ffin, 164–6, on meeting E. G. in London, 166–7, and in Paris with Maillol, 167–8; E. G.'s meeting with Robert Gibbings and work for the Golden Cockerel Press, 169–70; E. G.'s eroticism and relation to ecclesiastical authority, 170–2, 174–8, 179–81; diversity of E. G.'s reading, 182–3; meeting with Stanley Morison, Douglas Cleverdon and Denis Tegetmeier, 183; first work in typography, 185–6; visit to Rapallo and Rome, 188–90; Paris, Salies-de-Béarn and Chartres, 188–92; exhibition of sculpture at Goupil Gallery, 192–3; leaves Capel-y-ffin, and acquires Pigotts, 194–6.

Pigotts, 199–200; writing for *Order*, 200–2; estrangement from Fr. Vincent McNabb, 200; on sculptural ornament in architecture, 204; further work in typography, 206–8; visitors to Pigotts, 209; death of mother, 210; marriage of Petra Gill to Denis Teget-

2. WORKS

General Index